CRITICAL PRAISE FOR
THE SHERIFF OF BABYLON

"Of all the fantastic books writer Tom King has on the stands right now, this is by far the best. Not only standing above his own work, but towering above anything else being published at the moment. Gerads's coarse realism creates the perfect witness to danger and tension within this world. From his angles to his close-ups, he shows himself to be as much a cinematographer as a comic book artist from issue to issue."
—PATRICK HEALY, GRAPHICPOLICY.COM

"THE SHERIFF OF BABYLON is a thinking man's comic grounded in realpolitik horror, where the corpses of patriotism litter yesterday's battlefields."
—SEAN EDGAR, PASTE.COM

"The best military comic I've ever read. A perfect snapshot of 2003 Iraq and the murky dealings that followed the invasion."
—KEVIN MAURER, CO-AUTHOR OF *NO EASY DAY*

"A gritty window into a confusing time and place…the series drops the easy good guy/bad guy storylines found in so many comics to delve into a more nuanced world [King] hopes will ring true to those who served there."
—JON ANDERSON, *MILITARY TIMES*

"THE SHERIFF OF BABYLON is a comic book that'll be talked about for decades, the sort of thing you keep coming back to again and again to study and enjoy."
—BENJAMIN BAILEY, NERDIST.COM

"Quite possibly the best comic of the year."
—JOSHUA RIVERA, *GQ*

D1208812

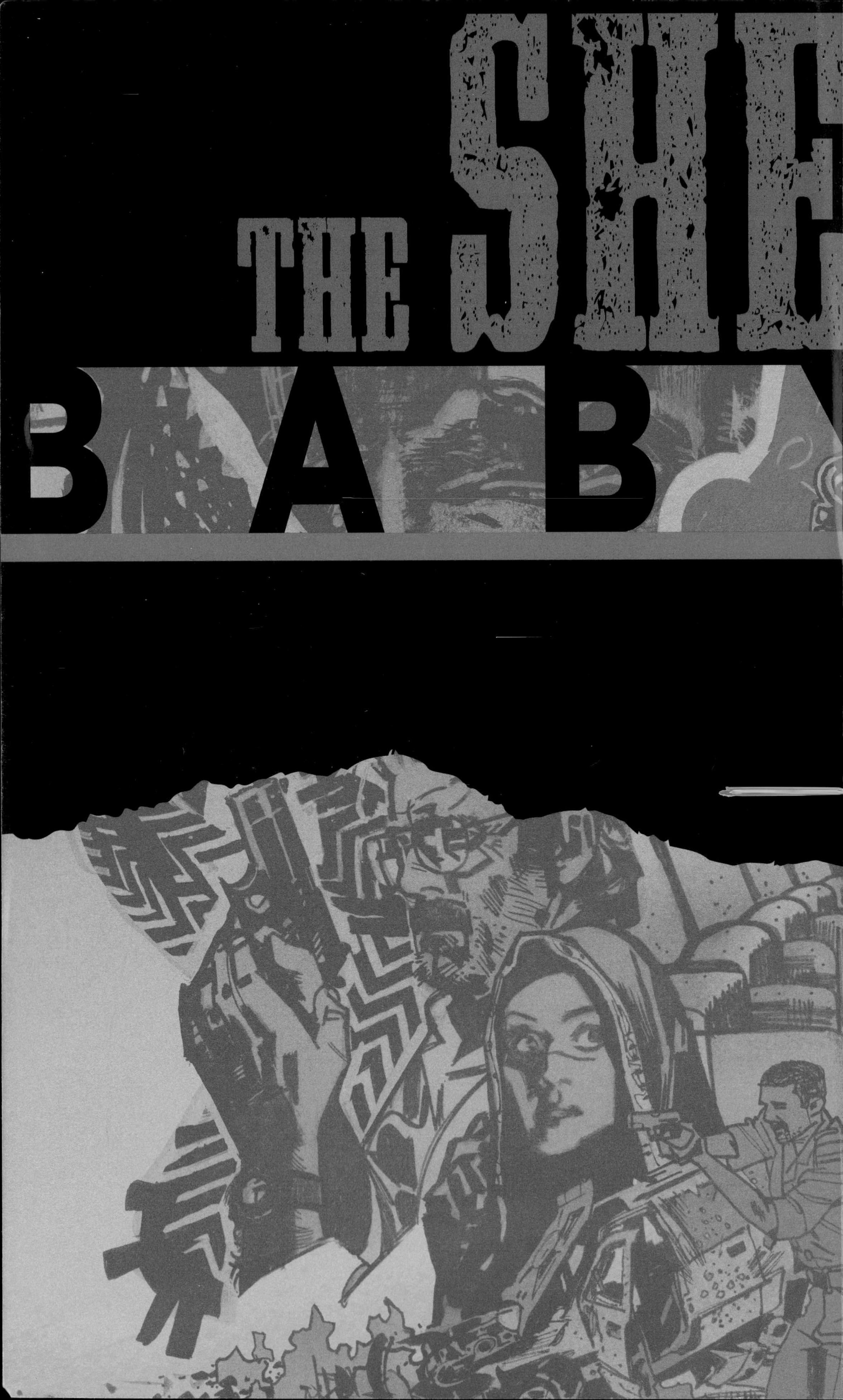
THE

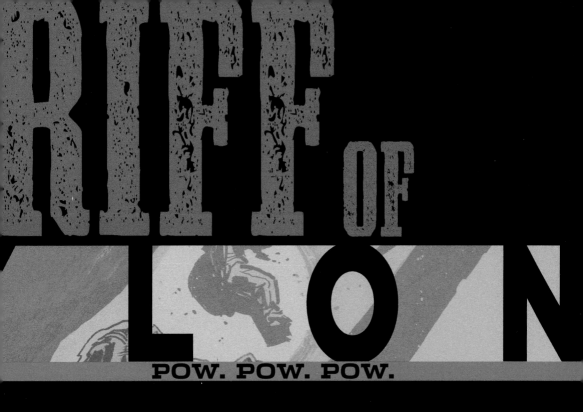

RIFF OF ZION

POW. POW. POW.

TOM KING
WRITER

MITCH GERADS
ART AND COLORS

TRAVIS LANHAM
LETTERING

JOHN PAUL LEON
COVER ART AND ORIGINAL SERIES COVERS

THE SHERIFF OF BABYLON CREATED BY
TOM KING **AND** MITCH GERADS

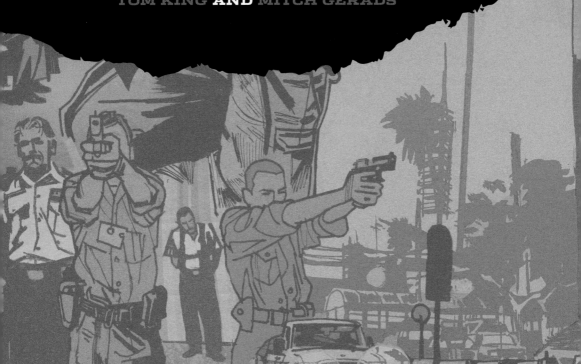

JAMIE S. RICH Group Editor – Vertigo Comics and Editor – Original Series
MOLLY MAHAN Associate Editor – Original Series
JEB WOODARD Group Editor – Collected Editions
SCOTT NYBAKKEN Editor – Collected Edition
STEVE COOK Design Director – Books
DAMIAN RYLAND Publication Design

DIANE NELSON President
DAN DiDIO Publisher
JIM LEE Publisher
GEOFF JOHNS President & Chief Creative Officer
AMIT DESAI Executive VP – Business & Marketing Strategy, Direct to Consumer & Global Franchise Management
SAM ADES Senior VP – Direct to Consumer
BOBBIE CHASE VP – Talent Development
MARK CHIARELLO Senior VP – Art, Design & Collected Editions
JOHN CUNNINGHAM Senior VP – Sales & Trade Marketing
ANNE DEPIES Senior VP – Business Strategy, Finance & Administration
DON FALLETTI VP – Manufacturing Operations
LAWRENCE GANEM VP – Editorial Administration & Talent Relations
ALISON GILL Senior VP – Manufacturing & Operations
HANK KANALZ Senior VP – Editorial Strategy & Administration
JAY KOGAN VP – Legal Affairs
THOMAS LOFTUS VP – Business Affairs
JACK MAHAN VP – Business Affairs
DAN MIRON VP – Sales Planning & Trade Development
NICK NAPOLITANO VP – Manufacturing Administration
EDDIE SCANNELL VP – Consumer Marketing
COURTNEY SIMMONS Senior VP – Publicity & Communications
JIM (SKI) SOKOLOWSKI VP – Comic Book Specialty Sales & Trade Marketing
NANCY SPEARS VP – Mass, Book, Digital Sales & Trade Marketing

Logo design by **MITCH GERADS**

THE SHERIFF OF BABYLON: POW. POW. POW.

DC Comics
2900 West Alameda Avenue
Burbank, CA 91505
Printed in the USA. First Printing.
ISBN: 978-1-4012-6726-1

Library of Congress Cataloging-in-Publication Data is available.

PEFC Certified

Printed on paper from
sustainably managed
forests, controlled
sources

PEFC/29-31-337   www.pefc.org

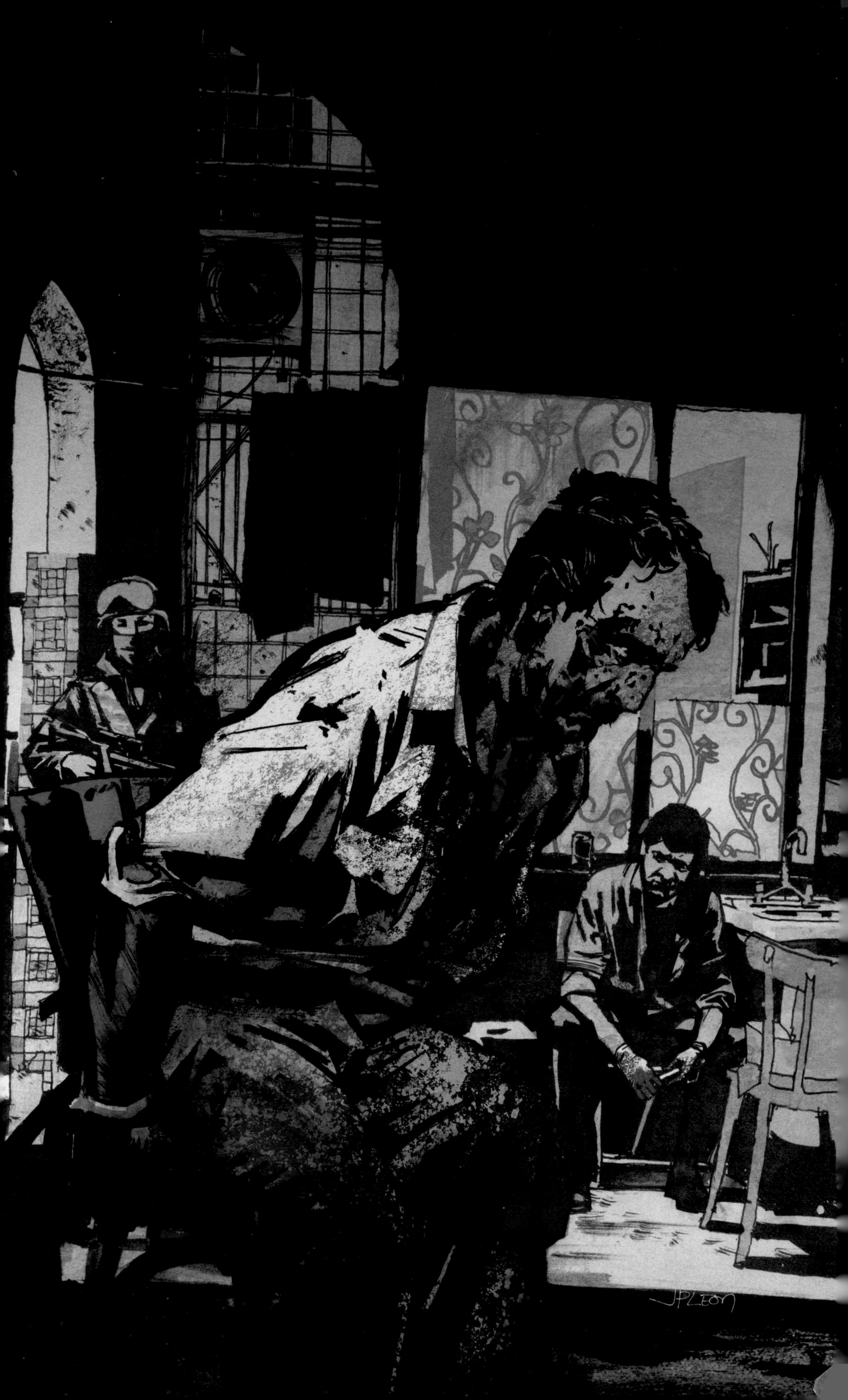
JPLEON

THE SHERIFF OF BABYLON

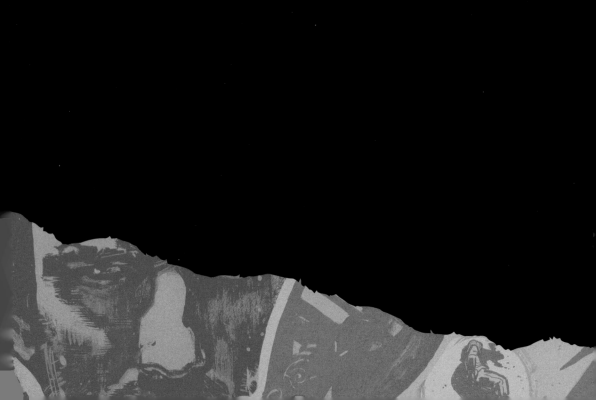

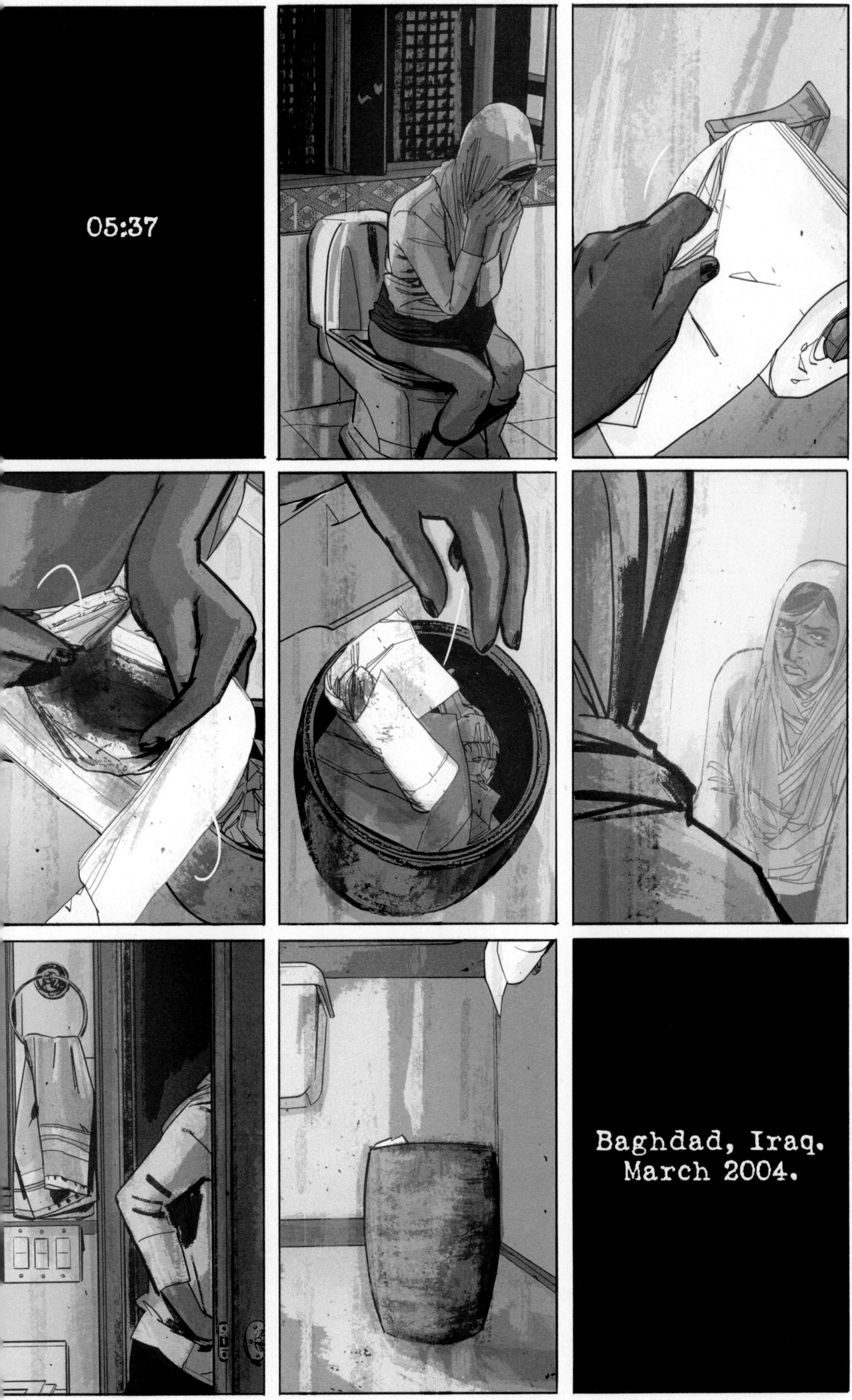
05:37
Baghdad, Iraq.
March 2004.

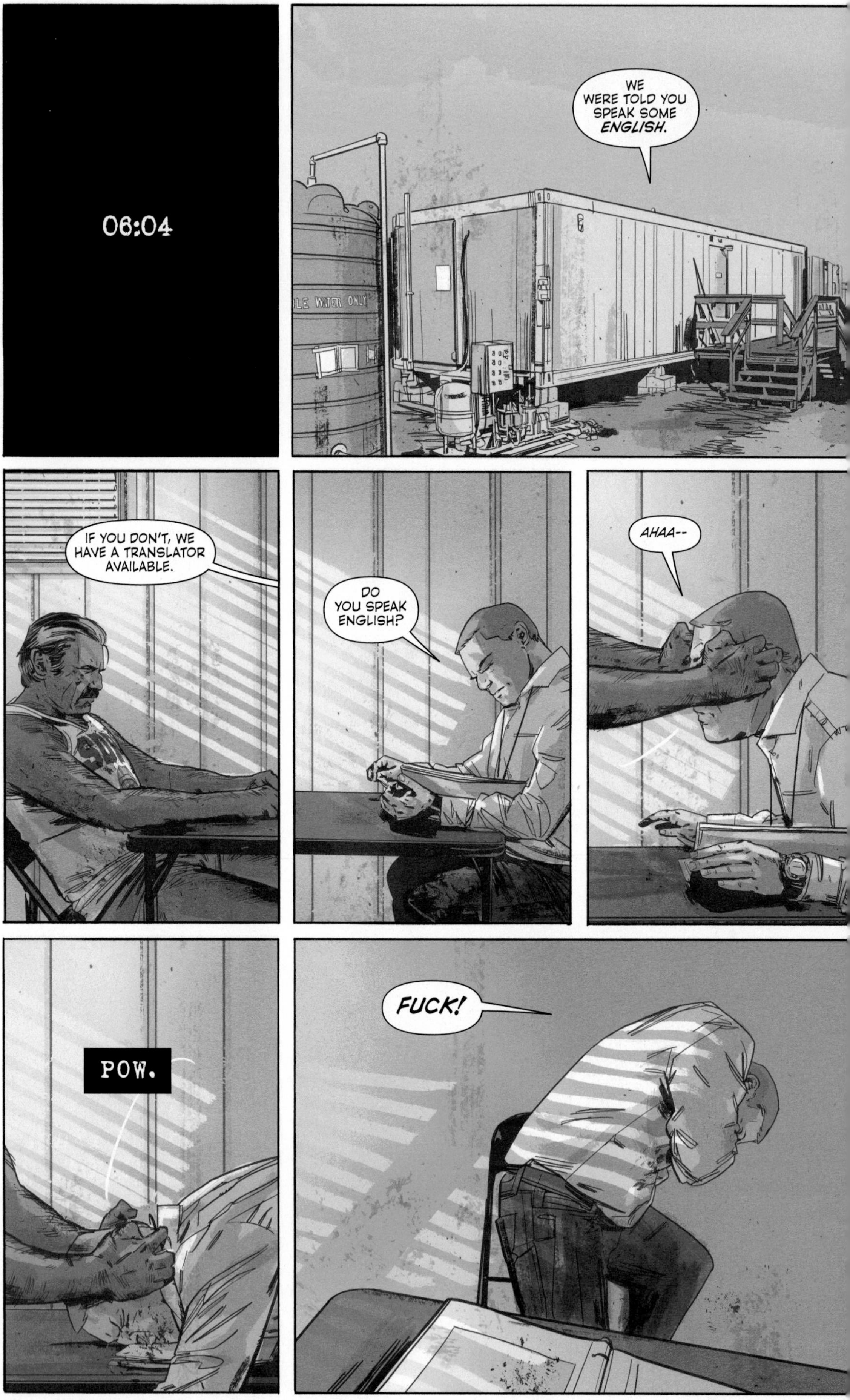
06:04
WE WERE TOLD YOU SPEAK SOME ENGLISH.
IF YOU DON'T, WE HAVE A TRANSLATOR AVAILABLE.
DO YOU SPEAK ENGLISH?
AHAA--
POW.
FUCK!

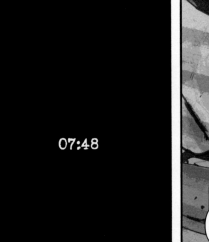

07:48

WE WANT TO TALK TO YOU.

BUT WE *CAN'T* TALK TO YOU IF YOU WANT THIS VIOLENCE TO GO ON.

ALL RIGHT.

THEY TOLD ME WHAT HAPPENED WITH YOUR WIFE. I'M SURE YOU'RE MAD.

BUT WE CAN'T HAVE YOU HURTING ANYONE. THESE PEOPLE DIDN'T DO THIS.

I UNDERSTAND.

ARE YOU READY TO TALK THEN?

OF COURSE.

I'M GOING TO HAVE TO BIND YOUR HANDS AND FEET.

IS THAT GOING TO BE A PROBLEM?

IT IS NOT A PROBLEM.

DO YOU HAVE A CIGARETTE?

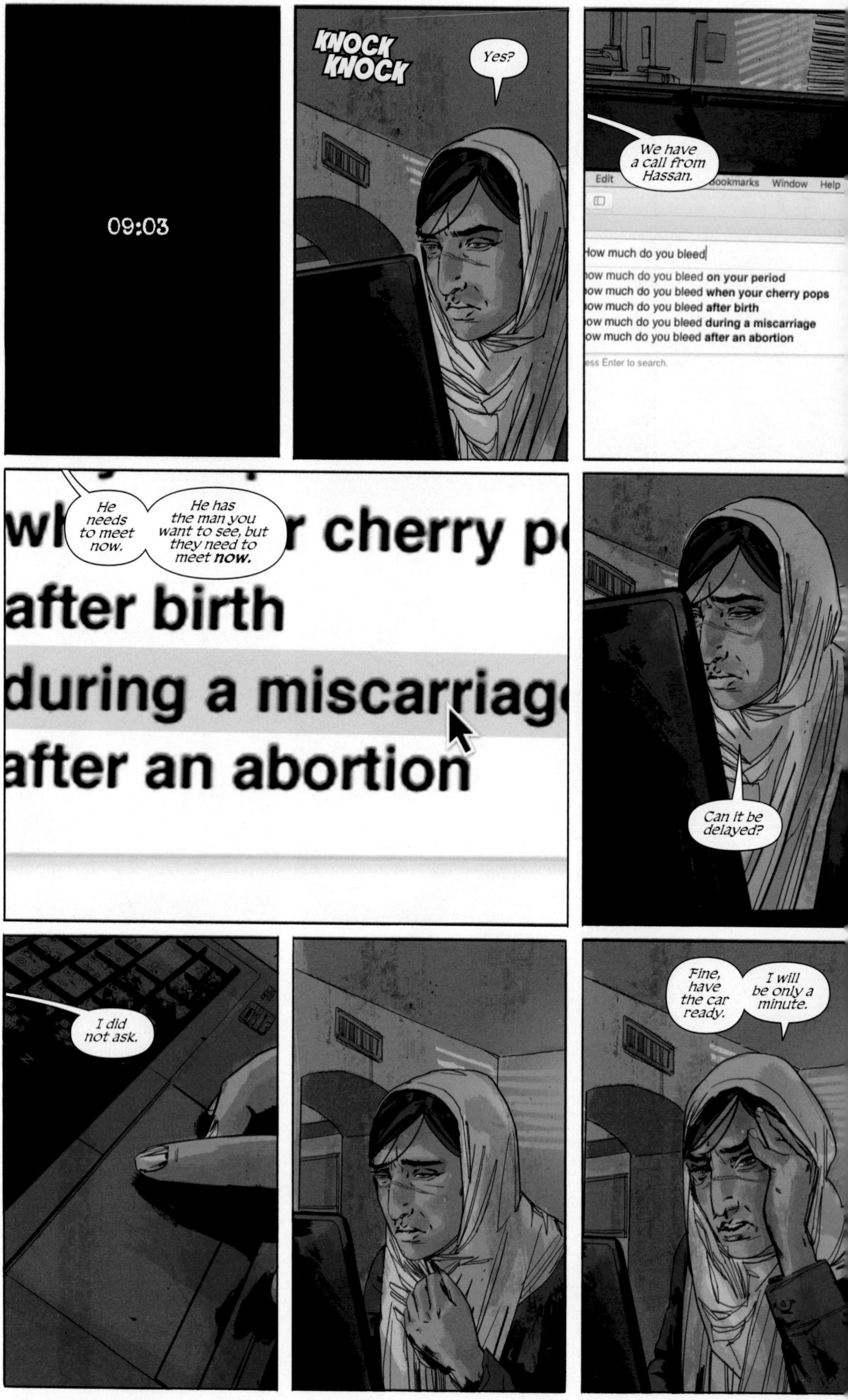
09:03
KNOCK KNOCK
Yes?
We have a call from Hassan.
Edit Bookmarks Window Help
How much do you bleed
ow much do you bleed on your period
ow much do you bleed when your cherry pops
ow much do you bleed after birth
ow much do you bleed during a miscarriage
ow much do you bleed after an abortion
ess Enter to search.
He needs to meet now.
He has the man you want to see, but they need to meet now.
r cherry p
after birth
during a miscarriag
after an abortion
Can it be delayed?
I did not ask.
Fine, have the car ready.
I will be only a minute.

10:17

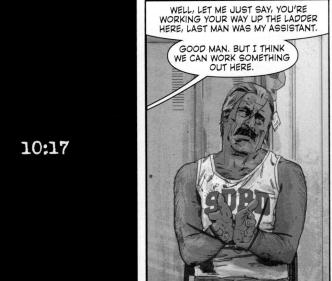

WELL, LET ME JUST SAY, YOU'RE WORKING YOUR WAY UP THE LADDER HERE, LAST MAN WAS MY ASSISTANT.

GOOD MAN. BUT I THINK WE CAN WORK SOMETHING OUT HERE.

THIS PROBLEM WITH YOUR WIFE.

IT'S IMPORTANT FOR YOU TO UNDERSTAND THAT THE PEOPLE--THE PEOPLE WHO ARE *RESPONSIBLE* FOR ALL OF THIS-- THEY WILL BE FOUND.

I WILL FIND THEM.

AND THEY WILL BE *PUNISHED*. FOR WHAT THEY DID, FOR ALL OF IT.

YOU HAVE MY WORD ON THAT, AND MY WORD MEANS SOMETHING.

BUT BEFORE THAT, WE HAVE TO TALK. WE HAVE TO TALK ABOUT A FEW THINGS.

MOST IMPORTANTLY, WE HAVE TO TALK ABOUT YOUR RELATIONSHIP WITH *ABU RAHIM*.

THIS EXTREMIST FELLOW YOU MET WITH BEFORE COMING ON OUR BASE.

WE KNOW ABOUT THAT NOW, AND I KNOW THAT YOU DON'T WANT TO TALK ABOUT IT.

I UNDERSTAND THAT, BUT WE *HAVE TO.*

BECAUSE OF A LOT OF THINGS THAT GO BEYOND ME AND THIS ROOM AND ALL OF IT.

WE HAVE TO TALK.

POW.

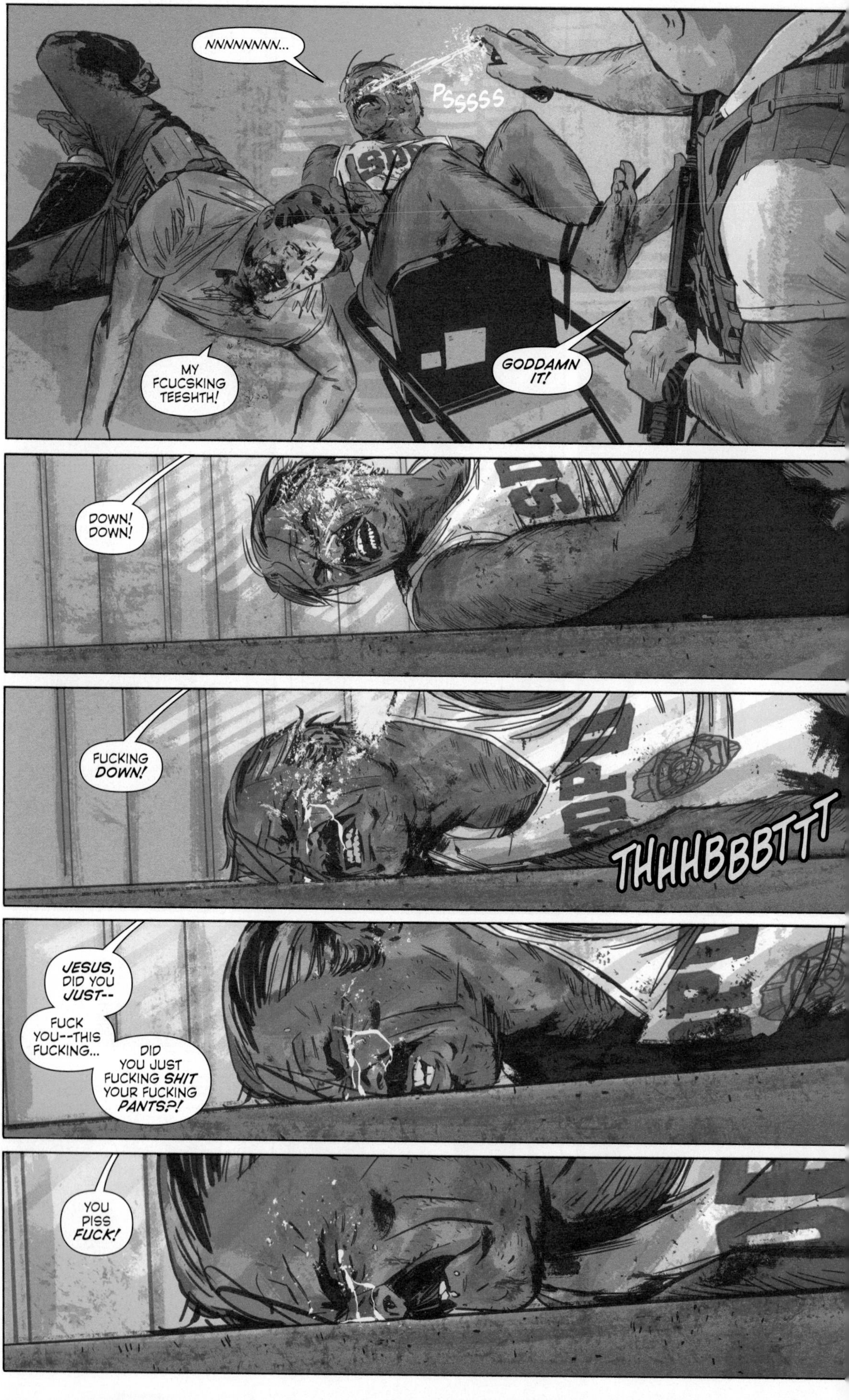
NNNNNNNN...
PSSSSS
MY FCUCSKING TEESHTH!
GODDAMN IT!
DOWN! DOWN!
FUCKING DOWN!
THHHBBBTTT
JESUS, DID YOU JUST--
FUCK YOU--THIS FUCKING...
DID YOU JUST FUCKING SHIT YOUR FUCKING PANTS?!
YOU PISS FUCK!

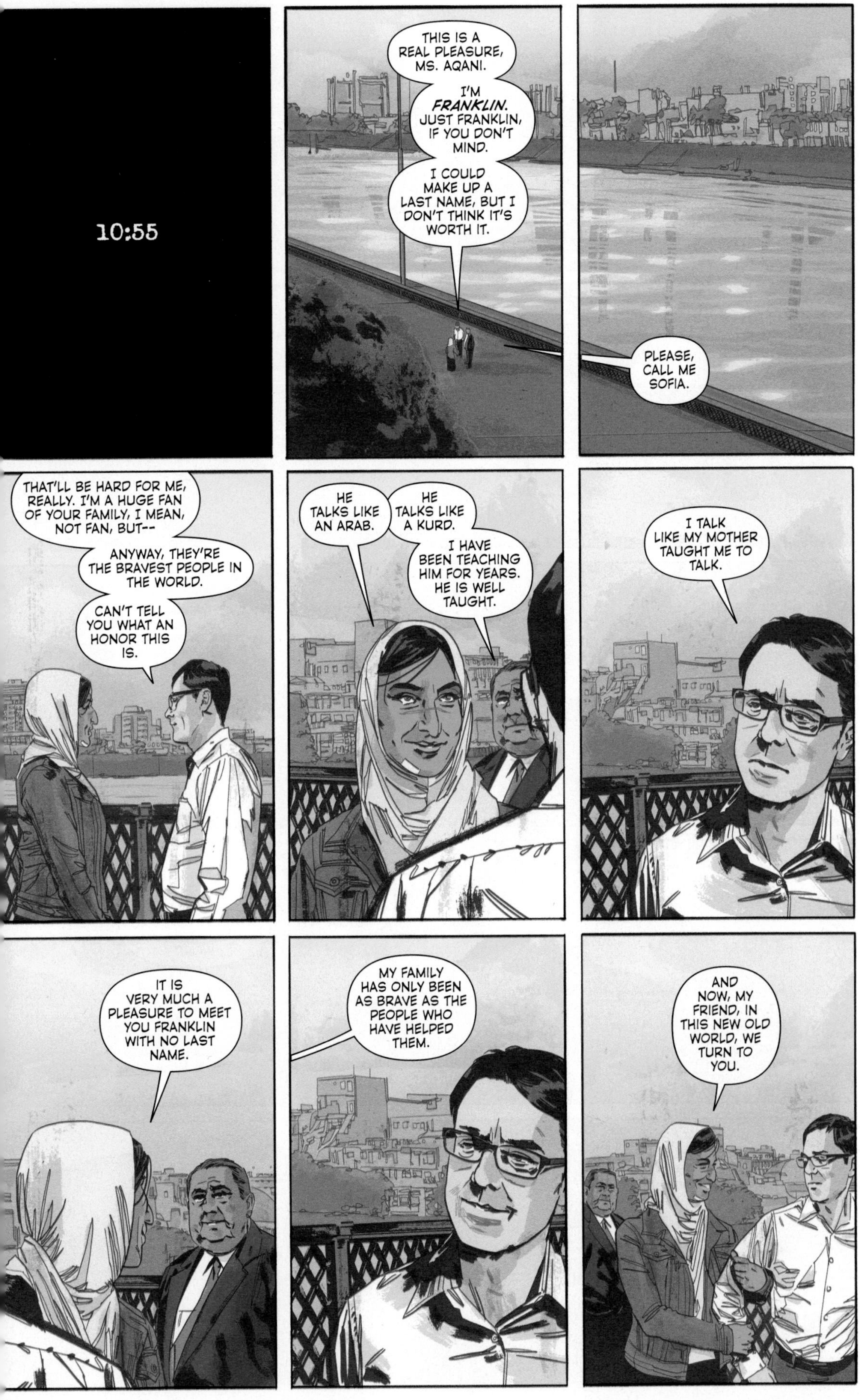
10:55
THIS IS A REAL PLEASURE, MS. AQANI.
I'M *FRANKLIN*. JUST FRANKLIN, IF YOU DON'T MIND.
I COULD MAKE UP A LAST NAME, BUT I DON'T THINK IT'S WORTH IT.
PLEASE, CALL ME SOFIA.
THAT'LL BE HARD FOR ME, REALLY. I'M A HUGE FAN OF YOUR FAMILY, I MEAN, NOT FAN, BUT--
ANYWAY, THEY'RE THE BRAVEST PEOPLE IN THE WORLD.
CAN'T TELL YOU WHAT AN HONOR THIS IS.
HE TALKS LIKE AN ARAB.
HE TALKS LIKE A KURD.
I HAVE BEEN TEACHING HIM FOR YEARS. HE IS WELL TAUGHT.
I TALK LIKE MY MOTHER TAUGHT ME TO TALK.
IT IS VERY MUCH A PLEASURE TO MEET YOU FRANKLIN WITH NO LAST NAME.
MY FAMILY HAS ONLY BEEN AS BRAVE AS THE PEOPLE WHO HAVE HELPED THEM.
AND NOW, MY FRIEND, IN THIS NEW OLD WORLD, WE TURN TO YOU.

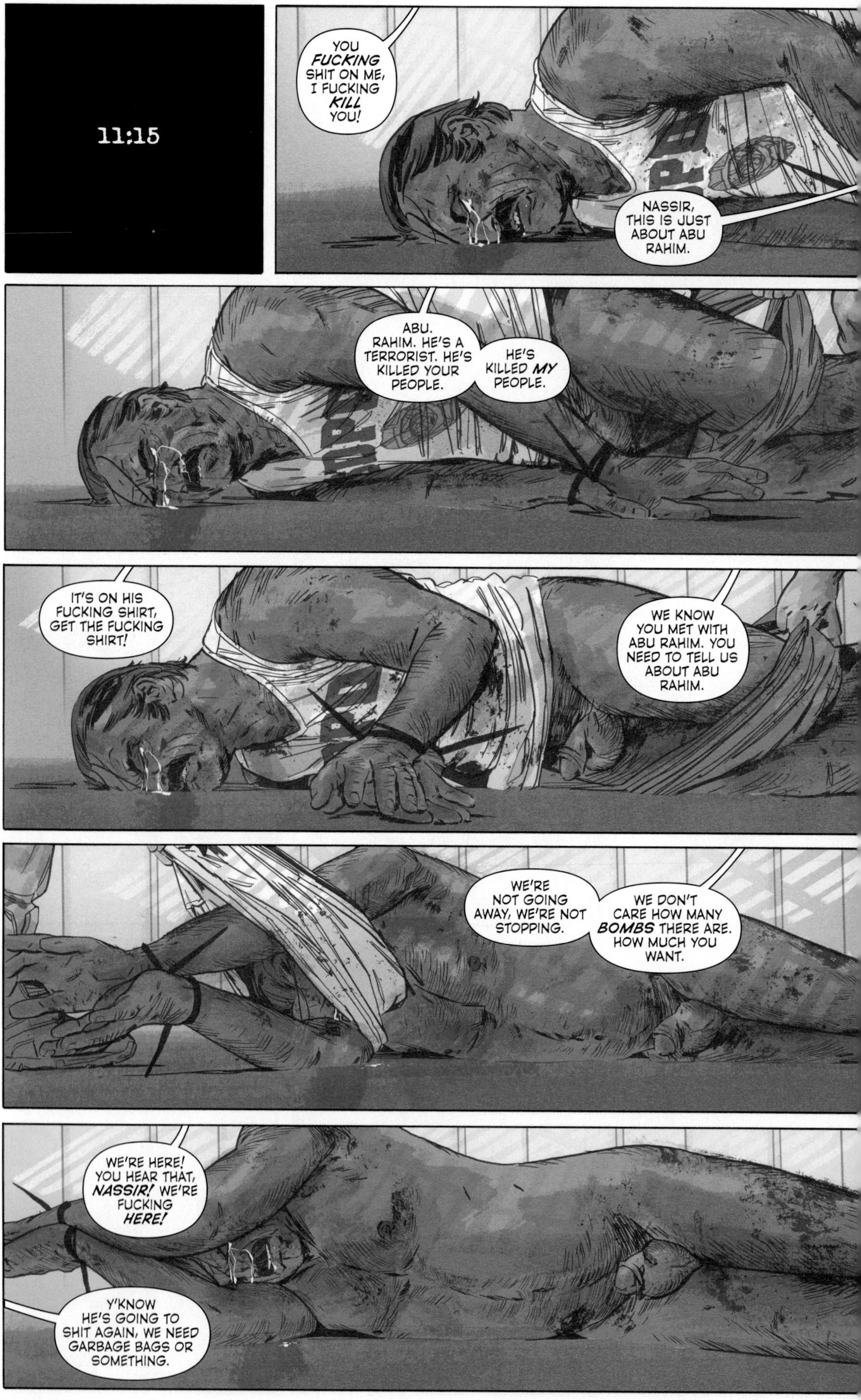

11:15
YOU FUCKING SHIT ON ME, I FUCKING KILL YOU!
NASSIR, THIS IS JUST ABOUT ABU RAHIM.
ABU. RAHIM. HE'S A TERRORIST. HE'S KILLED YOUR PEOPLE.
HE'S KILLED MY PEOPLE.
IT'S ON HIS FUCKING SHIRT, GET THE FUCKING SHIRT!
WE KNOW YOU MET WITH ABU RAHIM. YOU NEED TO TELL US ABOUT ABU RAHIM.
WE'RE NOT GOING AWAY, WE'RE NOT STOPPING.
WE DON'T CARE HOW MANY BOMBS THERE ARE. HOW MUCH YOU WANT.
WE'RE HERE! YOU HEAR THAT, NASSIR! WE'RE FUCKING HERE!
Y'KNOW HE'S GOING TO SHIT AGAIN, WE NEED GARBAGE BAGS OR SOMETHING.

11:38

I'VE WORKED FOR A WHILE WITH HASSAN.

SINCE BEFORE THE WAR, REALLY.

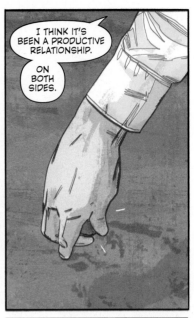

I THINK IT'S BEEN A PRODUCTIVE RELATIONSHIP.

ON BOTH SIDES.

BUT HONESTLY, PUT THAT ASIDE, IN THE END WHO CARES ABOUT PRODUCTIVITY?

HASSAN AND I, WE GO BEYOND THAT.

NNNNN...

WE'RE *FAMILY* NOW.

WE HELP EACH OTHER LIKE FAMILY HELPS EACH OTHER.

GRNNNN...

I KNOW YOU'VE WORKED WITH OTHER AMERICANS ON THIS WAR.

GENERAL HOLLAND, AND ALL THOSE WASHINGTON PEOPLE.

I KNOW THEY HAVE AGENDAS. *EVERYONE* HAS AGENDAS.

I HAVE AGENDAS. YOU HAVE THEM.

BUT I HOPE YOU'LL SEE, I HOPE YOU *CAN* SEE...

THAT IF--WHEN YOU'RE WORKING WITH ME, IT'S NOT *ALWAYS* ABOUT THE AGENDAS.

IT'S ABOUT BUILDING SOMETHING LIKE FAMILY.

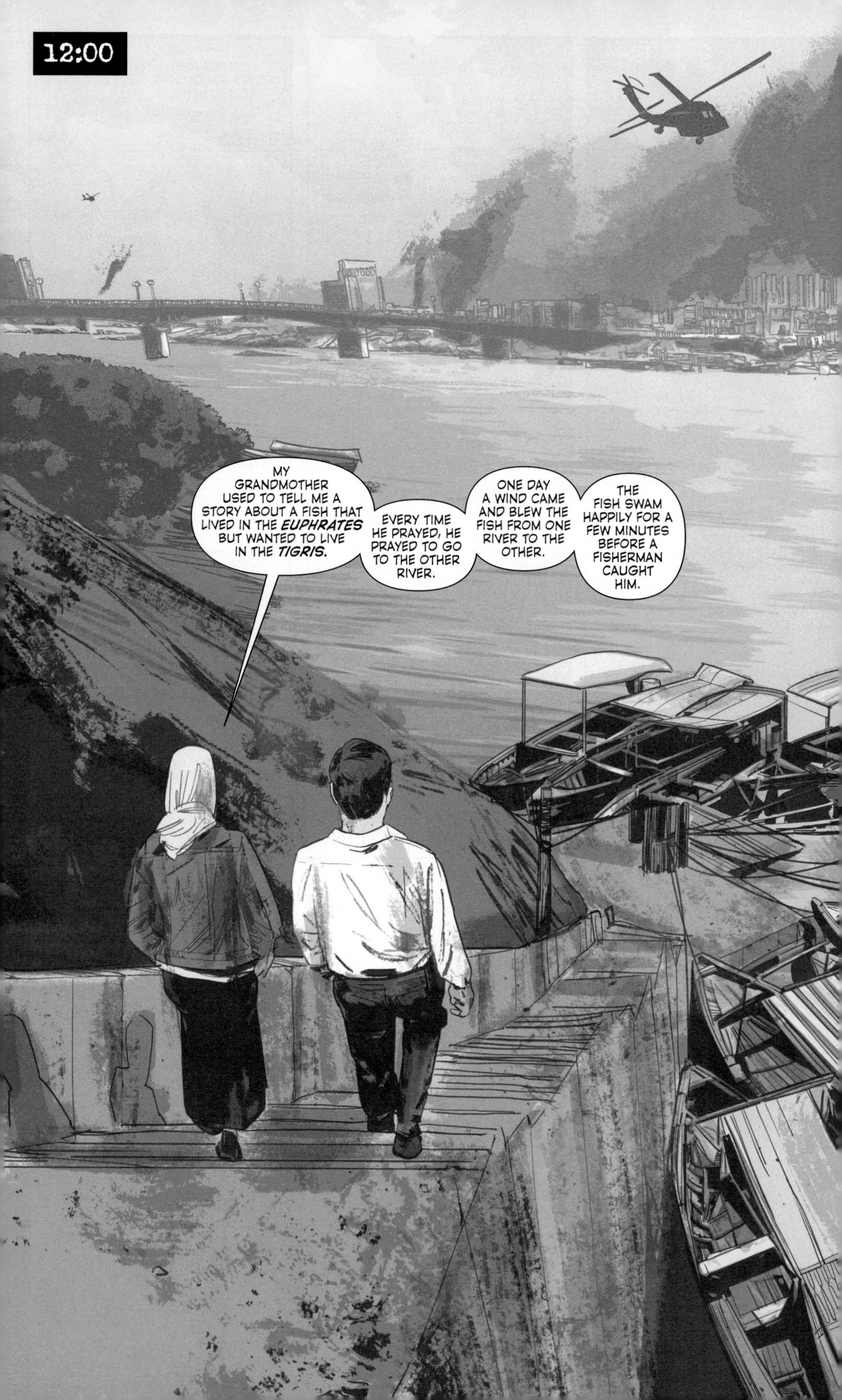
12:00
MY GRANDMOTHER USED TO TELL ME A STORY ABOUT A FISH THAT LIVED IN THE *EUPHRATES* BUT WANTED TO LIVE IN THE *TIGRIS*.
EVERY TIME HE PRAYED, HE PRAYED TO GO TO THE OTHER RIVER.
ONE DAY A WIND CAME AND BLEW THE FISH FROM ONE RIVER TO THE OTHER.
THE FISH SWAM HAPPILY FOR A FEW MINUTES BEFORE A FISHERMAN CAUGHT HIM.

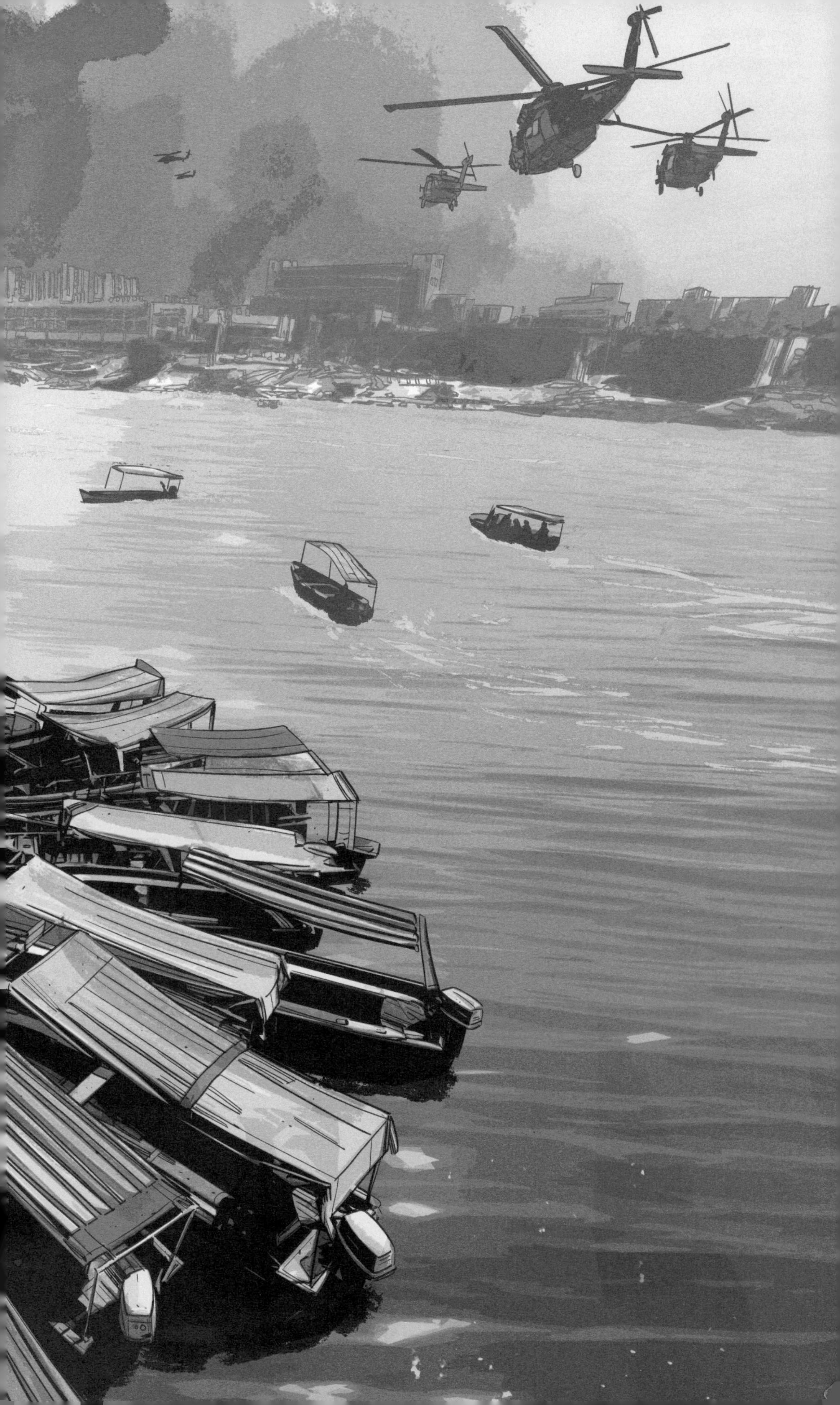

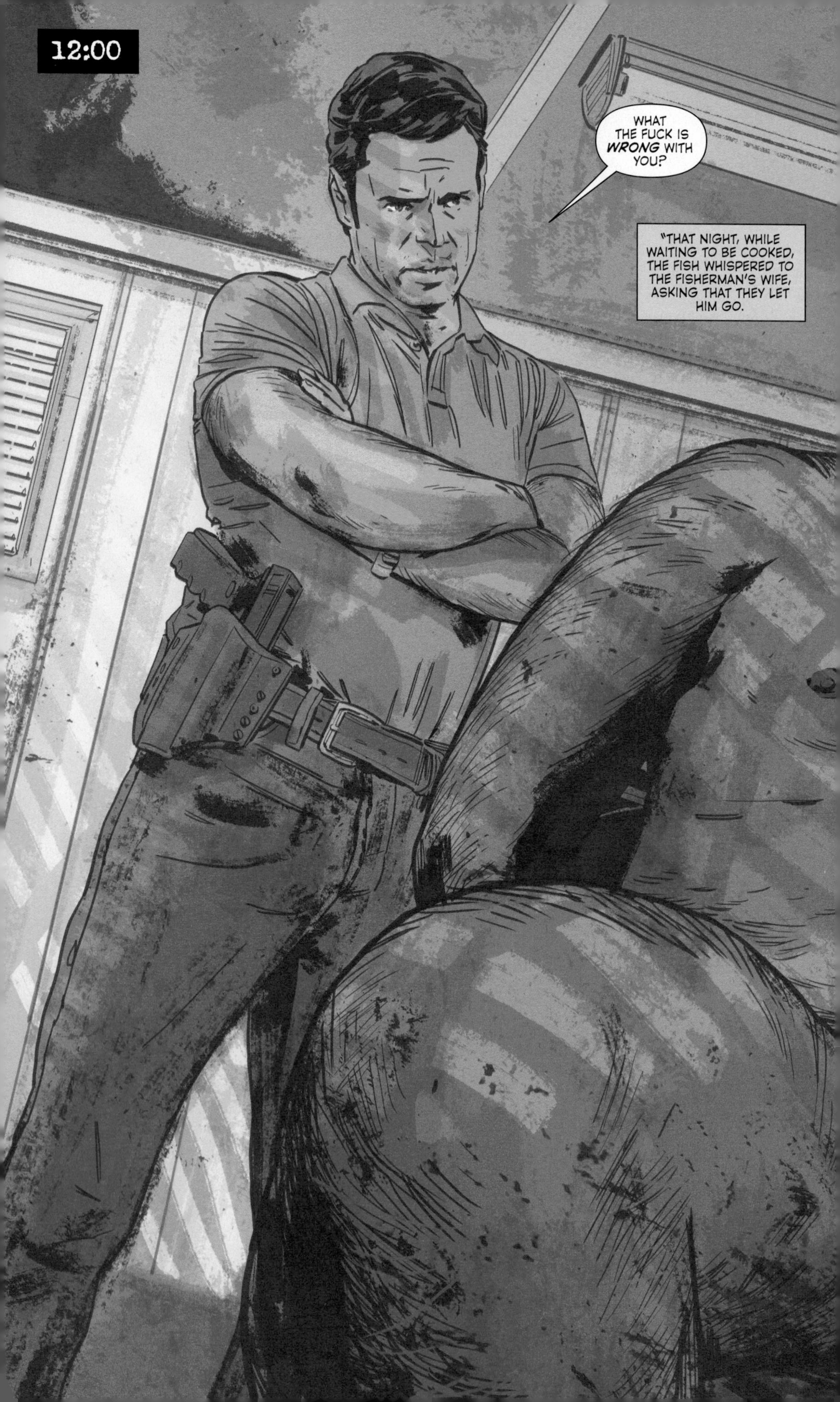
12:00
WHAT THE FUCK IS WRONG WITH YOU?
"THAT NIGHT, WHILE WAITING TO BE COOKED, THE FISH WHISPERED TO THE FISHERMAN'S WIFE, ASKING THAT THEY LET HIM GO.

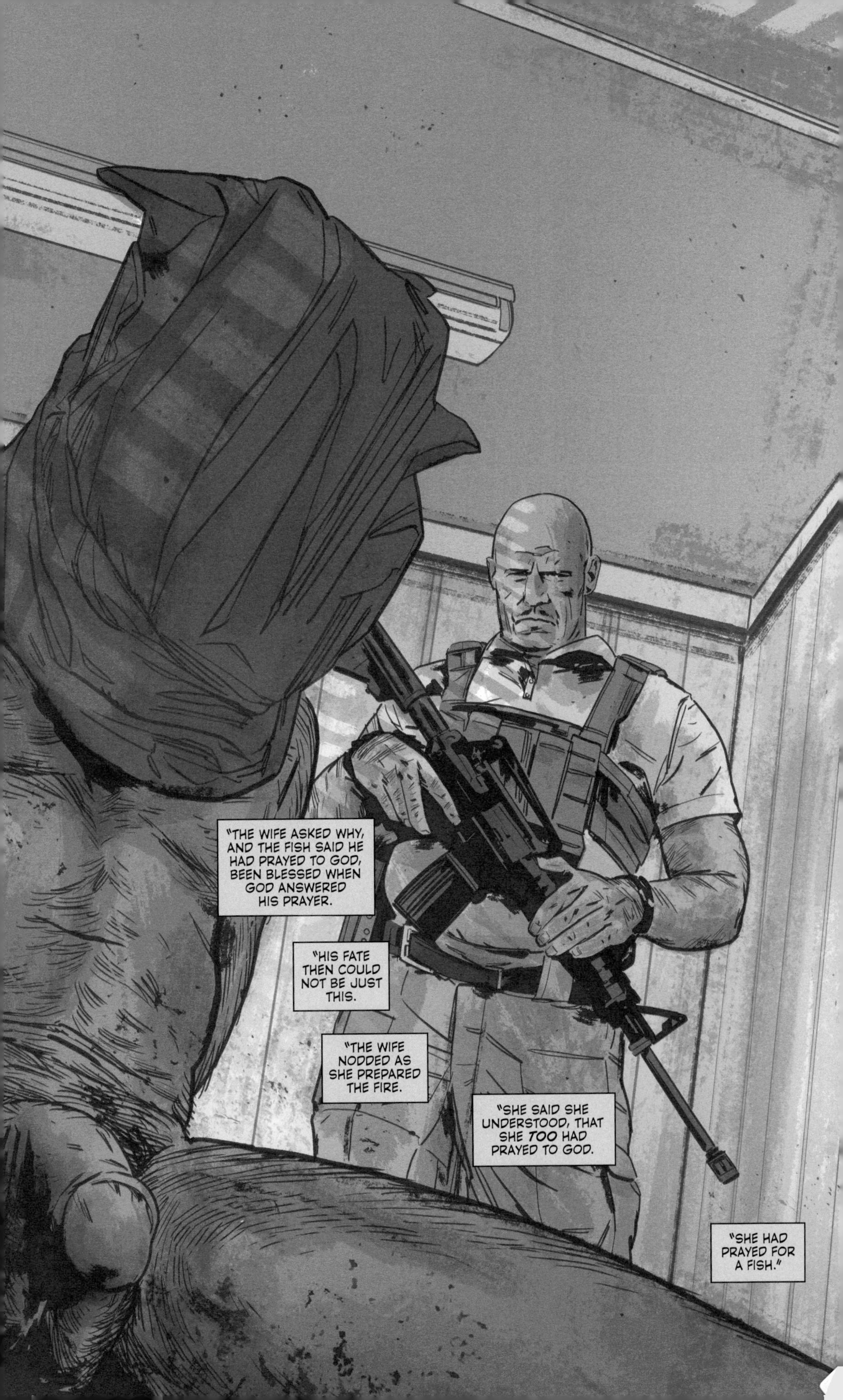
"THE WIFE ASKED WHY, AND THE FISH SAID HE HAD PRAYED TO GOD, BEEN BLESSED WHEN GOD ANSWERED HIS PRAYER.
"HIS FATE THEN COULD NOT BE JUST THIS.
"THE WIFE NODDED AS SHE PREPARED THE FIRE.
"SHE SAID SHE UNDERSTOOD, THAT SHE TOO HAD PRAYED TO GOD.
"SHE HAD PRAYED FOR A FISH."

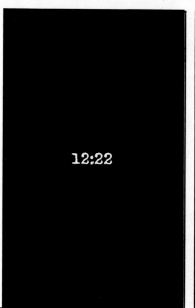

12:22

WE SHOULD TALK ABOUT THIS EXTREMIST, THE ONE YOU REPORTED ON.

WHO KILLED THE POLICE TRAINEE.

"ABU RAHIM."

HE'S WELL KNOWN. AN AMERICAN CIT', ACTUALLY. BUT BORN IN JORDAN.

DAD WORKED FOR *EXXON.* HE MOVED TO AMERICA WHEN HE WAS IN HIS TEENS. LEFT THERE IN THE EARLY '90S.

WHY IS HE HERE?

I DON'T KNOW, WANTS TO BLOW THINGS UP, I GUESS.

AFTER AMERICA, HE GOT HOOKED UP WITH SOME *AL-QA'IDA* KIND OF PEOPLE.

AND THERE'S LOTS OF THINGS FOR HIM TO DO UP HERE. *BLOW UP,* YOU KNOW?

HE DID IT TO YOU.

"I MEAN, HE WAS THE ONE WHO ORDERED THE ATTACK ON YOUR CAR."

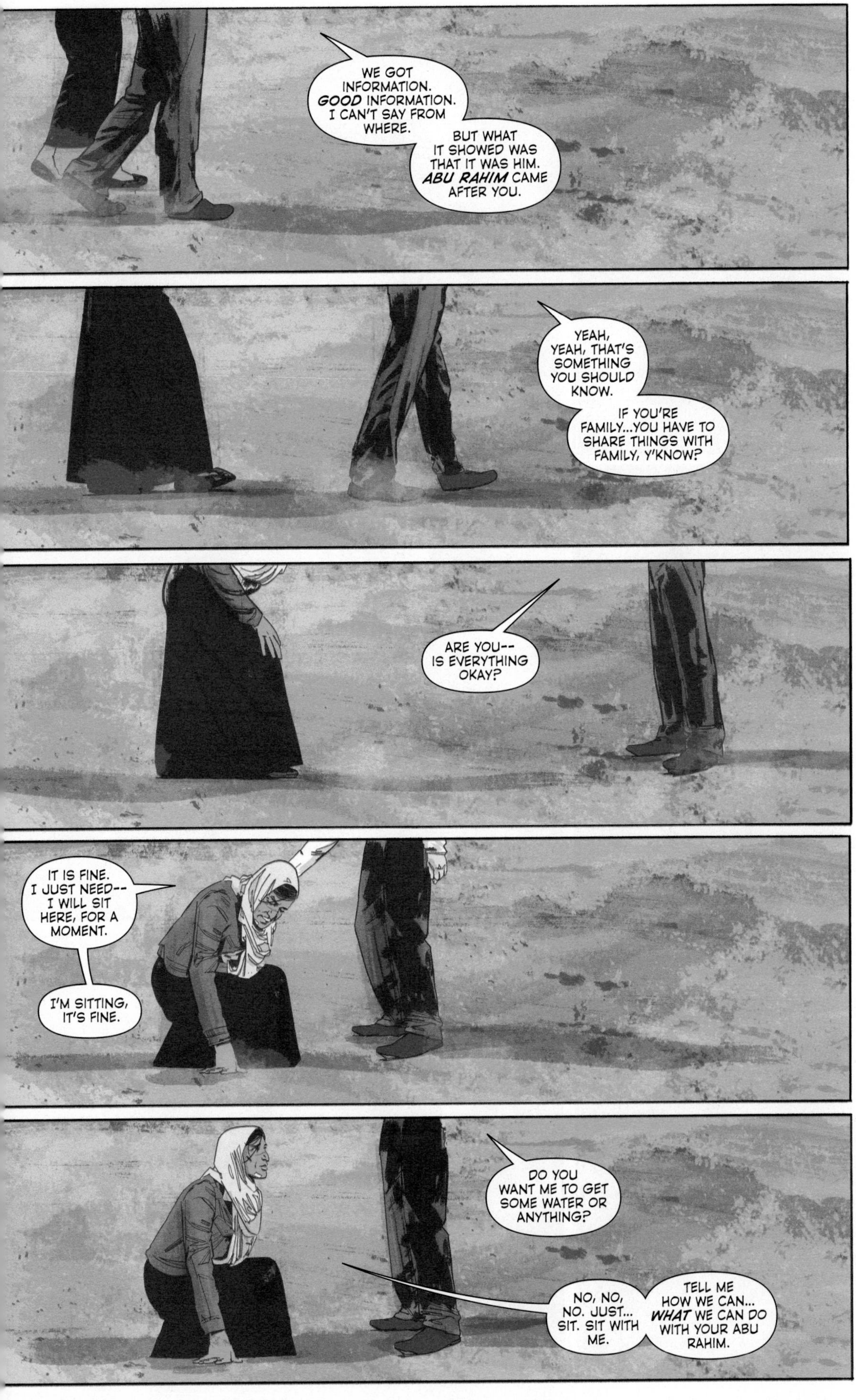
WE GOT INFORMATION. GOOD INFORMATION. I CAN'T SAY FROM WHERE.
BUT WHAT IT SHOWED WAS THAT IT WAS HIM. ABU RAHIM CAME AFTER YOU.
YEAH, YEAH, THAT'S SOMETHING YOU SHOULD KNOW.
IF YOU'RE FAMILY...YOU HAVE TO SHARE THINGS WITH FAMILY, Y'KNOW?
ARE YOU-- IS EVERYTHING OKAY?
IT IS FINE. I JUST NEED-- I WILL SIT HERE, FOR A MOMENT.
I'M SITTING, IT'S FINE.
DO YOU WANT ME TO GET SOME WATER OR ANYTHING?
NO, NO, NO. JUST... SIT. SIT WITH ME.
TELL ME HOW WE CAN... WHAT WE CAN DO WITH YOUR ABU RAHIM.

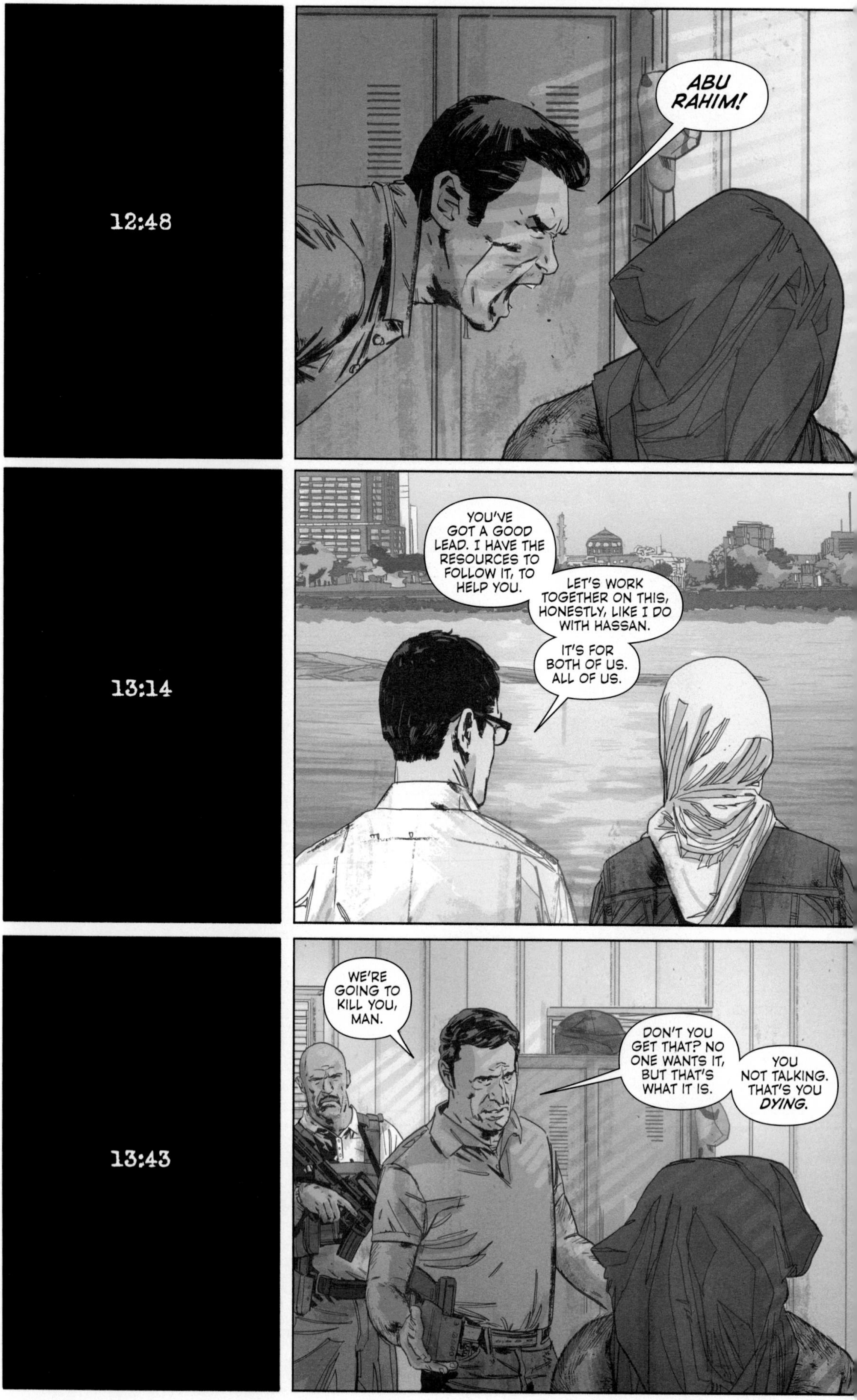
12:48
ABU RAHIM!
13:14
YOU'VE GOT A GOOD LEAD. I HAVE THE RESOURCES TO FOLLOW IT, TO HELP YOU.
LET'S WORK TOGETHER ON THIS, HONESTLY, LIKE I DO WITH HASSAN.
IT'S FOR BOTH OF US. ALL OF US.
13:43
WE'RE GOING TO KILL YOU, MAN.
DON'T YOU GET THAT? NO ONE WANTS IT, BUT THAT'S WHAT IT IS.
YOU NOT TALKING. THAT'S YOU *DYING.*

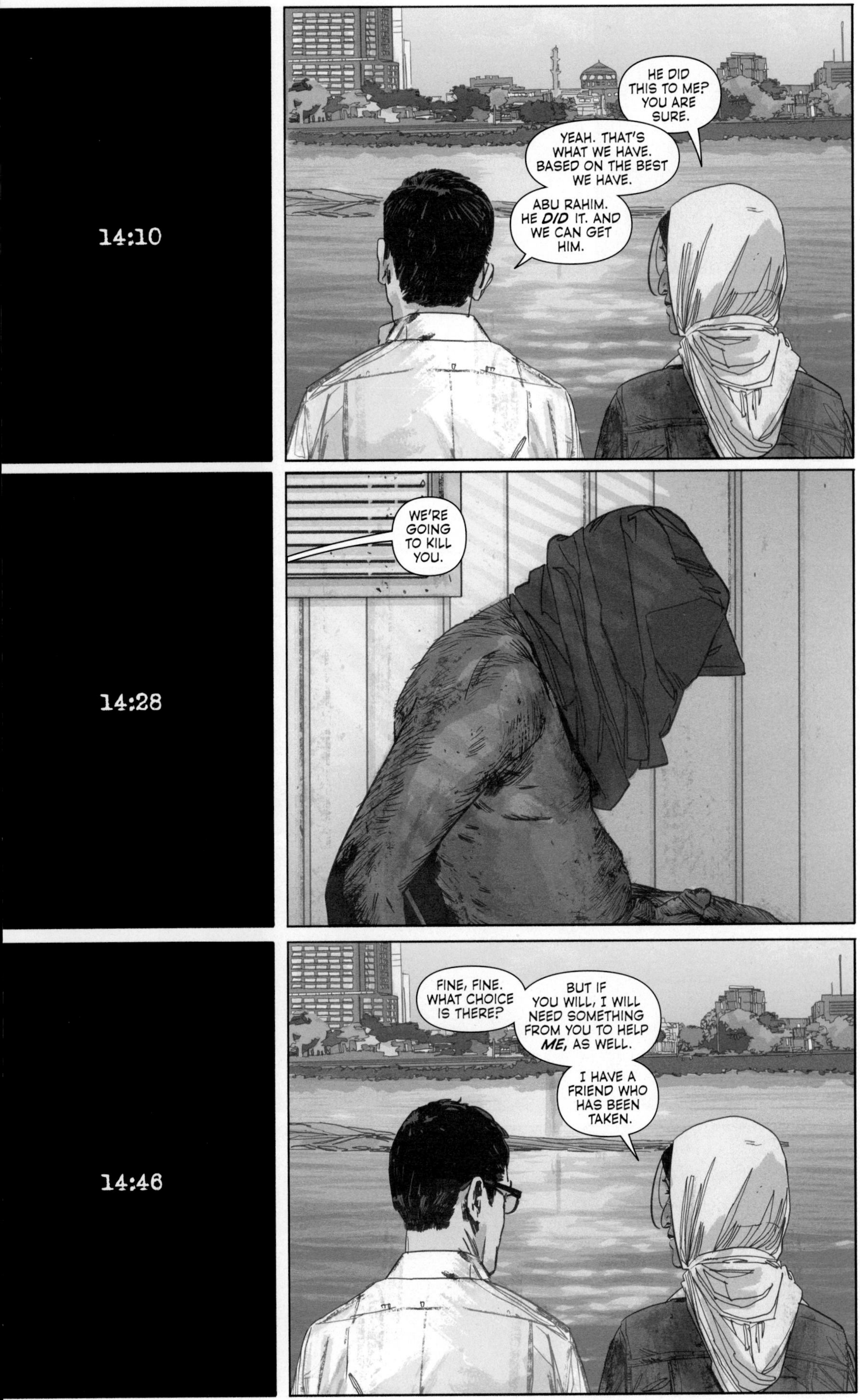
14:10
HE DID THIS TO ME? YOU ARE SURE.
YEAH. THAT'S WHAT WE HAVE. BASED ON THE BEST WE HAVE.
ABU RAHIM. HE *DID* IT. AND WE CAN GET HIM.
14:28
WE'RE GOING TO KILL YOU.
14:46
FINE, FINE. WHAT CHOICE IS THERE?
BUT IF YOU WILL, I WILL NEED SOMETHING FROM YOU TO HELP *ME,* AS WELL.
I HAVE A FRIEND WHO HAS BEEN TAKEN.

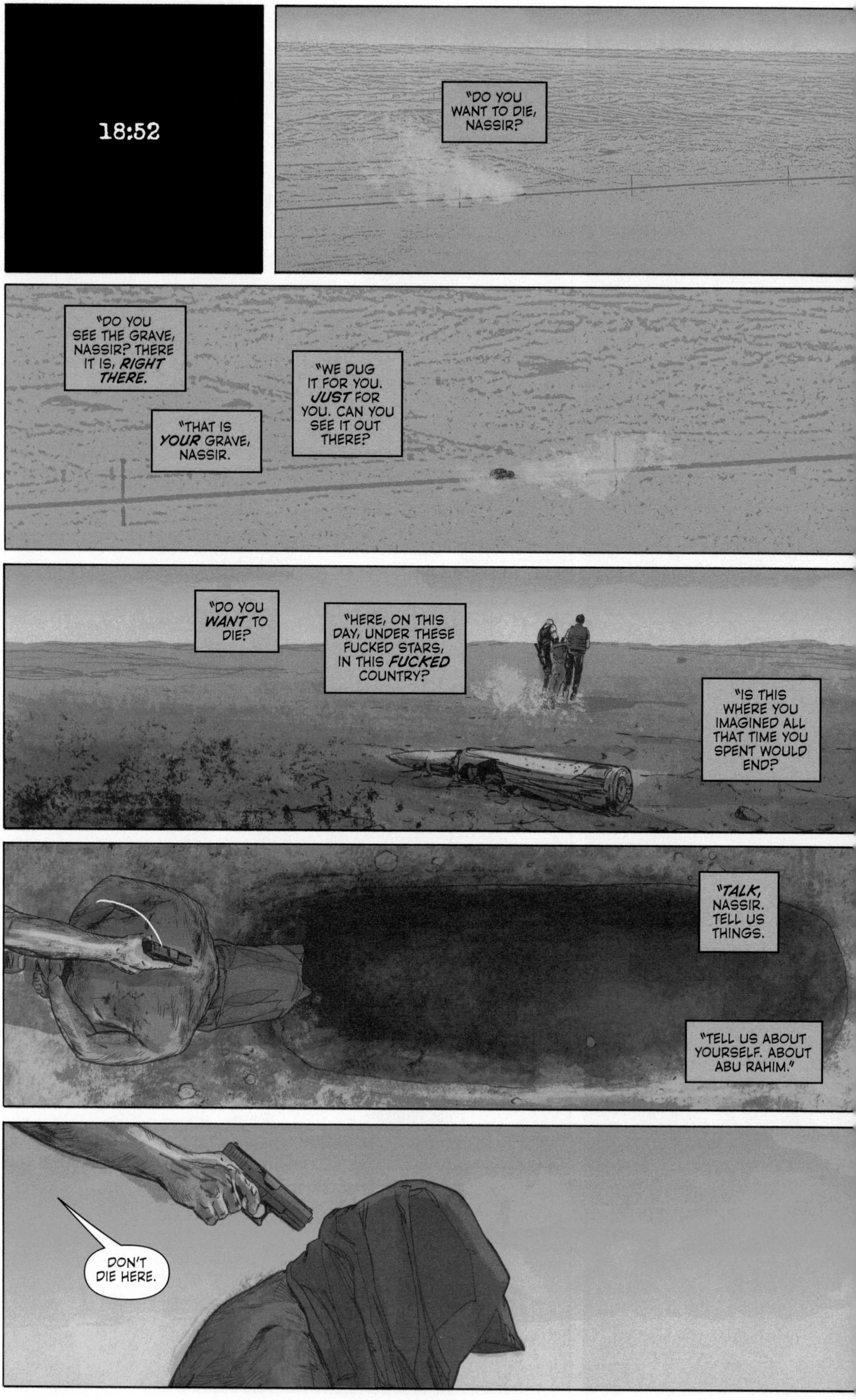
18:52
"DO YOU WANT TO DIE, NASSIR?
"DO YOU SEE THE GRAVE, NASSIR? THERE IT IS, RIGHT THERE.
"THAT IS YOUR GRAVE, NASSIR.
"WE DUG IT FOR YOU. JUST FOR YOU. CAN YOU SEE IT OUT THERE?
"DO YOU WANT TO DIE?
"HERE, ON THIS DAY, UNDER THESE FUCKED STARS, IN THIS FUCKED COUNTRY?
"IS THIS WHERE YOU IMAGINED ALL THAT TIME YOU SPENT WOULD END?
"TALK, NASSIR. TELL US THINGS.
"TELL US ABOUT YOURSELF. ABOUT ABU RAHIM."
DON'T DIE HERE.

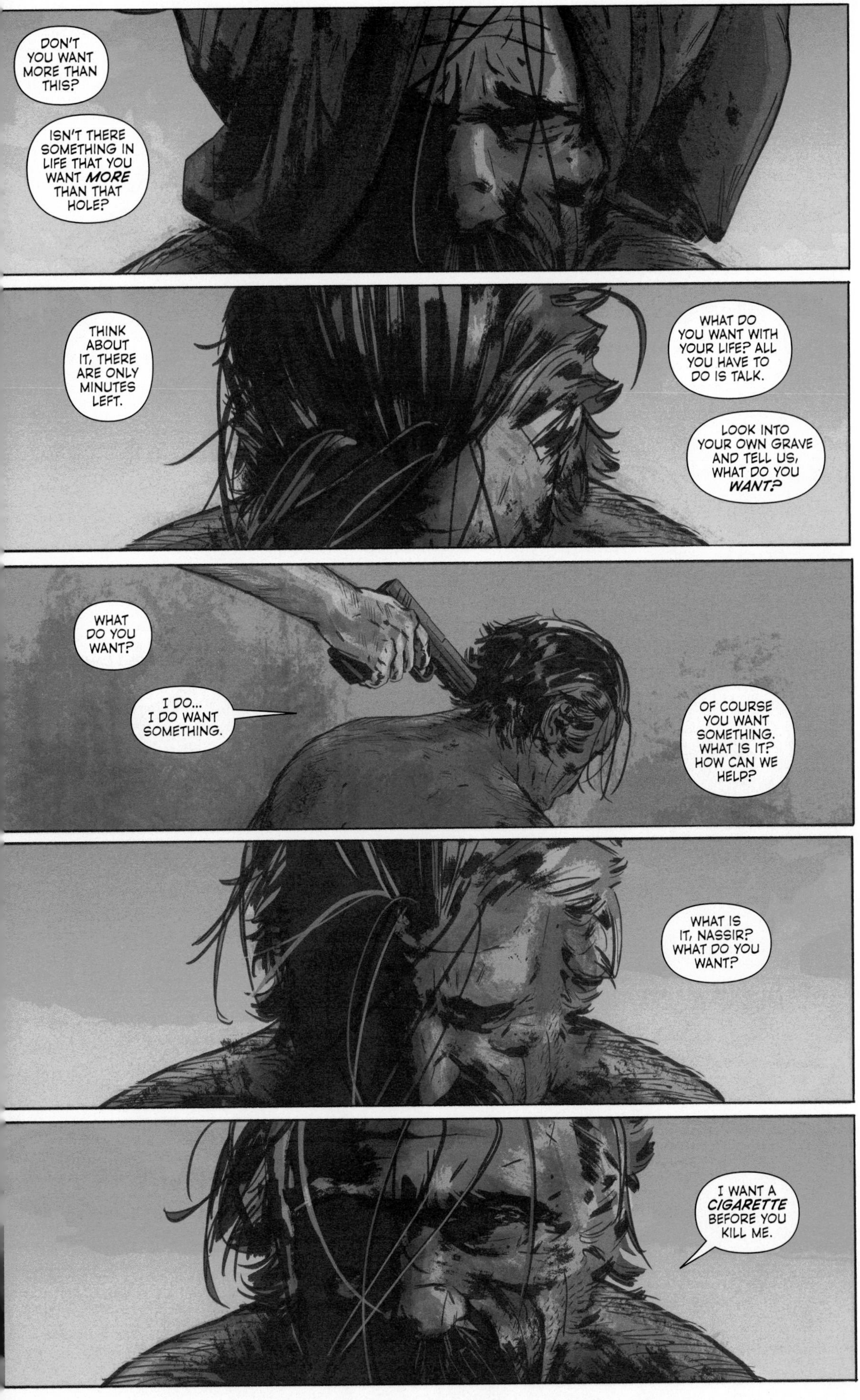
DON'T YOU WANT MORE THAN THIS?
ISN'T THERE SOMETHING IN LIFE THAT YOU WANT *MORE* THAN THAT HOLE?
THINK ABOUT IT, THERE ARE ONLY MINUTES LEFT.
WHAT DO YOU WANT WITH YOUR LIFE? ALL YOU HAVE TO DO IS TALK.
LOOK INTO YOUR OWN GRAVE AND TELL US, WHAT DO YOU *WANT?*
WHAT DO YOU WANT?
I DO... I DO WANT SOMETHING.
OF COURSE YOU WANT SOMETHING. WHAT IS IT? HOW CAN WE HELP?
WHAT IS IT, NASSIR? WHAT DO YOU WANT?
I WANT A *CIGARETTE* BEFORE YOU KILL ME.

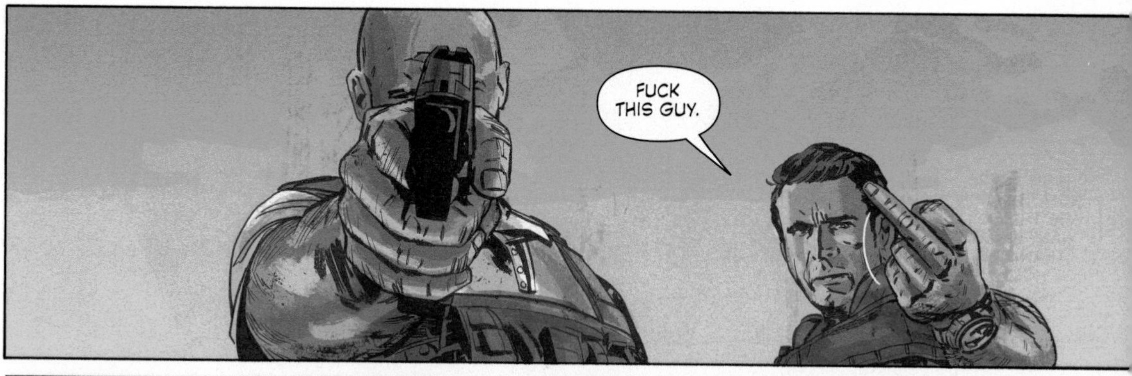
FUCK THIS GUY.

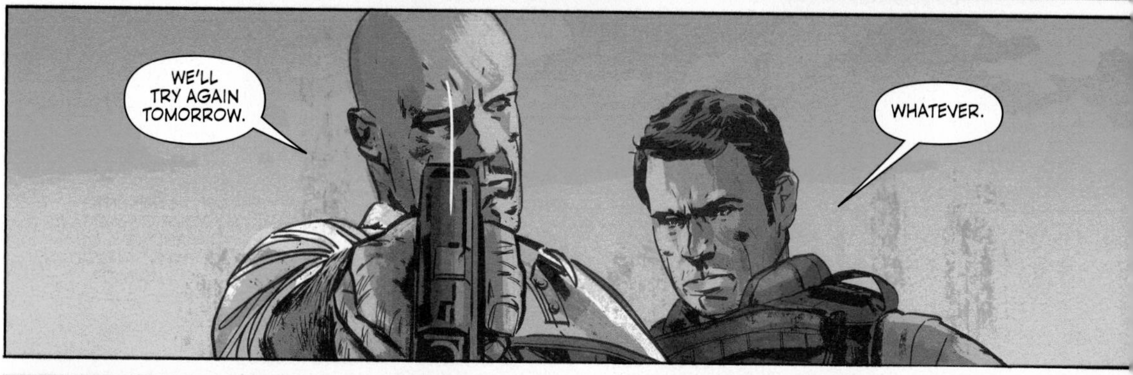
WE'LL TRY AGAIN TOMORROW.
WHATEVER.

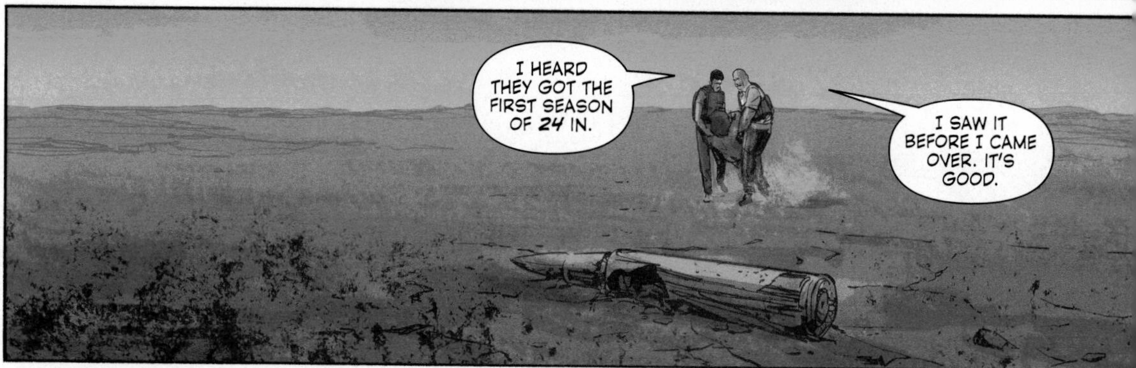
I HEARD THEY GOT THE FIRST SEASON OF 24 IN.
I SAW IT BEFORE I CAME OVER. IT'S GOOD.

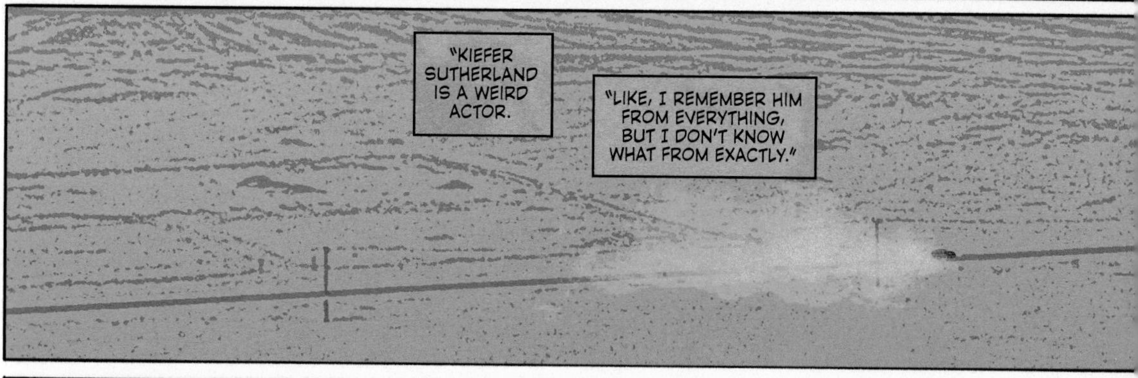
"KIEFER SUTHERLAND IS A WEIRD ACTOR.
"LIKE, I REMEMBER HIM FROM EVERYTHING, BUT I DON'T KNOW WHAT FROM EXACTLY."

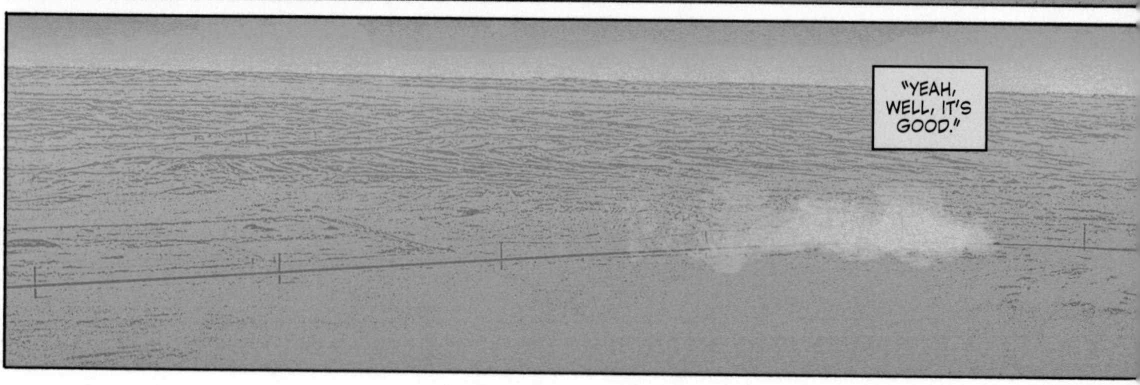
"YEAH, WELL, IT'S GOOD."

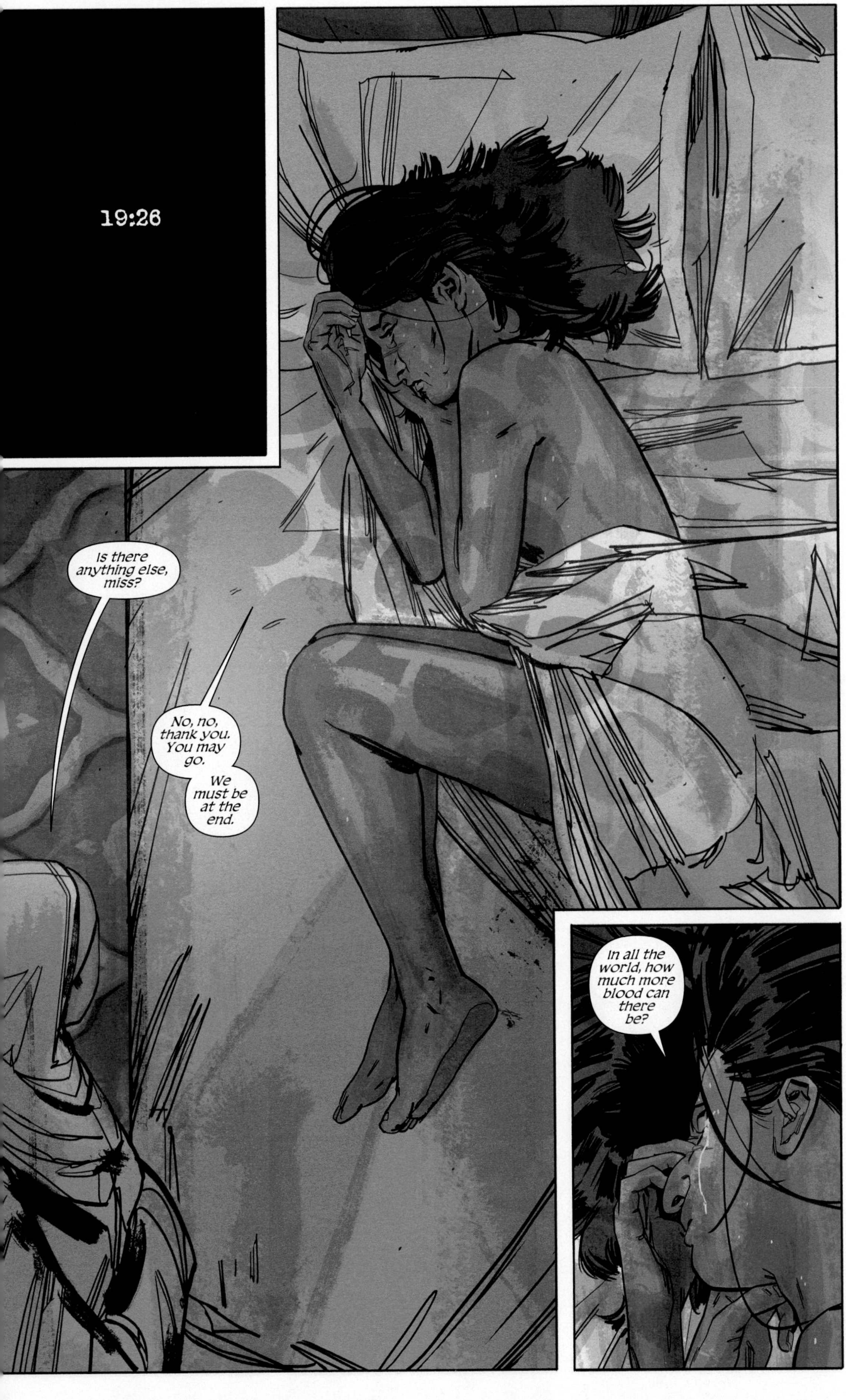
19:26
Is there anything else, miss?
No, no, thank you. You may go.
We must be at the end.
In all the world, how much more blood can there be?

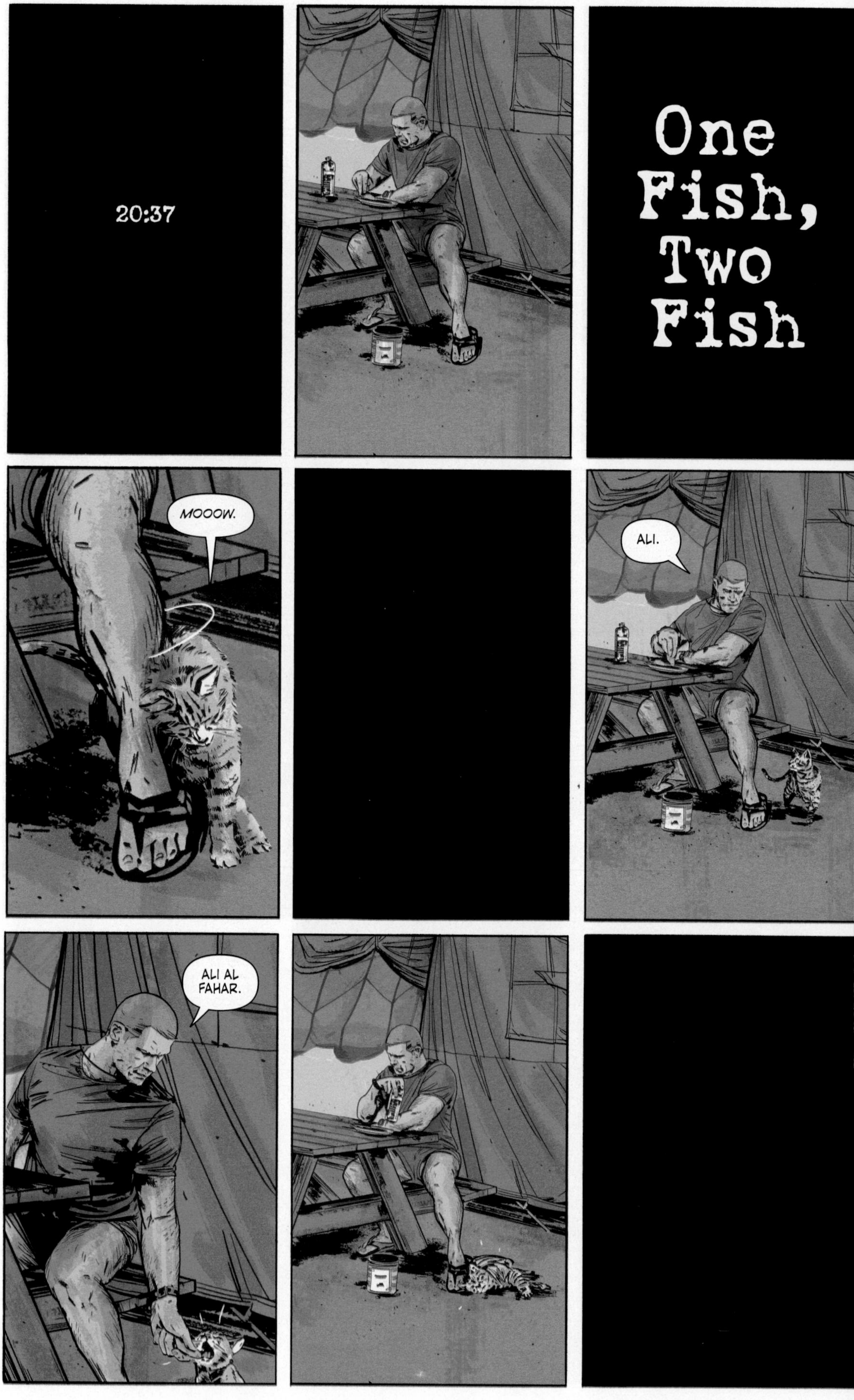
20:37
One Fish, Two Fish
MOOOW.
ALI.
ALI AL FAHAR.

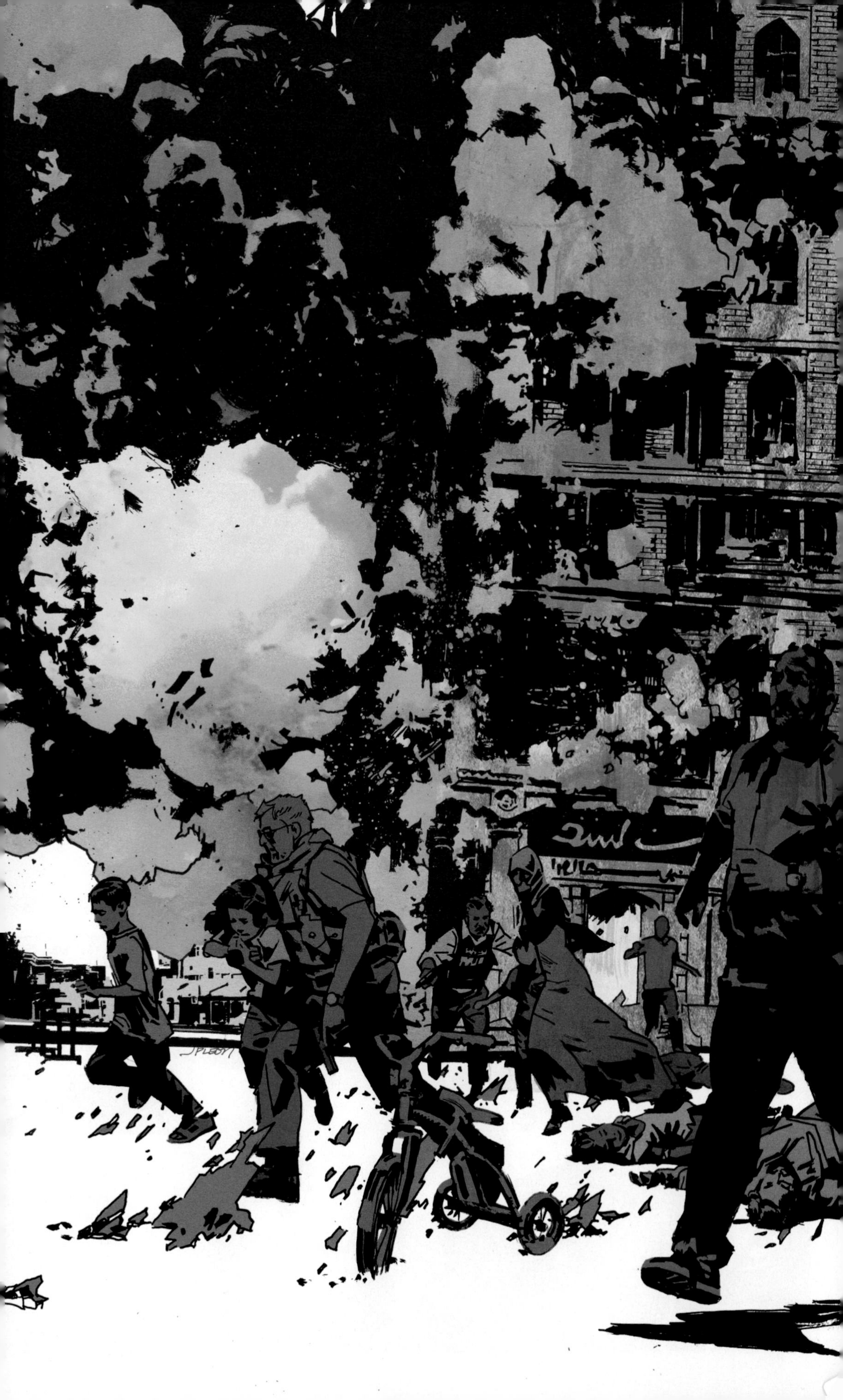

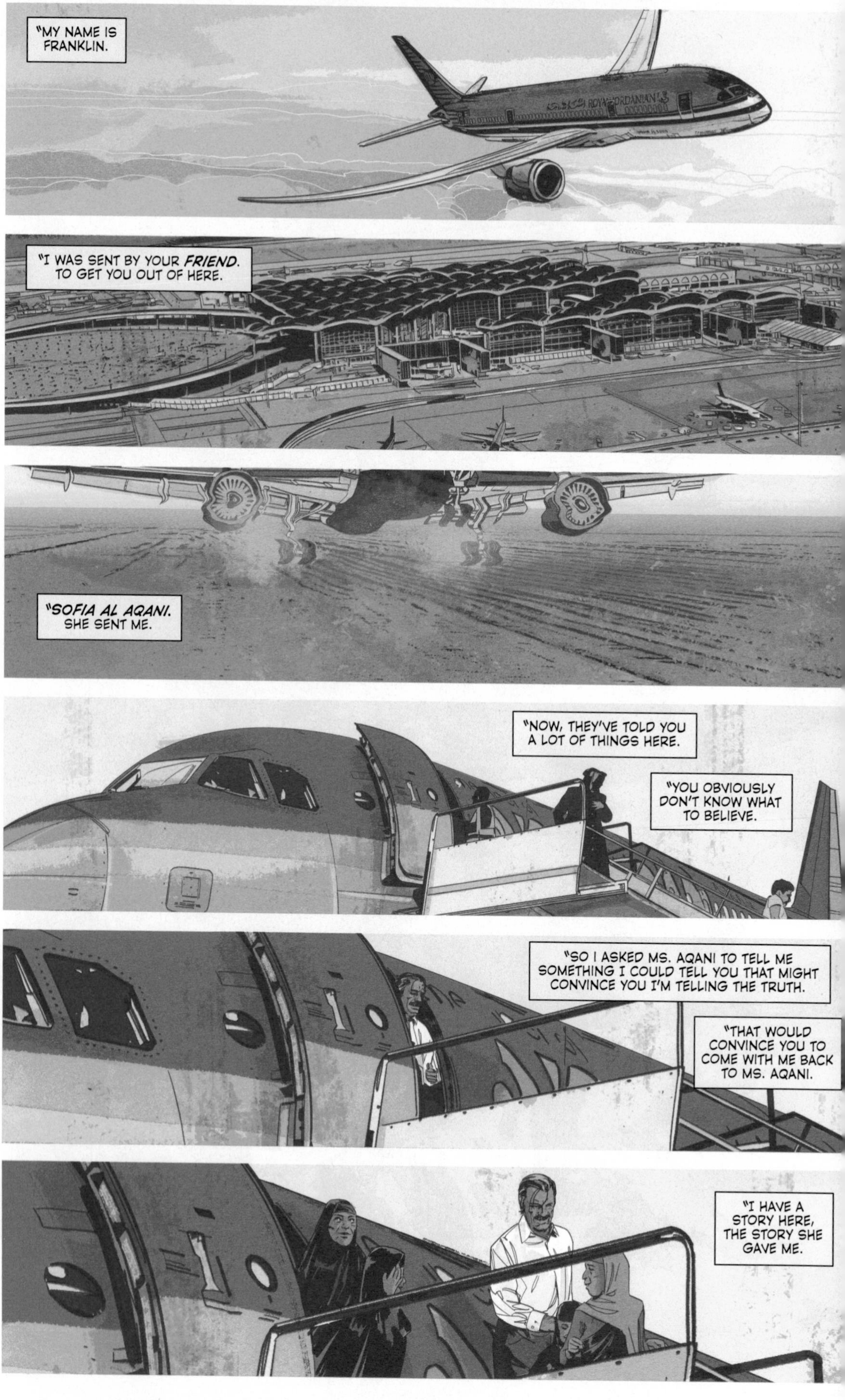
"MY NAME IS FRANKLIN.
ROYAL JORDANIAN
"I WAS SENT BY YOUR *FRIEND*. TO GET YOU OUT OF HERE.
"*SOFIA AL AQANI.* SHE SENT ME.
"NOW, THEY'VE TOLD YOU A LOT OF THINGS HERE.
"YOU OBVIOUSLY DON'T KNOW WHAT TO BELIEVE.
"SO I ASKED MS. AQANI TO TELL ME SOMETHING I COULD TELL YOU THAT MIGHT CONVINCE YOU I'M TELLING THE TRUTH.
"THAT WOULD CONVINCE YOU TO COME WITH ME BACK TO MS. AQANI.
"I HAVE A STORY HERE, THE STORY SHE GAVE ME.

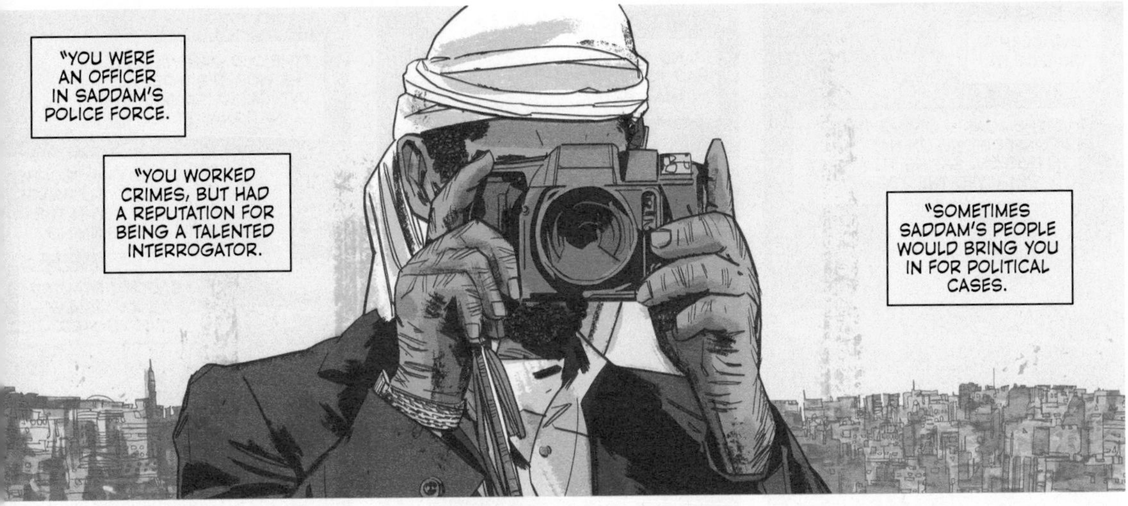
"YOU WERE AN OFFICER IN SADDAM'S POLICE FORCE.
"YOU WORKED CRIMES, BUT HAD A REPUTATION FOR BEING A TALENTED INTERROGATOR.
"SOMETIMES SADDAM'S PEOPLE WOULD BRING YOU IN FOR POLITICAL CASES.

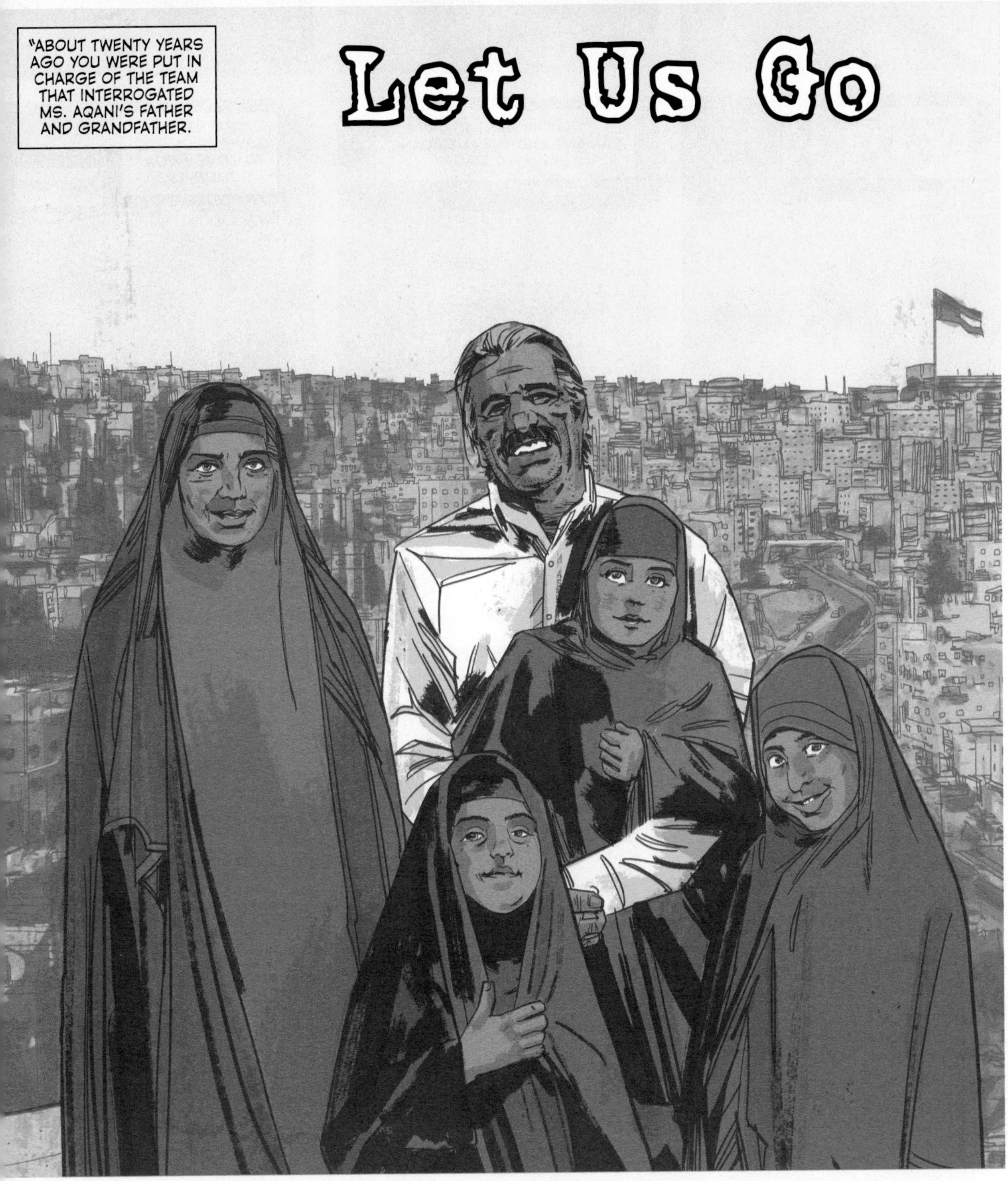
"ABOUT TWENTY YEARS AGO YOU WERE PUT IN CHARGE OF THE TEAM THAT INTERROGATED MS. AQANI'S FATHER AND GRANDFATHER.
Let Us Go

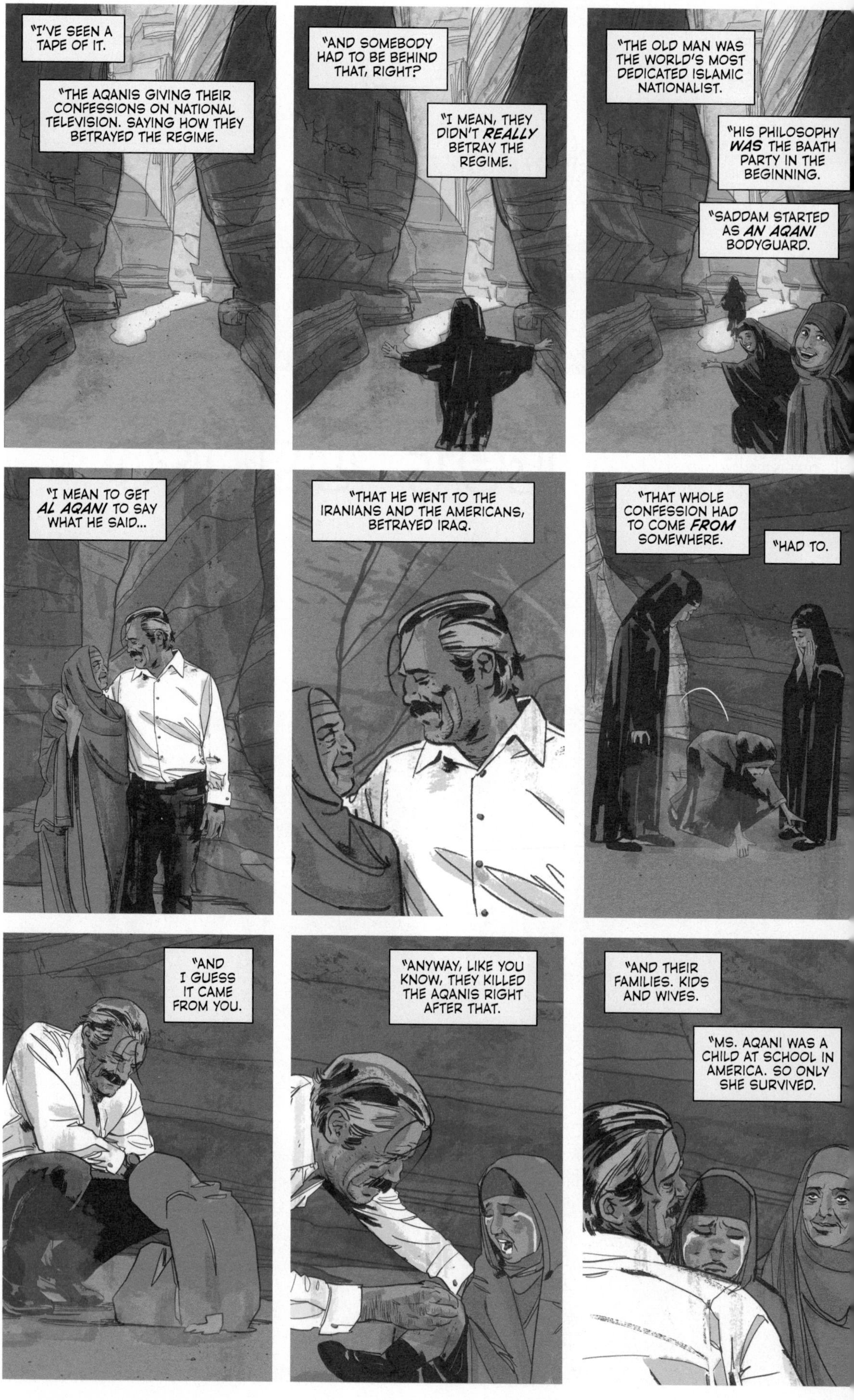
"I'VE SEEN A TAPE OF IT.
"THE AQANIS GIVING THEIR CONFESSIONS ON NATIONAL TELEVISION. SAYING HOW THEY BETRAYED THE REGIME.
"AND SOMEBODY HAD TO BE BEHIND THAT, RIGHT?
"I MEAN, THEY DIDN'T *REALLY* BETRAY THE REGIME.
"THE OLD MAN WAS THE WORLD'S MOST DEDICATED ISLAMIC NATIONALIST.
"HIS PHILOSOPHY *WAS* THE BAATH PARTY IN THE BEGINNING.
"SADDAM STARTED AS *AN AQANI* BODYGUARD.
"I MEAN TO GET *AL AQANI* TO SAY WHAT HE SAID...
"THAT HE WENT TO THE IRANIANS AND THE AMERICANS, BETRAYED IRAQ.
"THAT WHOLE CONFESSION HAD TO COME *FROM* SOMEWHERE.
"HAD TO.
"AND I GUESS IT CAME FROM YOU.
"ANYWAY, LIKE YOU KNOW, THEY KILLED THE AQANIS RIGHT AFTER THAT.
"AND THEIR FAMILIES. KIDS AND WIVES.
"MS. AQANI WAS A CHILD AT SCHOOL IN AMERICA. SO ONLY SHE SURVIVED.

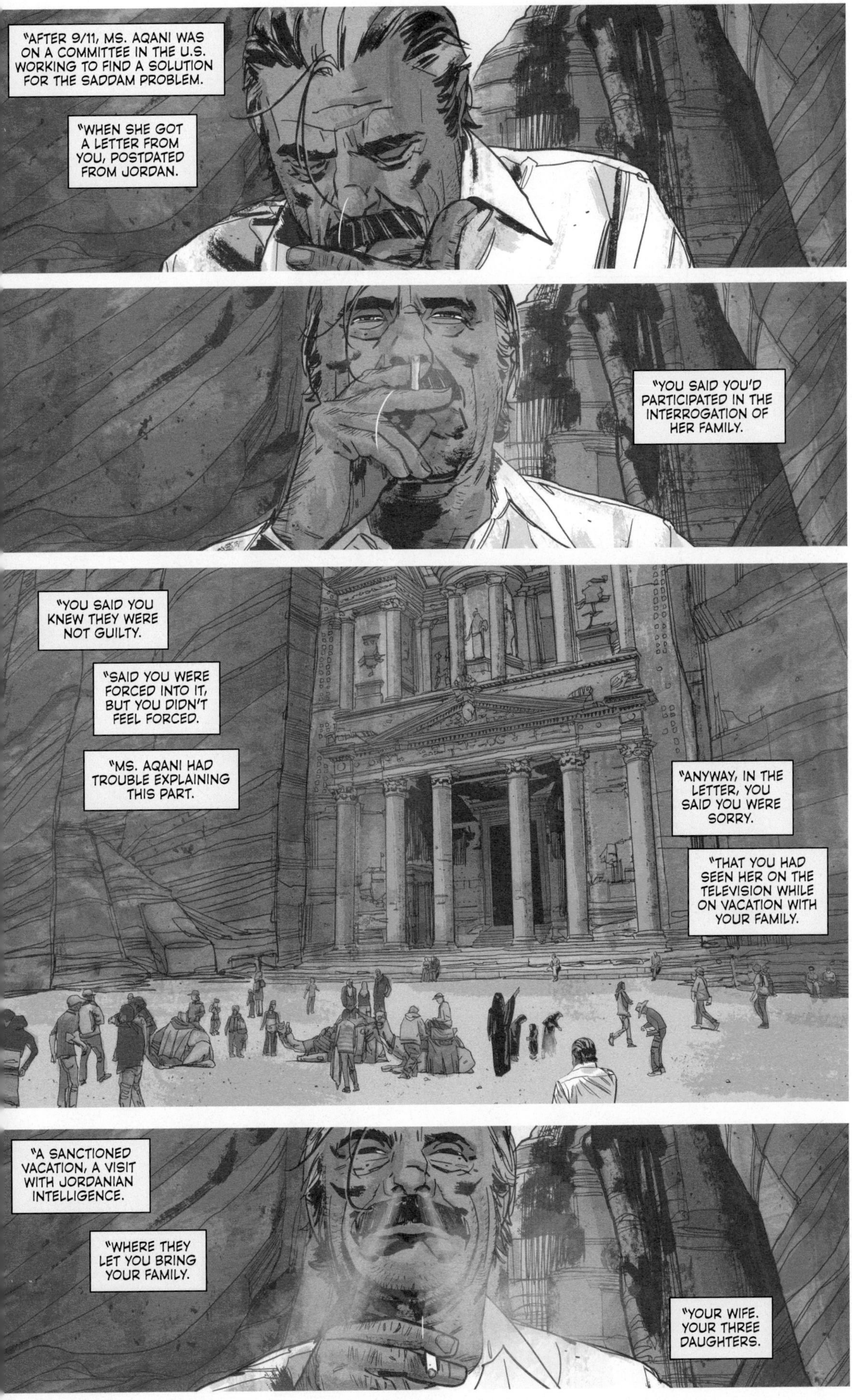
"AFTER 9/11, MS. AQANI WAS ON A COMMITTEE IN THE U.S. WORKING TO FIND A SOLUTION FOR THE SADDAM PROBLEM.
"WHEN SHE GOT A LETTER FROM YOU, POSTDATED FROM JORDAN.
"YOU SAID YOU'D PARTICIPATED IN THE INTERROGATION OF HER FAMILY.
"YOU SAID YOU KNEW THEY WERE NOT GUILTY.
"SAID YOU WERE FORCED INTO IT, BUT YOU DIDN'T FEEL FORCED.
"MS. AQANI HAD TROUBLE EXPLAINING THIS PART.
"ANYWAY, IN THE LETTER, YOU SAID YOU WERE SORRY.
"THAT YOU HAD SEEN HER ON THE TELEVISION WHILE ON VACATION WITH YOUR FAMILY.
"A SANCTIONED VACATION, A VISIT WITH JORDANIAN INTELLIGENCE.
"WHERE THEY LET YOU BRING YOUR FAMILY.
"YOUR WIFE. YOUR THREE DAUGHTERS.

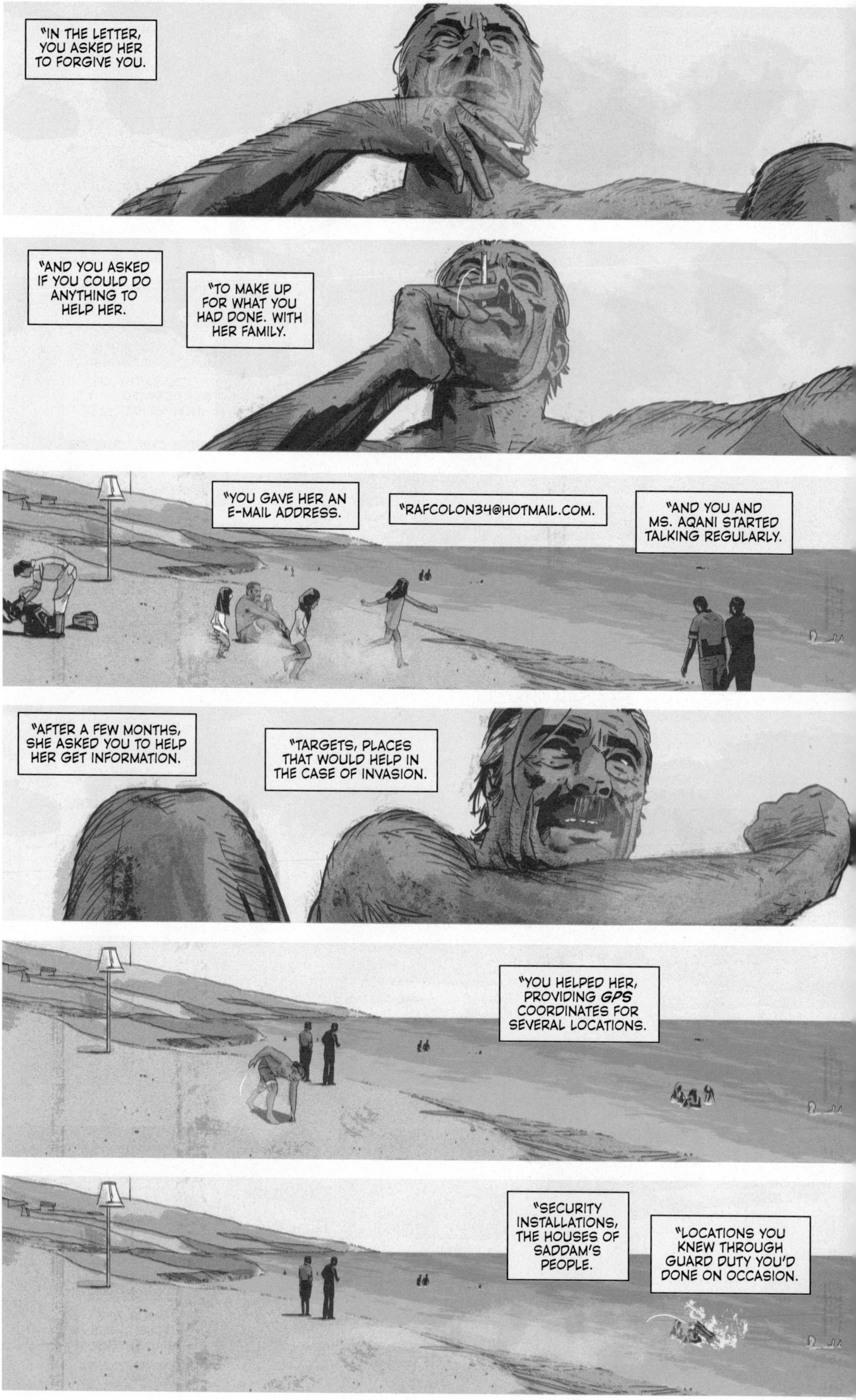
"IN THE LETTER, YOU ASKED HER TO FORGIVE YOU.
"AND YOU ASKED IF YOU COULD DO ANYTHING TO HELP HER.
"TO MAKE UP FOR WHAT YOU HAD DONE. WITH HER FAMILY.
"YOU GAVE HER AN E-MAIL ADDRESS.
"RAFCOLON34@HOTMAIL.COM.
"AND YOU AND MS. AQANI STARTED TALKING REGULARLY.
"AFTER A FEW MONTHS, SHE ASKED YOU TO HELP HER GET INFORMATION.
"TARGETS, PLACES THAT WOULD HELP IN THE CASE OF INVASION.
"YOU HELPED HER, PROVIDING GPS COORDINATES FOR SEVERAL LOCATIONS.
"SECURITY INSTALLATIONS, THE HOUSES OF SADDAM'S PEOPLE.
"LOCATIONS YOU KNEW THROUGH GUARD DUTY YOU'D DONE ON OCCASION.

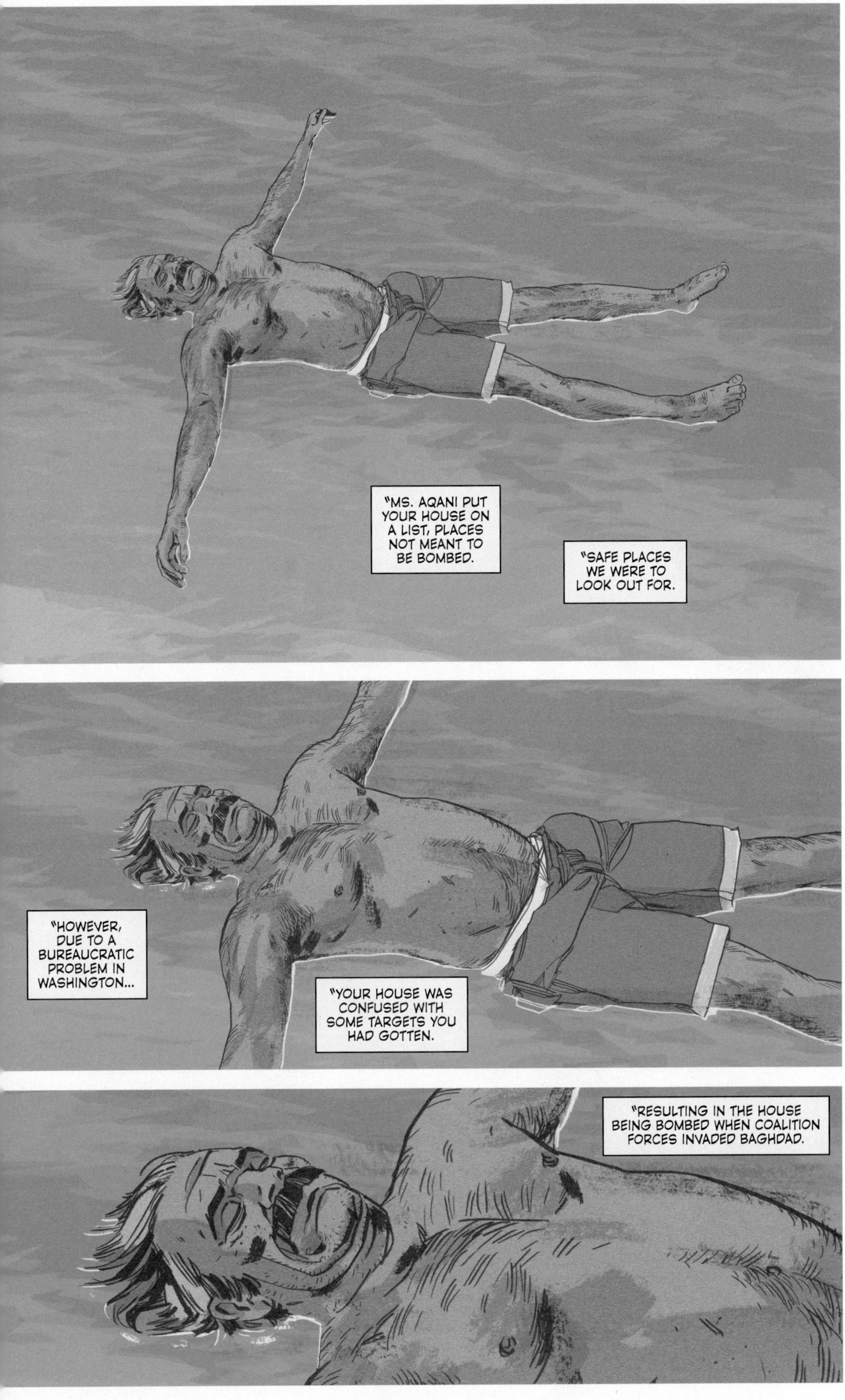
"MS. AQANI PUT YOUR HOUSE ON A LIST, PLACES NOT MEANT TO BE BOMBED.
"SAFE PLACES WE WERE TO LOOK OUT FOR.
"HOWEVER, DUE TO A BUREAUCRATIC PROBLEM IN WASHINGTON...
"YOUR HOUSE WAS CONFUSED WITH SOME TARGETS YOU HAD GOTTEN.
"RESULTING IN THE HOUSE BEING BOMBED WHEN COALITION FORCES INVADED BAGHDAD.

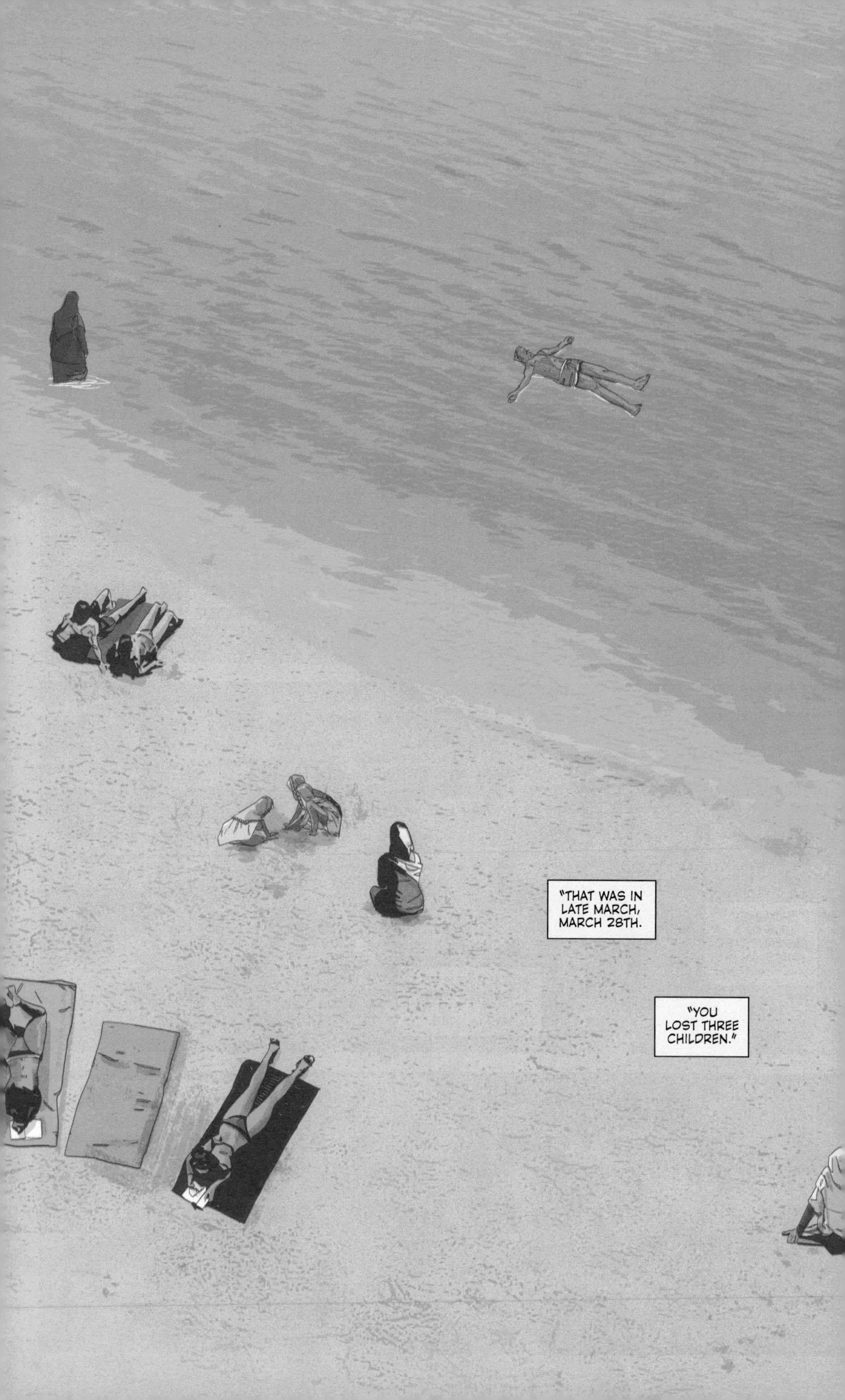
"THAT WAS IN LATE MARCH, MARCH 28TH.
"YOU LOST THREE CHILDREN."

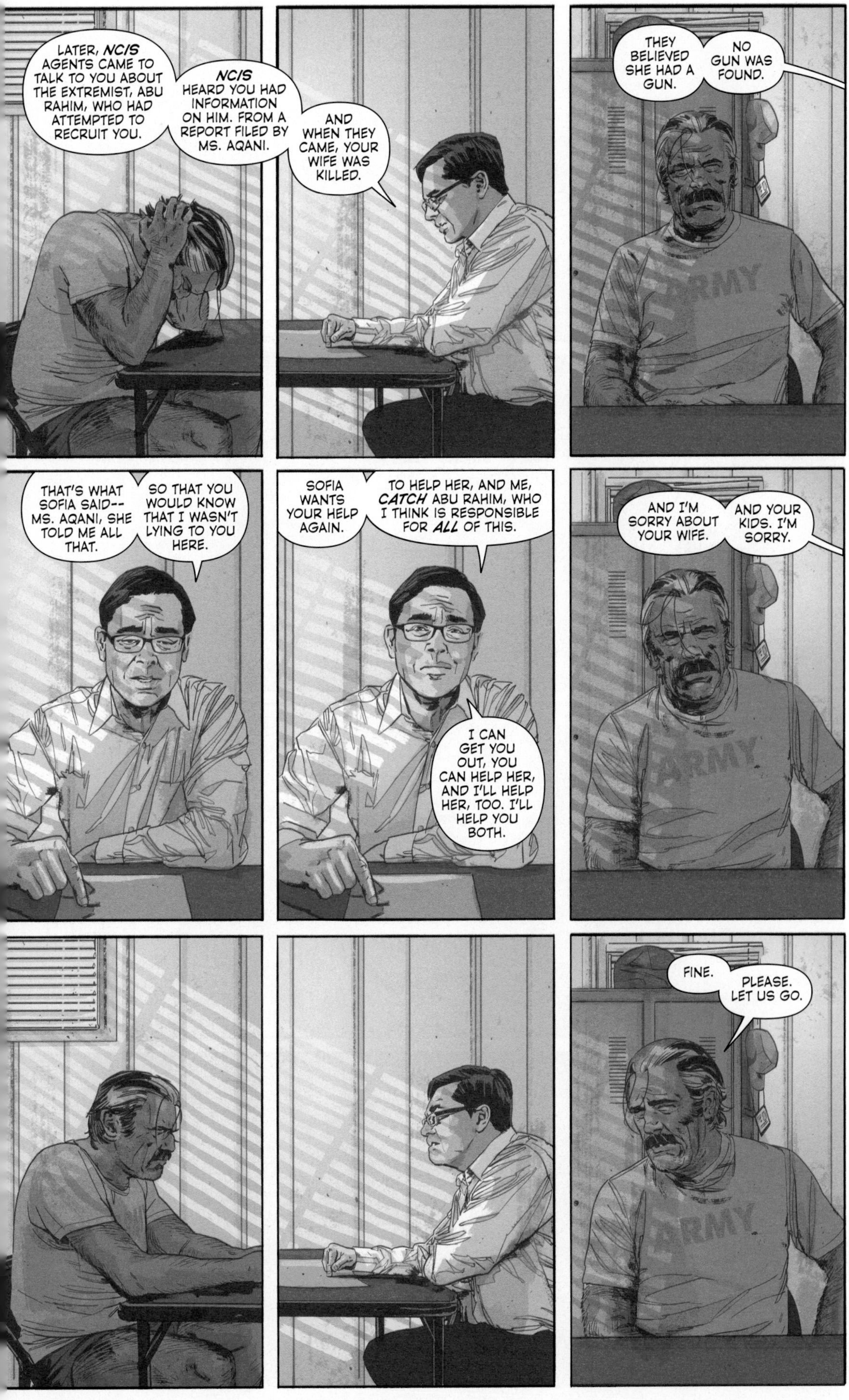
LATER, NCIS AGENTS CAME TO TALK TO YOU ABOUT THE EXTREMIST, ABU RAHIM, WHO HAD ATTEMPTED TO RECRUIT YOU.
NCIS HEARD YOU HAD INFORMATION ON HIM. FROM A REPORT FILED BY MS. AQANI.
AND WHEN THEY CAME, YOUR WIFE WAS KILLED.
THEY BELIEVED SHE HAD A GUN.
NO GUN WAS FOUND.
THAT'S WHAT SOFIA SAID-- MS. AQANI, SHE TOLD ME ALL THAT.
SO THAT YOU WOULD KNOW THAT I WASN'T LYING TO YOU HERE.
SOFIA WANTS YOUR HELP AGAIN.
TO HELP HER, AND ME, CATCH ABU RAHIM, WHO I THINK IS RESPONSIBLE FOR ALL OF THIS.
I CAN GET YOU OUT, YOU CAN HELP HER, AND I'LL HELP HER, TOO. I'LL HELP YOU BOTH.
AND I'M SORRY ABOUT YOUR WIFE.
AND YOUR KIDS. I'M SORRY.
FINE.
PLEASE. LET US GO.

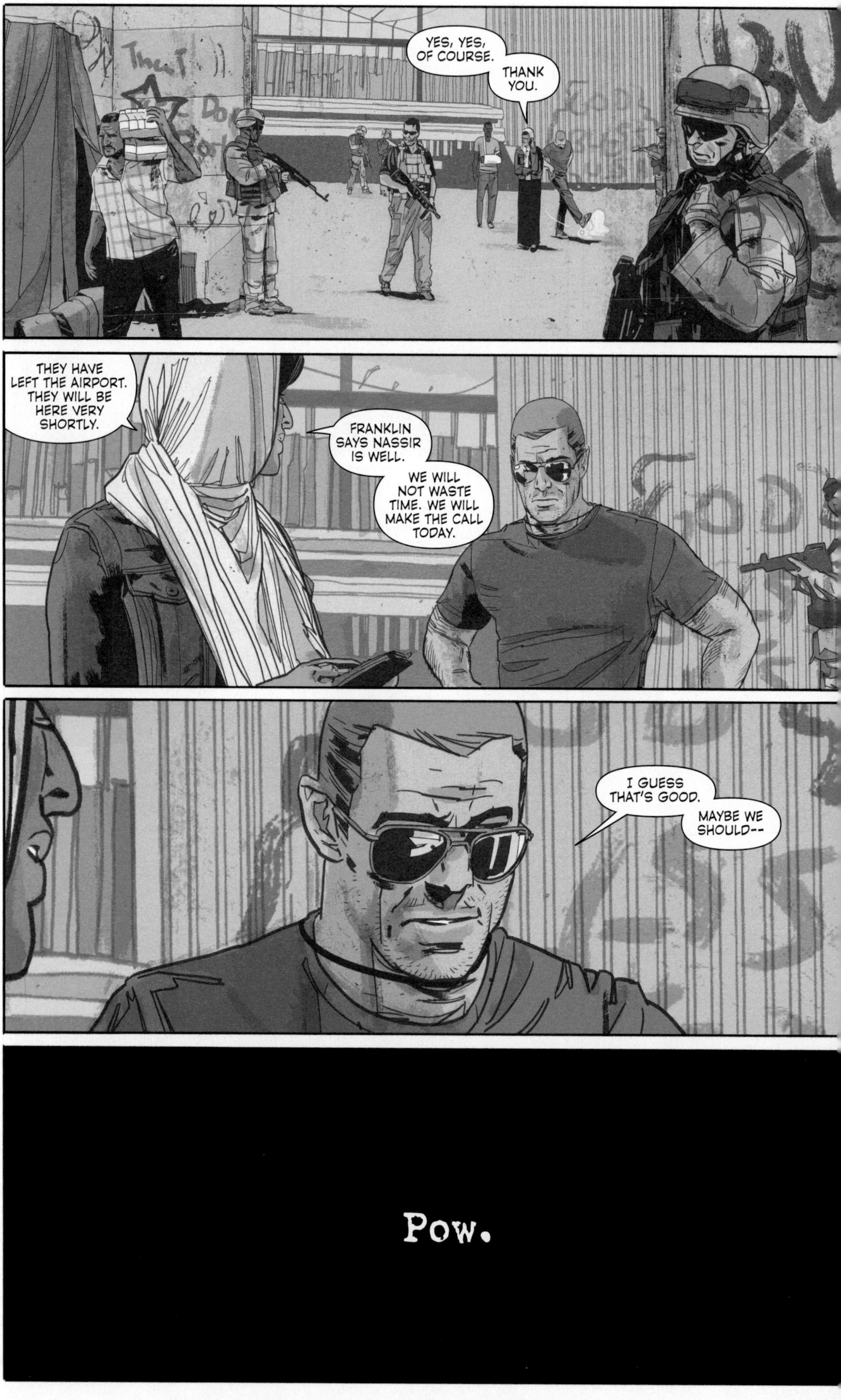

YES, YES, OF COURSE.
THANK YOU.
THEY HAVE LEFT THE AIRPORT. THEY WILL BE HERE VERY SHORTLY.
FRANKLIN SAYS NASSIR IS WELL.
WE WILL NOT WASTE TIME. WE WILL MAKE THE CALL TODAY.
I GUESS THAT'S GOOD.
MAYBE WE SHOULD--
Pow.

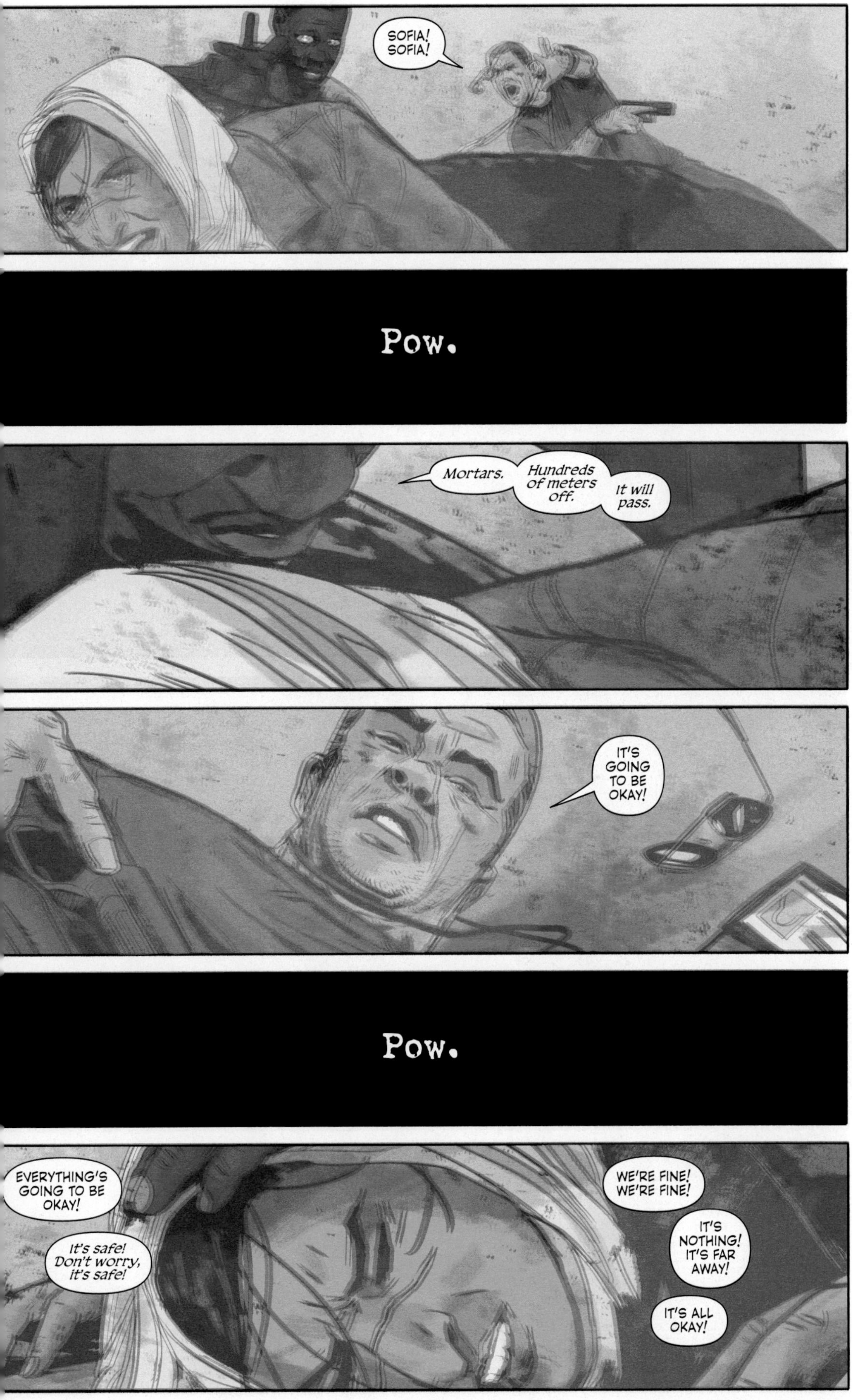
SOFIA! SOFIA!
Pow.
Mortars.
Hundreds of meters off.
It will pass.
IT'S GOING TO BE OKAY!
Pow.
EVERYTHING'S GOING TO BE OKAY!
It's safe! Don't worry, it's safe!
WE'RE FINE! WE'RE FINE!
IT'S NOTHING! IT'S FAR AWAY!
IT'S ALL OKAY!

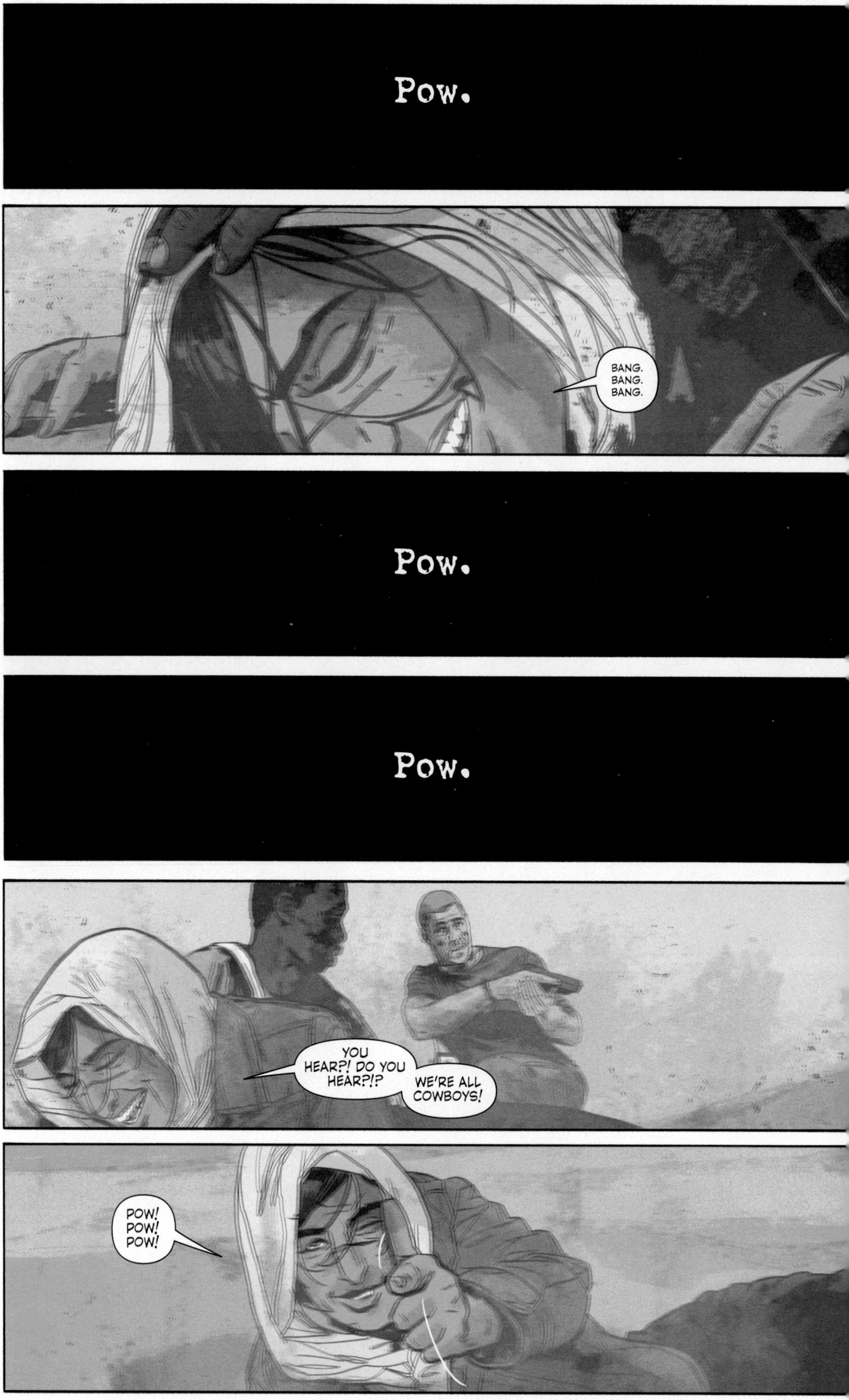
Pow.
BANG. BANG. BANG.
Pow.
Pow.
YOU HEAR?! DO YOU HEAR?!?
WE'RE ALL COWBOYS!
POW! POW! POW!

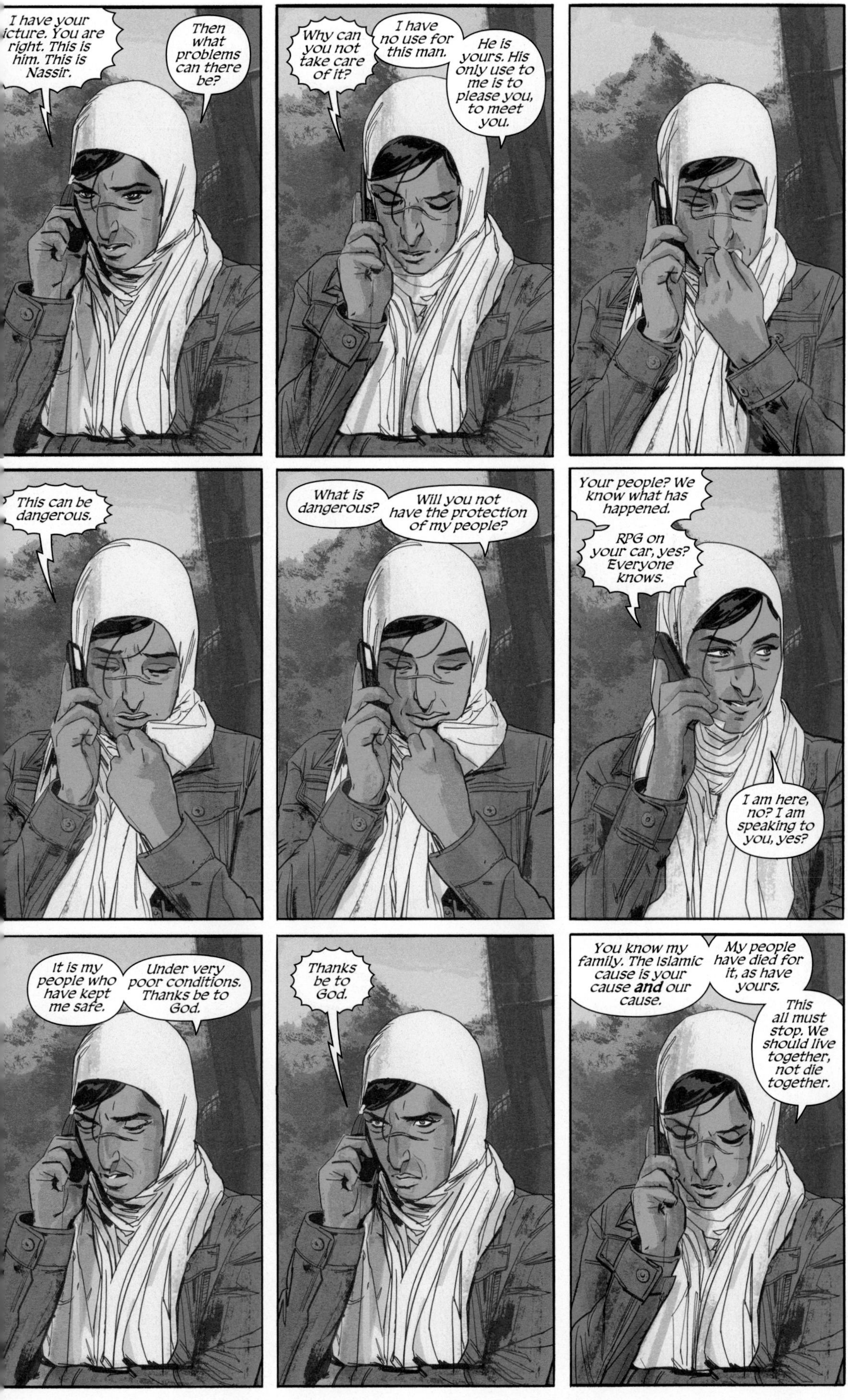
I have your icture. You are right. This is him. This is Nassir.
Then what problems can there be?
Why can you not take care of it?
I have no use for this man.
He is yours. His only use to me is to please you, to meet you.
This can be dangerous.
What is dangerous?
Will you not have the protection of my people?
Your people? We know what has happened.
RPG on your car, yes? Everyone knows.
I am here, no? I am speaking to you, yes?
It is my people who have kept me safe.
Under very poor conditions. Thanks be to God.
Thanks be to God.
You know my family. The Islamic cause is your cause **and** our cause.
My people have died for it, as have yours.
This all must stop. We should live together, not die together.

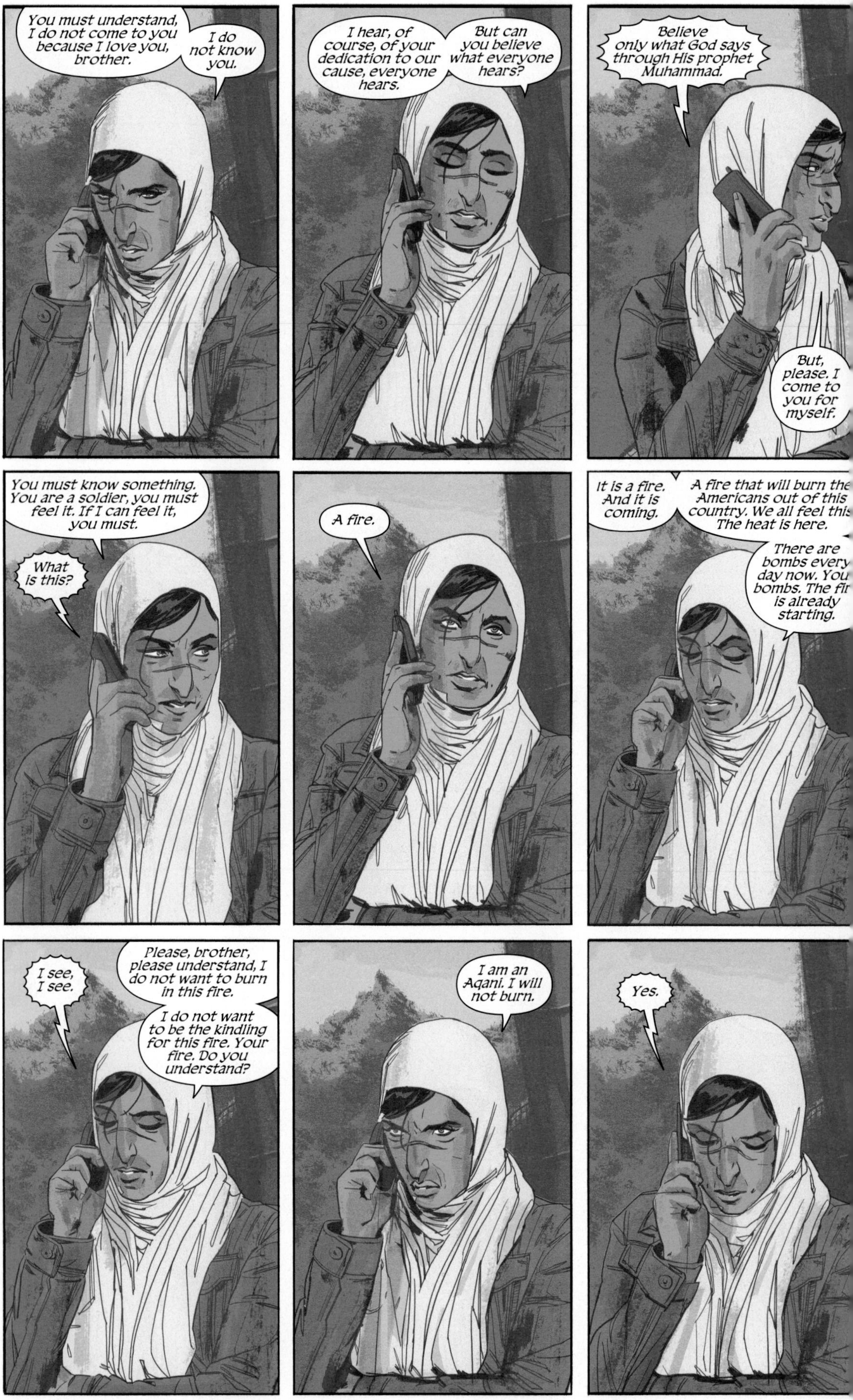
You must understand, I do not come to you because I love you, brother.
I do not know you.
I hear, of course, of your dedication to our cause, everyone hears.
But can you believe what everyone hears?
Believe only what God says through His prophet Muhammad.
But, please. I come to you for myself.
You must know something. You are a soldier, you must feel it. If I can feel it, you must.
What is this?
A fire.
It is a fire. And it is coming.
A fire that will burn the Americans out of this country. We all feel this. The heat is here.
There are bombs every day now. You bombs. The fire is already starting.
I see, I see.
Please, brother, please understand, I do not want to burn in this fire.
I do not want to be the kindling for this fire. Your fire. Do you understand?
I am an Aqani. I will not burn.
Yes.

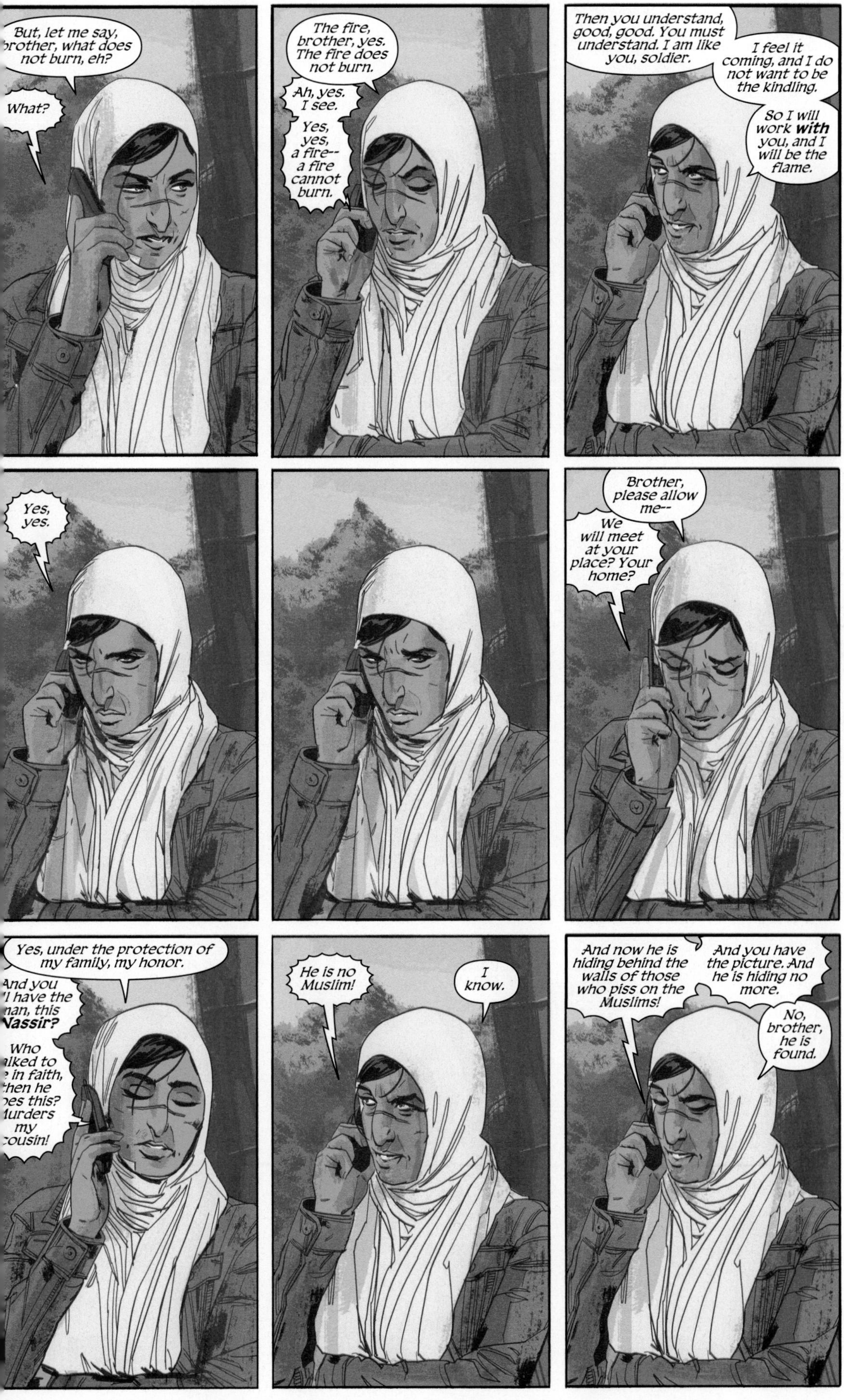

But, let me say, brother, what does not burn, eh?
What?
The fire, brother, yes. The fire does not burn.
Ah, yes. I see.
Yes, yes, a fire-- a fire cannot burn.
Then you understand, good, good. You must understand. I am like you, soldier.
I feel it coming, and I do not want to be the kindling.
So I will work **with** you, and I will be the flame.
Yes, yes.
Brother, please allow me--
We will meet at your place? Your home?
Yes, under the protection of my family, my honor.
And you 'l have the nan, this Nassir?
Who alked to e in faith, then he oes this? Murders my cousin!
He is no Muslim!
I know.
And now he is hiding behind the walls of those who piss on the Muslims!
And you have the picture. And he is hiding no more.
No, brother, he is found.

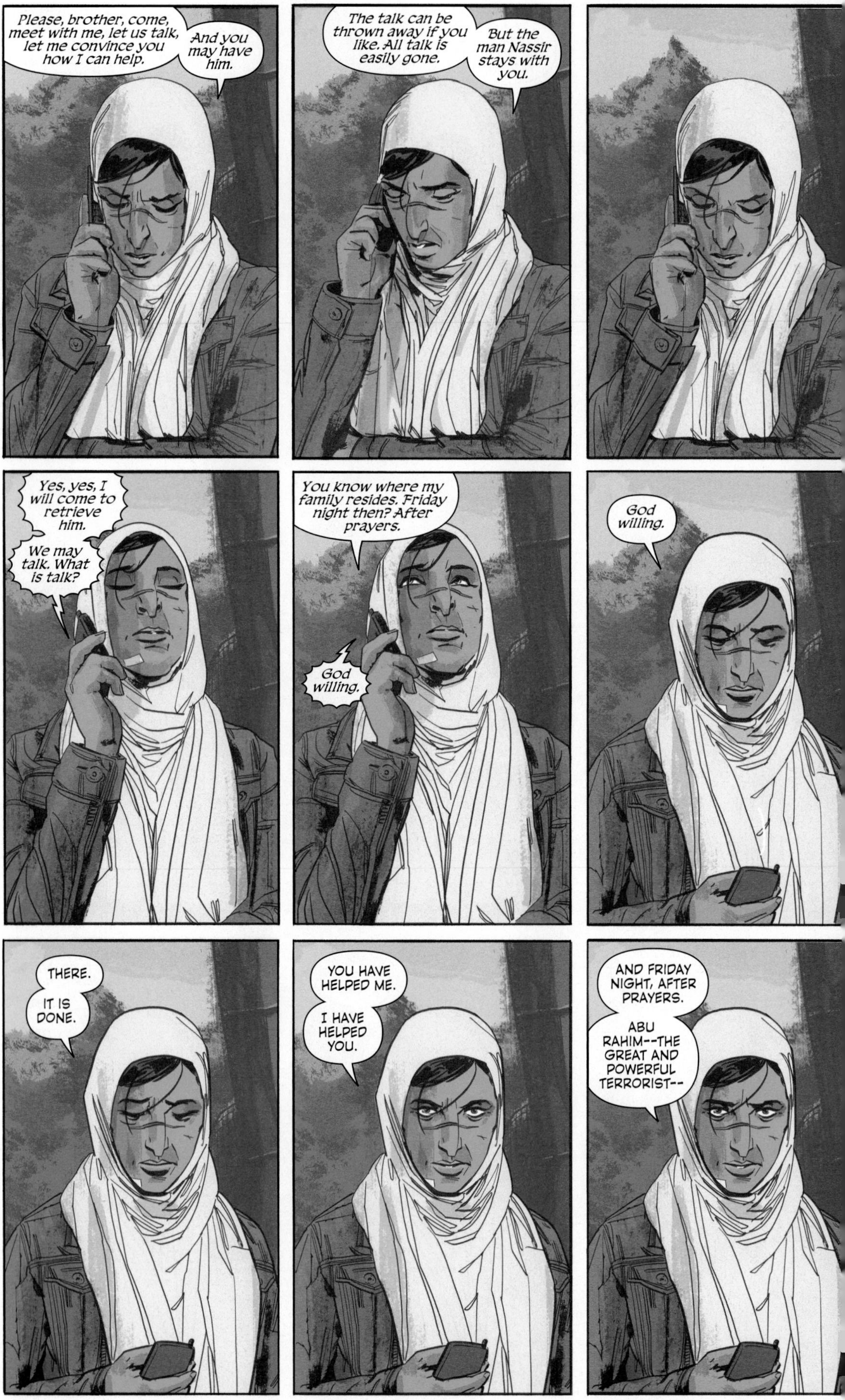

Please, brother, come, meet with me, let us talk, let me convince you how I can help.
And you may have him.
The talk can be thrown away if you like. All talk is easily gone.
But the man Nassir stays with you.
Yes, yes, I will come to retrieve him.
We may talk. What is talk?
You know where my family resides. Friday night then? After prayers.
God willing.
God willing.
THERE.
IT IS DONE.
YOU HAVE HELPED ME.
I HAVE HELPED YOU.
AND FRIDAY NIGHT, AFTER PRAYERS.
ABU RAHIM--THE GREAT AND POWERFUL TERRORIST--

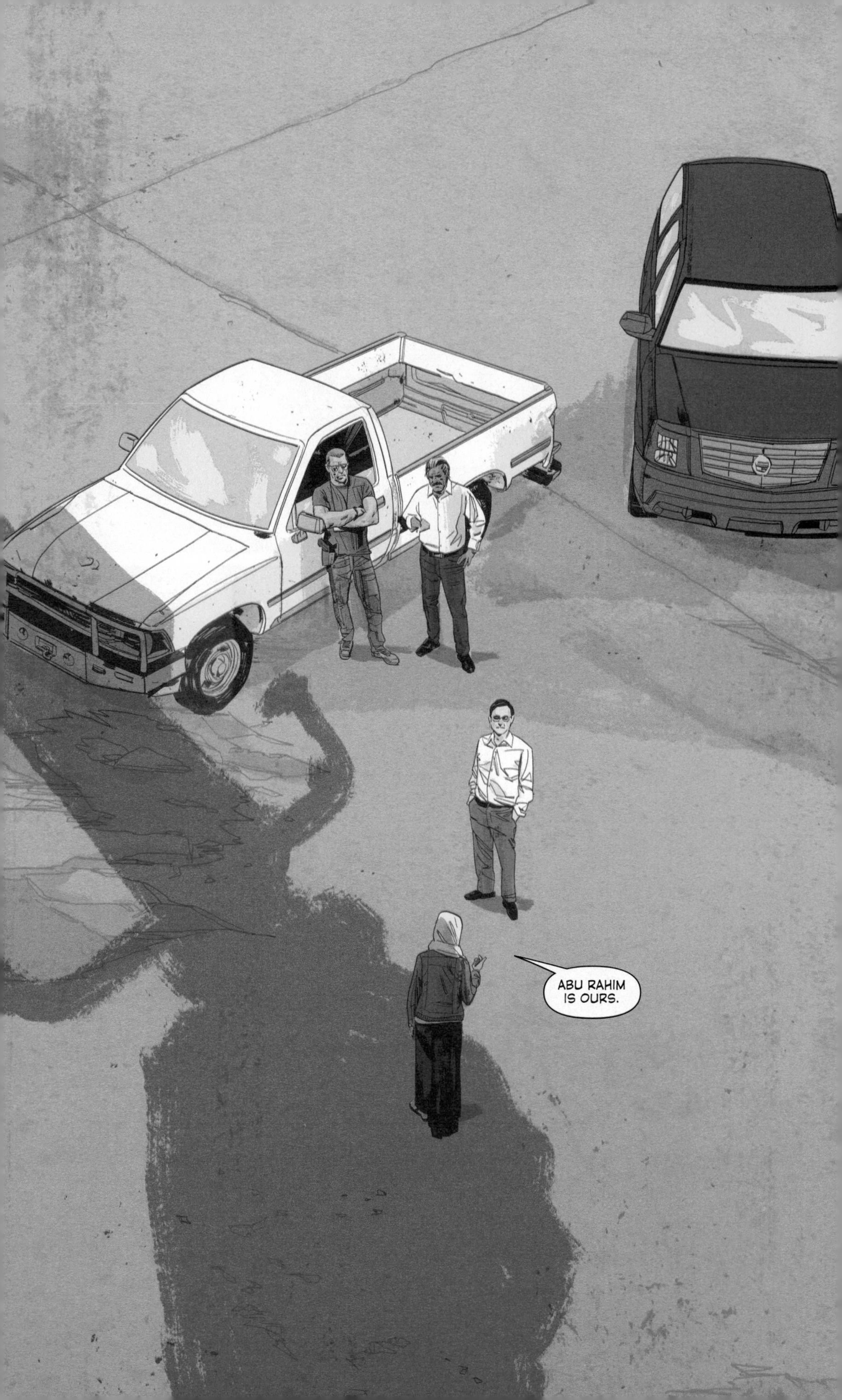
ABU RAHIM IS OURS.

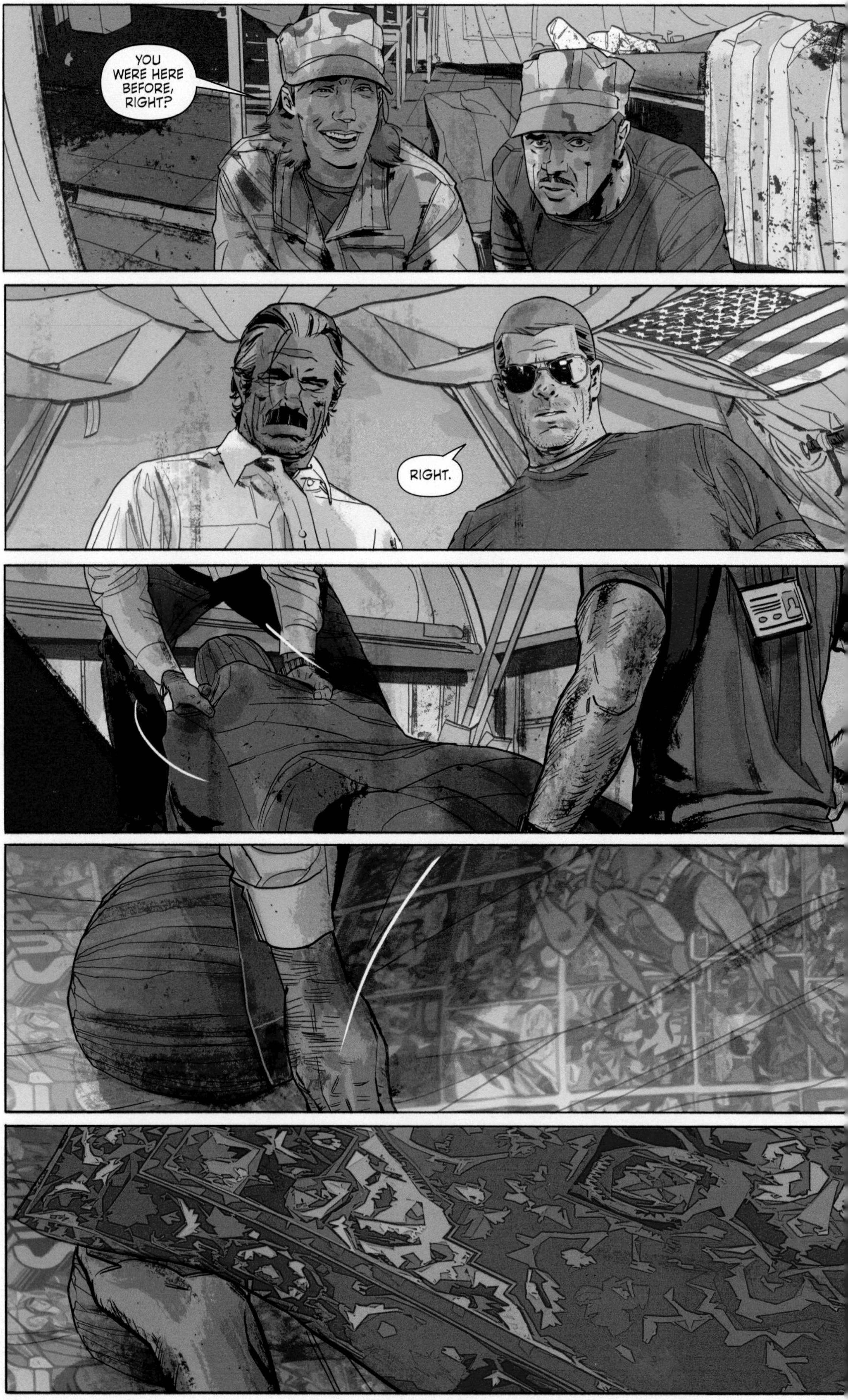
YOU WERE HERE BEFORE, RIGHT?
RIGHT.

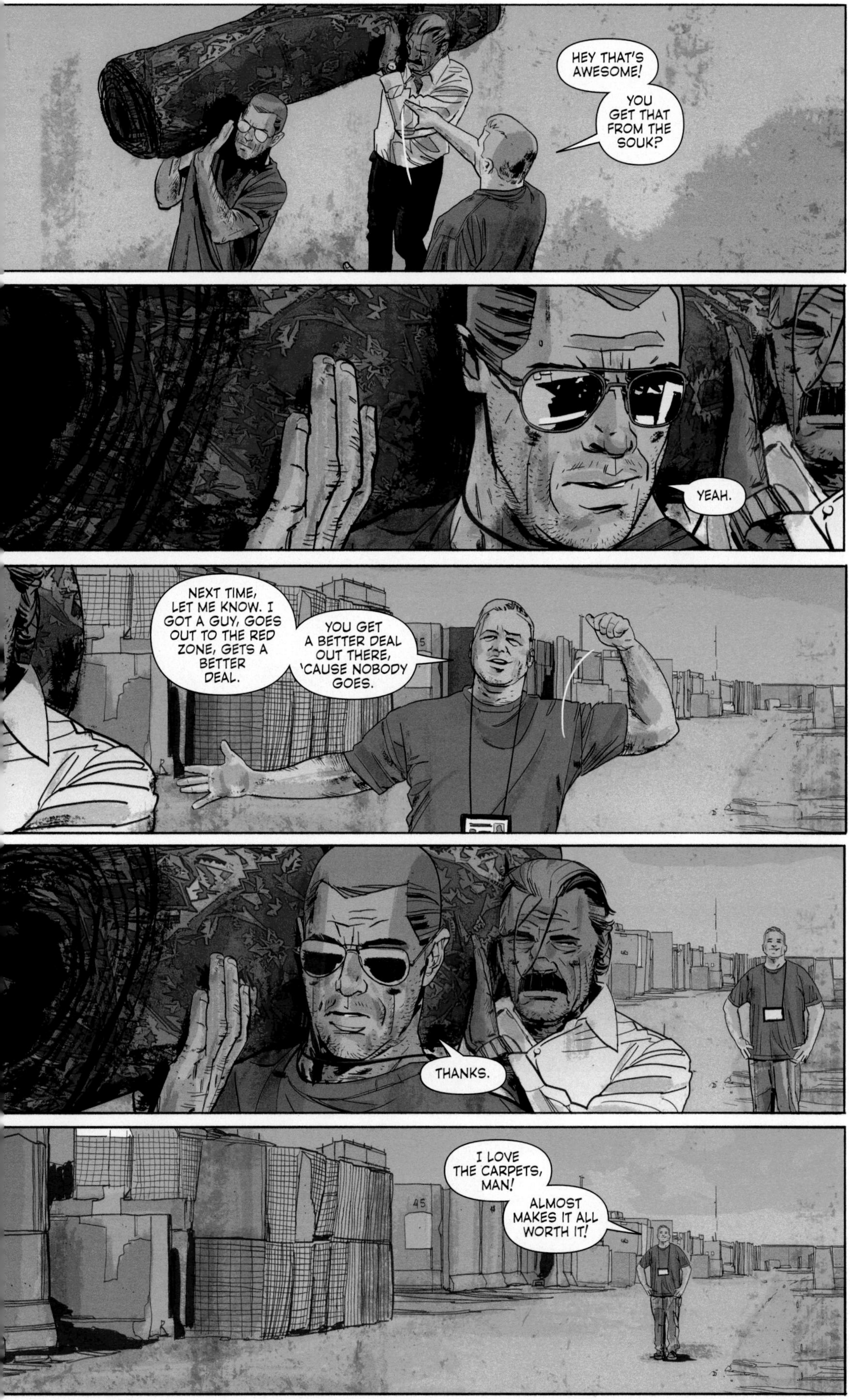
HEY THAT'S AWESOME!
YOU GET THAT FROM THE SOUK?
YEAH.
NEXT TIME, LET ME KNOW. I GOT A GUY, GOES OUT TO THE RED ZONE, GETS A BETTER DEAL.
YOU GET A BETTER DEAL OUT THERE, 'CAUSE NOBODY GOES.
THANKS.
I LOVE THE CARPETS, MAN!
ALMOST MAKES IT ALL WORTH IT!

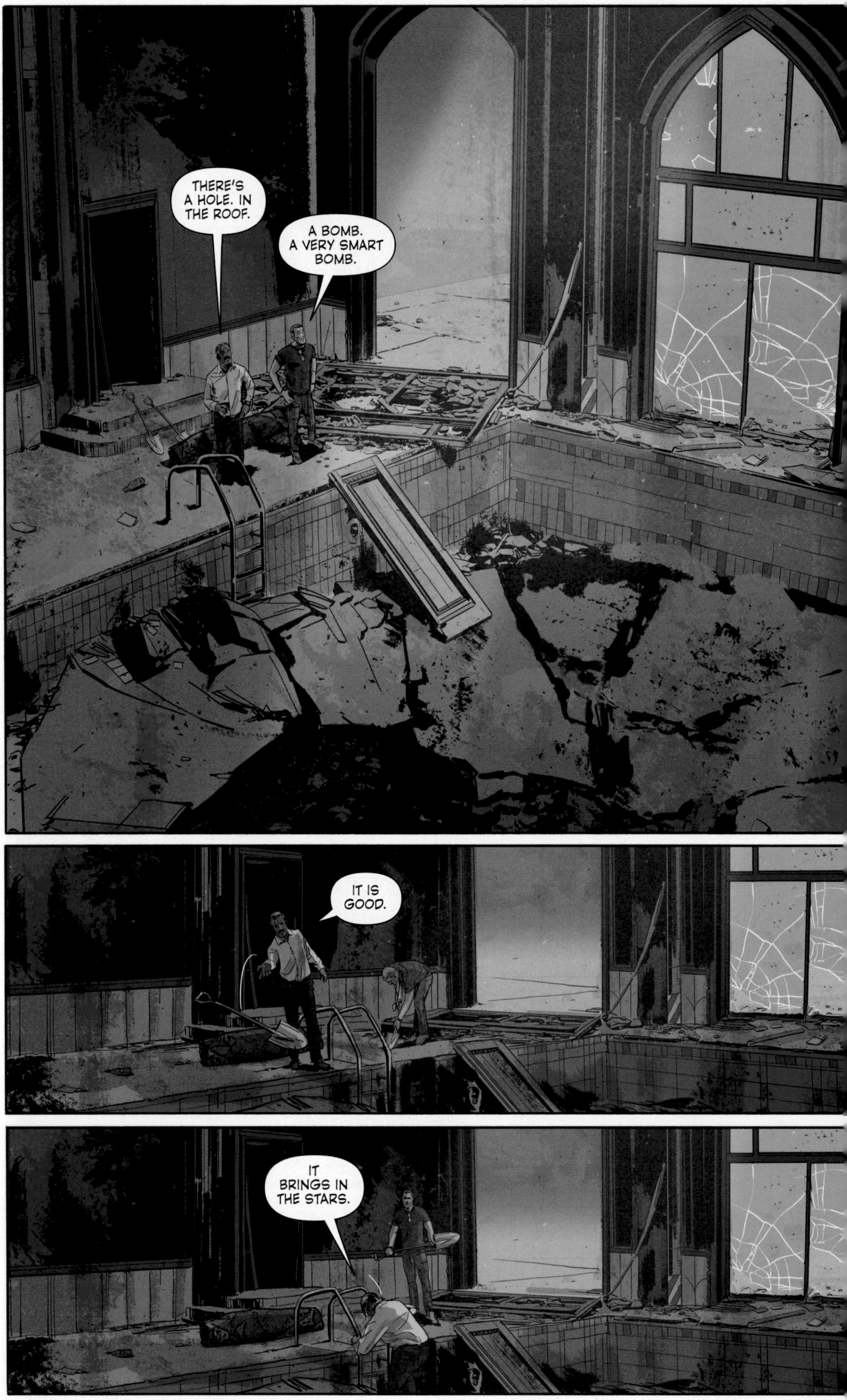
THERE'S A HOLE. IN THE ROOF.
A BOMB. A VERY SMART BOMB.
IT IS GOOD.
IT BRINGS IN THE STARS.

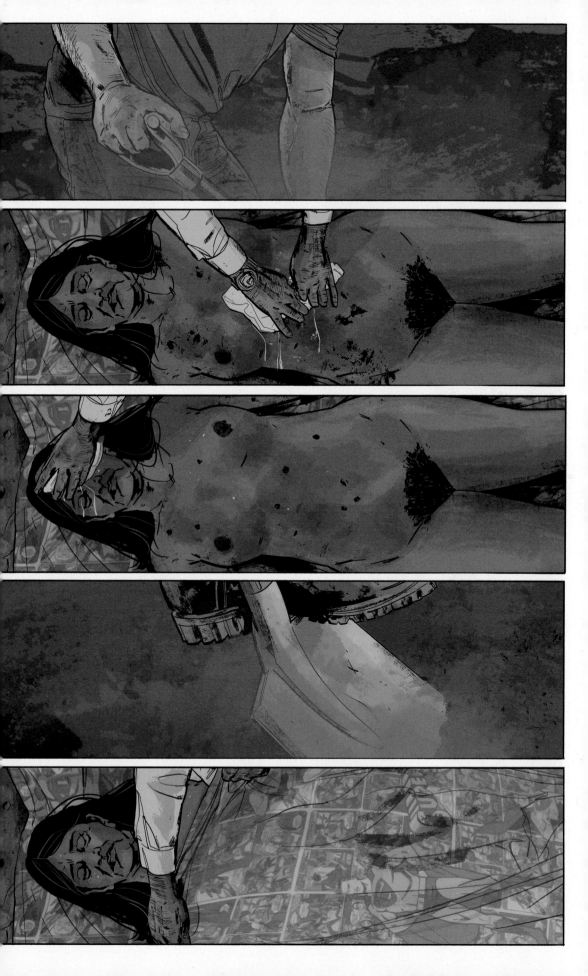

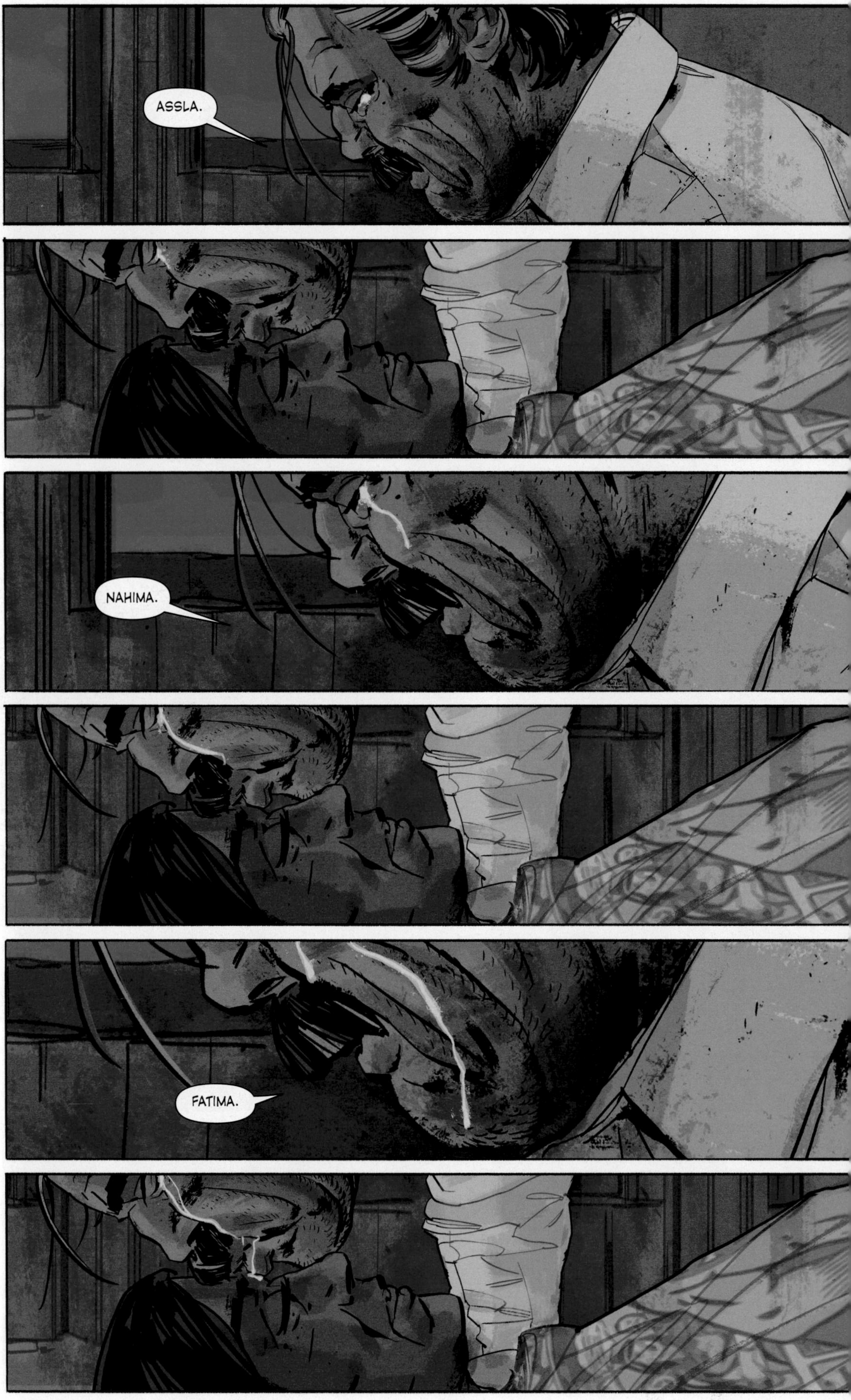
ASSLA.
NAHIMA.
FATIMA.

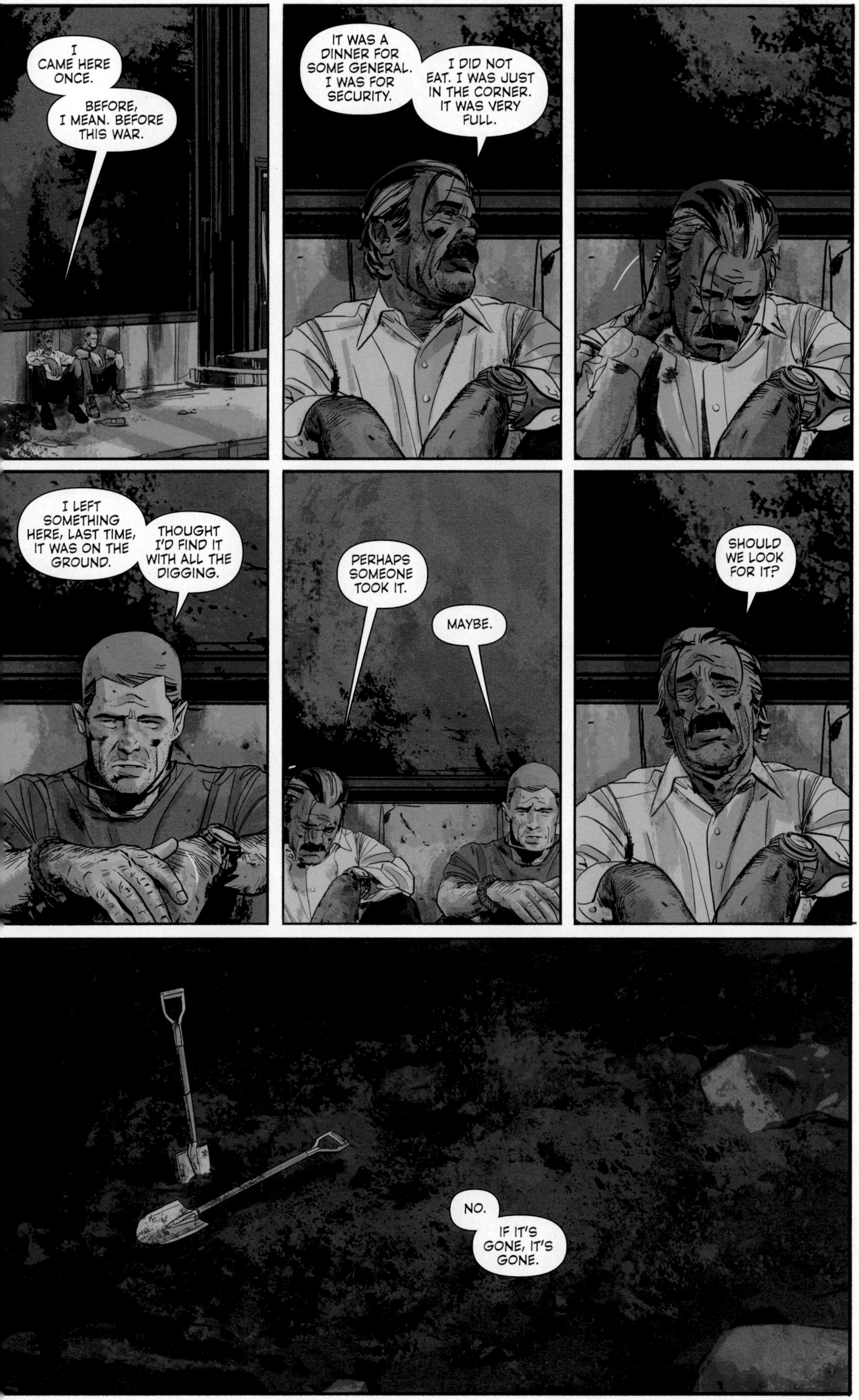
I CAME HERE ONCE.
BEFORE, I MEAN. BEFORE THIS WAR.
IT WAS A DINNER FOR SOME GENERAL. I WAS FOR SECURITY.
I DID NOT EAT. I WAS JUST IN THE CORNER. IT WAS VERY FULL.
I LEFT SOMETHING HERE, LAST TIME, IT WAS ON THE GROUND.
THOUGHT I'D FIND IT WITH ALL THE DIGGING.
PERHAPS SOMEONE TOOK IT.
MAYBE.
SHOULD WE LOOK FOR IT?
NO.
IF IT'S GONE, IT'S GONE.

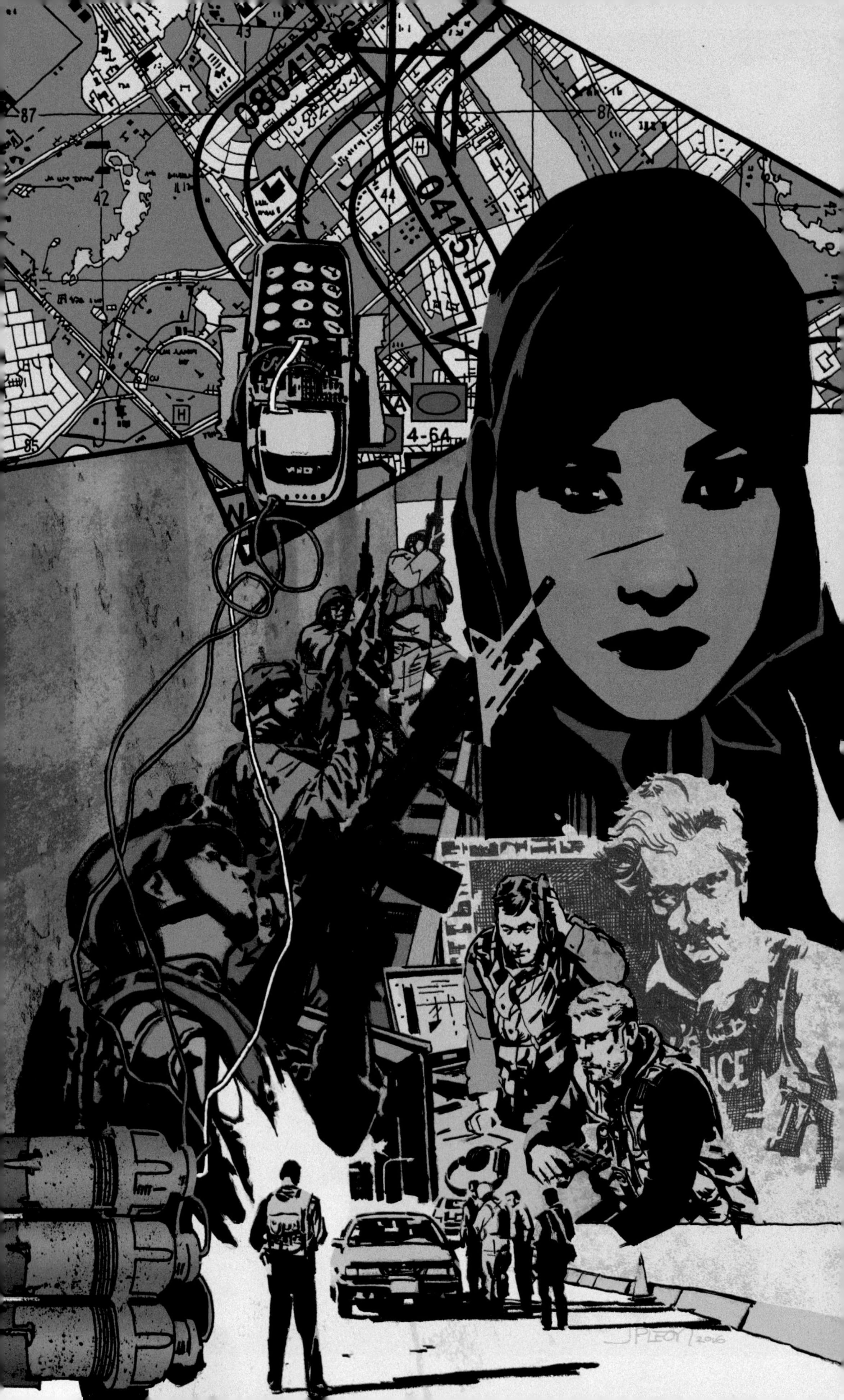
4-64

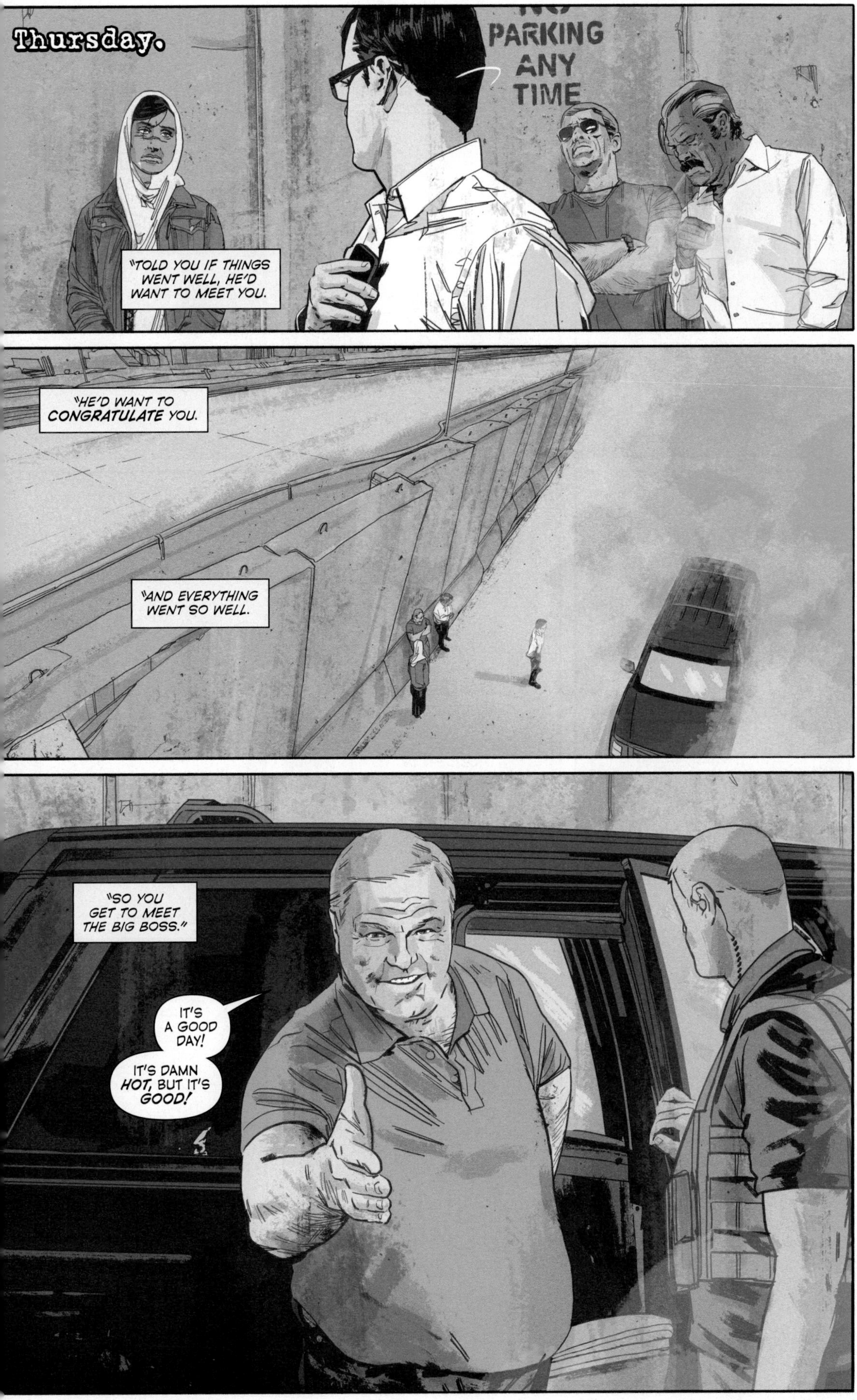
Thursday.
PARKING
ANY
TIME
"TOLD YOU IF THINGS WENT WELL, HE'D WANT TO MEET YOU.
"HE'D WANT TO CONGRATULATE YOU.
"AND EVERYTHING WENT SO WELL.
"SO YOU GET TO MEET THE BIG BOSS."
IT'S A GOOD DAY!
IT'S DAMN HOT, BUT IT'S GOOD!

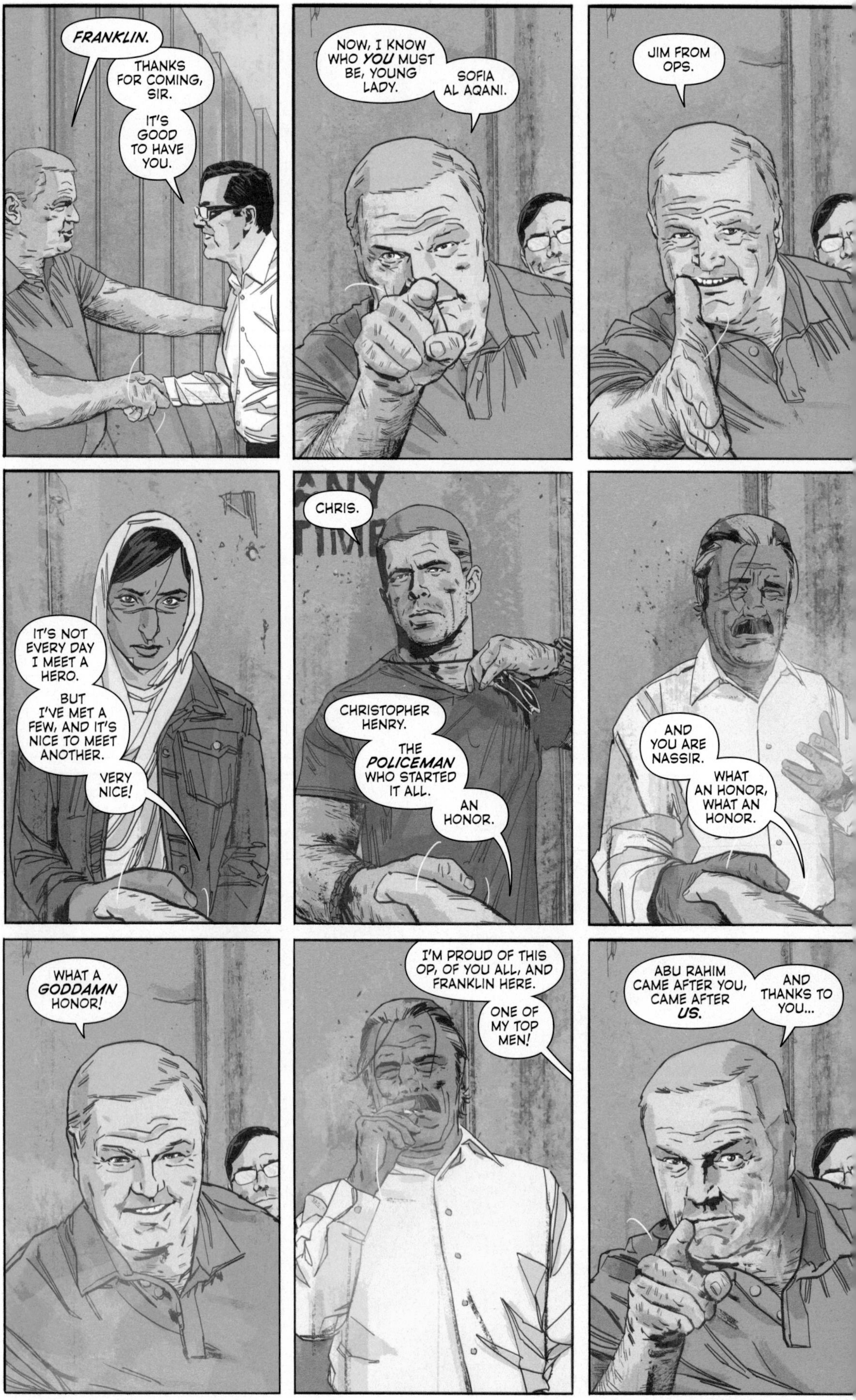
FRANKLIN.
THANKS FOR COMING, SIR.
IT'S GOOD TO HAVE YOU.
NOW, I KNOW WHO YOU MUST BE, YOUNG LADY.
SOFIA AL AQANI.
JIM FROM OPS.
IT'S NOT EVERY DAY I MEET A HERO.
BUT I'VE MET A FEW, AND IT'S NICE TO MEET ANOTHER.
VERY NICE!
CHRIS.
CHRISTOPHER HENRY.
THE POLICEMAN WHO STARTED IT ALL.
AN HONOR.
AND YOU ARE NASSIR.
WHAT AN HONOR, WHAT AN HONOR.
WHAT A GODDAMN HONOR!
I'M PROUD OF THIS OP, OF YOU ALL, AND FRANKLIN HERE.
ONE OF MY TOP MEN!
ABU RAHIM CAME AFTER YOU, CAME AFTER US.
AND THANKS TO YOU...

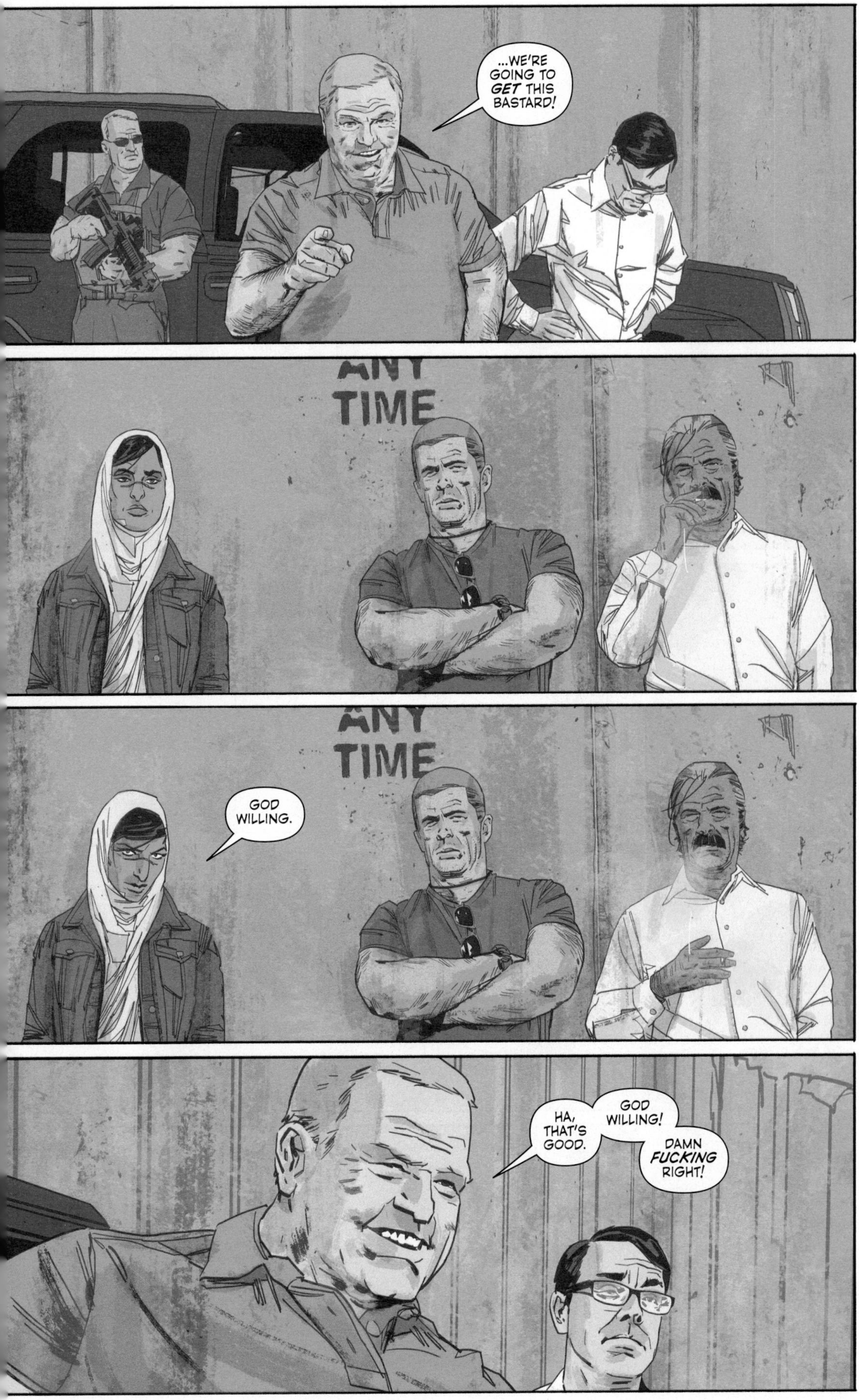
...WE'RE GOING TO GET THIS BASTARD!
ANY TIME
ANY TIME
GOD WILLING.
HA, THAT'S GOOD.
GOD WILLING!
DAMN FUCKING RIGHT!

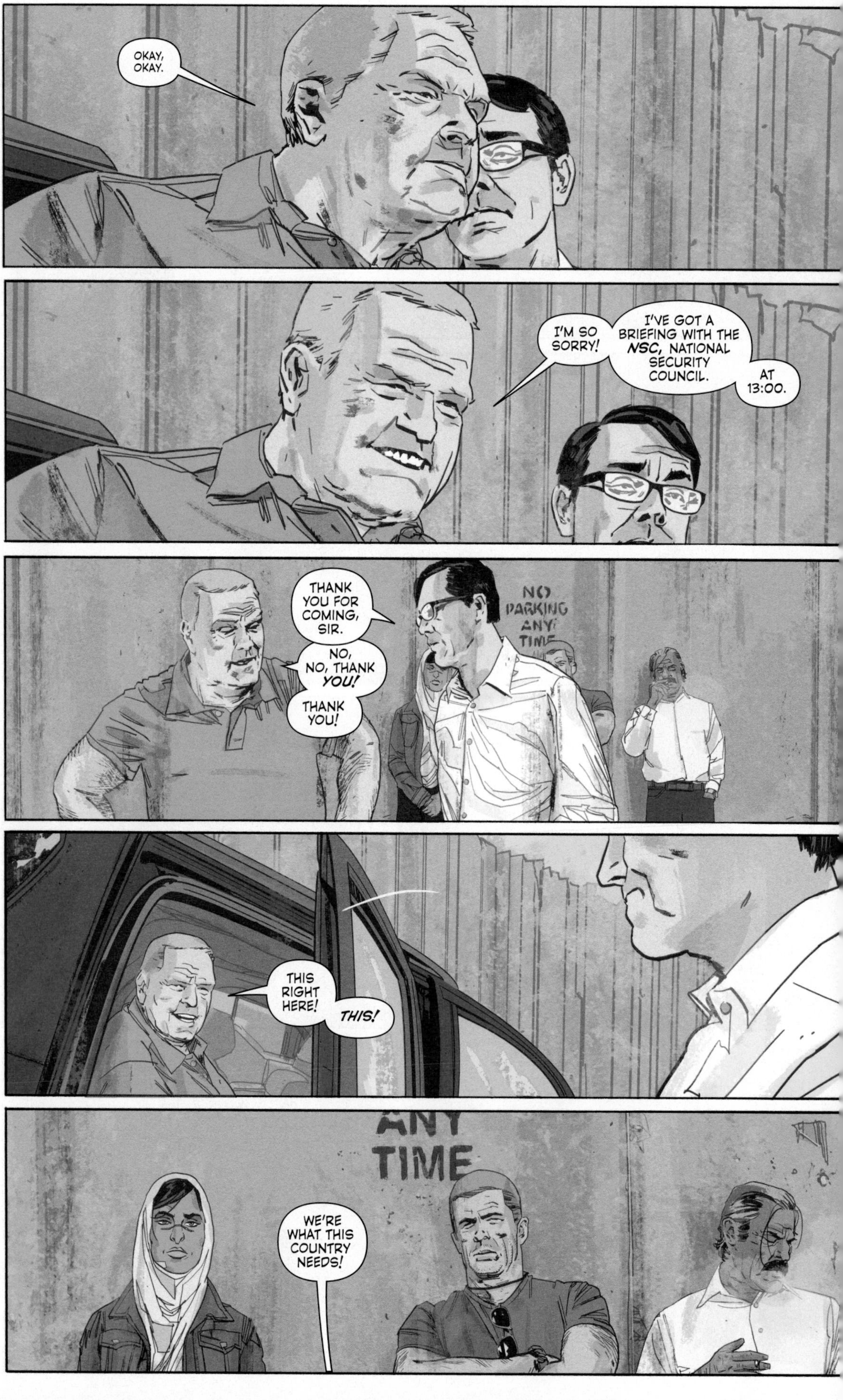
OKAY, OKAY.
I'M SO SORRY!
I'VE GOT A BRIEFING WITH THE NSC, NATIONAL SECURITY COUNCIL.
AT 13:00.
THANK YOU FOR COMING, SIR.
NO PARKING ANY TIME
NO, NO, THANK YOU!
THANK YOU!
THIS RIGHT HERE!
THIS!
ANY TIME
WE'RE WHAT THIS COUNTRY NEEDS!

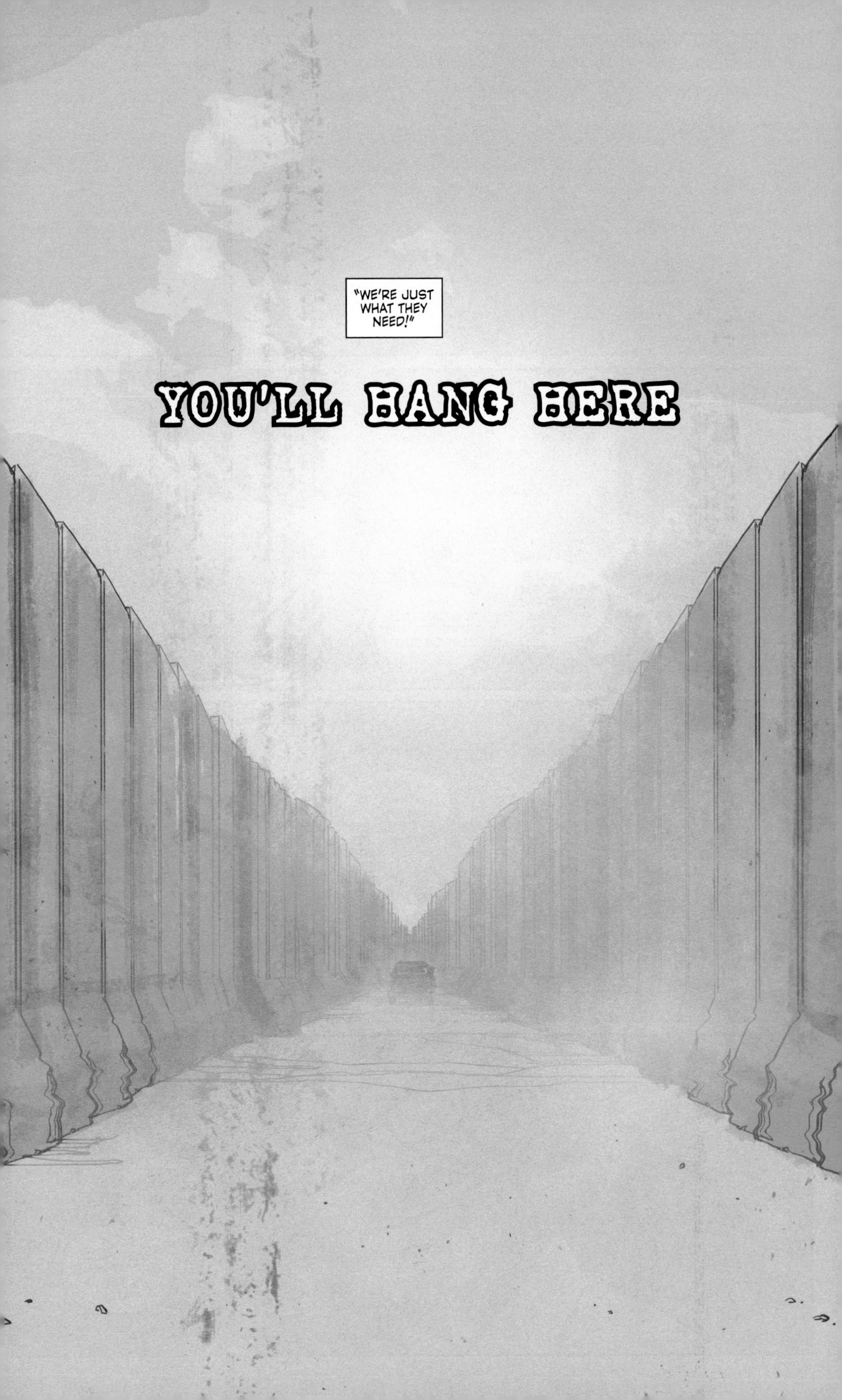
"WE'RE JUST WHAT THEY NEED!"
YOU'LL HANG HERE

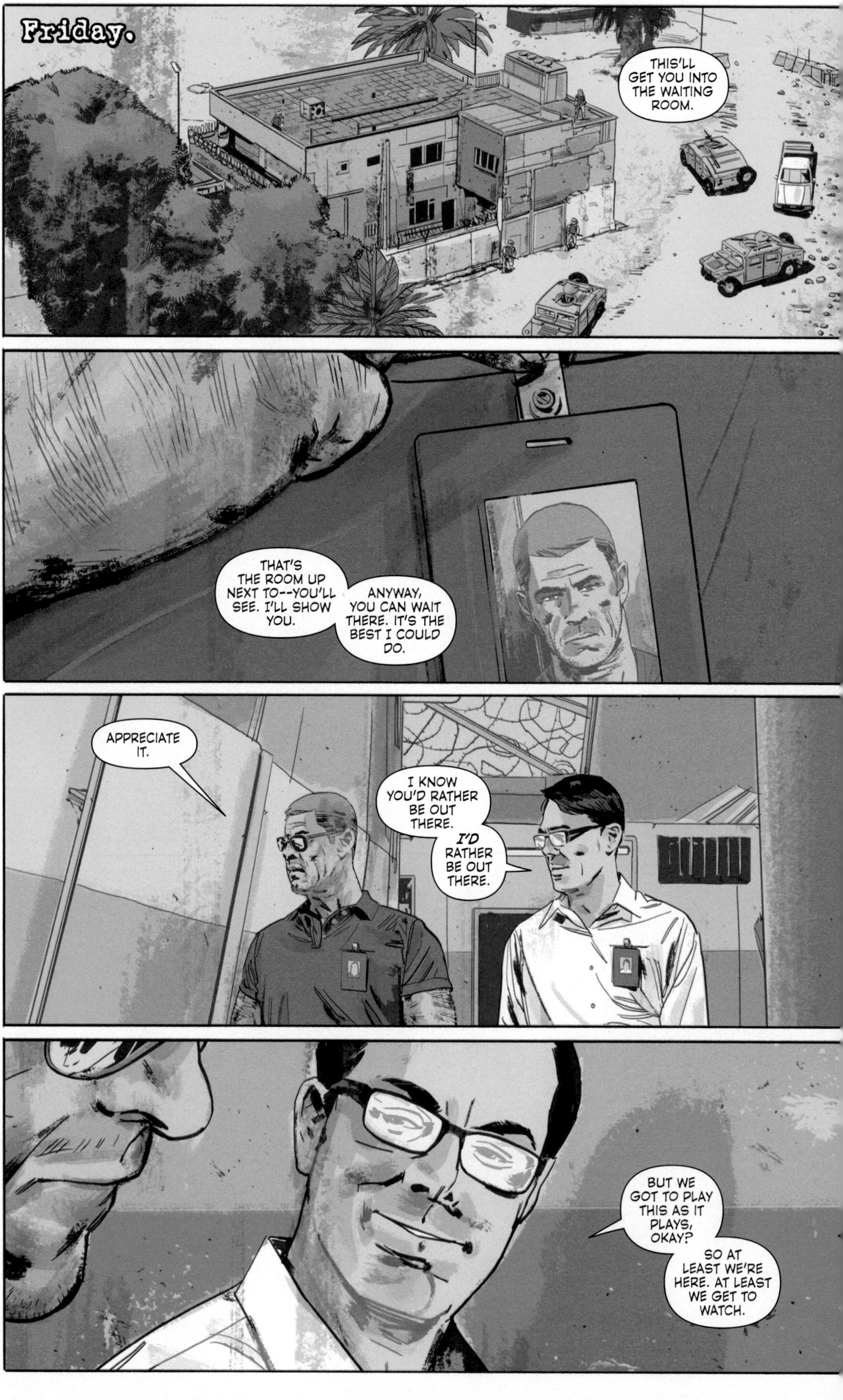
Friday.
THIS'LL GET YOU INTO THE WAITING ROOM.
THAT'S THE ROOM UP NEXT TO--YOU'LL SEE. I'LL SHOW YOU.
ANYWAY, YOU CAN WAIT THERE. IT'S THE BEST I COULD DO.
APPRECIATE IT.
I KNOW YOU'D RATHER BE OUT THERE.
I'D RATHER BE OUT THERE.
BUT WE GOT TO PLAY THIS AS IT PLAYS, OKAY?
SO AT LEAST WE'RE HERE. AT LEAST WE GET TO WATCH.

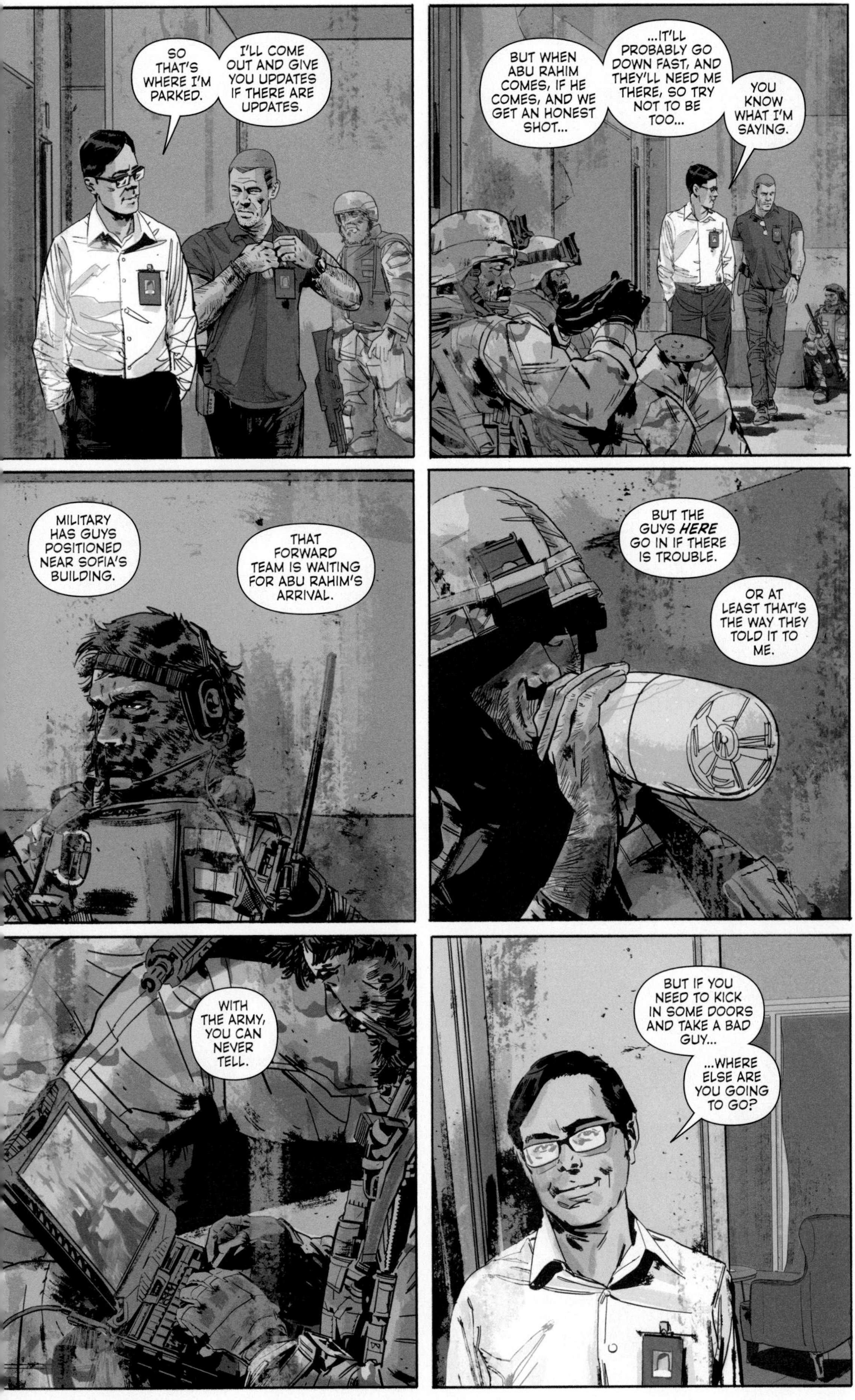
SO THAT'S WHERE I'M PARKED.
I'LL COME OUT AND GIVE YOU UPDATES IF THERE ARE UPDATES.
BUT WHEN ABU RAHIM COMES, IF HE COMES, AND WE GET AN HONEST SHOT...
...IT'LL PROBABLY GO DOWN FAST, AND THEY'LL NEED ME THERE, SO TRY NOT TO BE TOO...
YOU KNOW WHAT I'M SAYING.
MILITARY HAS GUYS POSITIONED NEAR SOFIA'S BUILDING.
THAT FORWARD TEAM IS WAITING FOR ABU RAHIM'S ARRIVAL.
BUT THE GUYS HERE GO IN IF THERE IS TROUBLE.
OR AT LEAST THAT'S THE WAY THEY TOLD IT TO ME.
WITH THE ARMY, YOU CAN NEVER TELL.
BUT IF YOU NEED TO KICK IN SOME DOORS AND TAKE A BAD GUY...
...WHERE ELSE ARE YOU GOING TO GO?

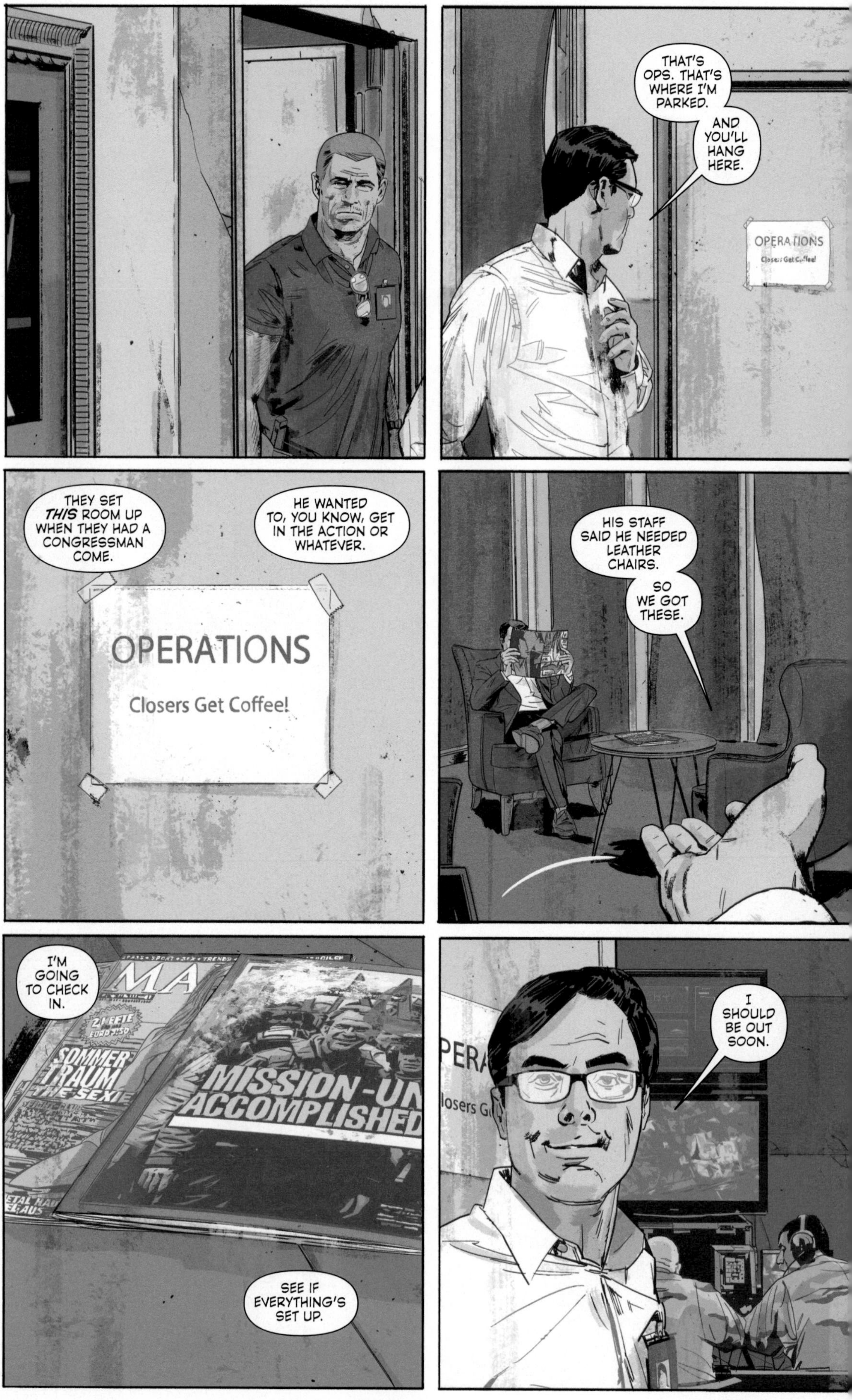
THAT'S OPS. THAT'S WHERE I'M PARKED.
AND YOU'LL HANG HERE.
OPERATIONS
Closers Get Coffee!
THEY SET THIS ROOM UP WHEN THEY HAD A CONGRESSMAN COME.
HE WANTED TO, YOU KNOW, GET IN THE ACTION OR WHATEVER.
OPERATIONS
Closers Get Coffee!
HIS STAFF SAID HE NEEDED LEATHER CHAIRS.
SO WE GOT THESE.
I'M GOING TO CHECK IN.
SOMMER TRAUM
MISSION-UN ACCOMPLISHED
SEE IF EVERYTHING'S SET UP.
I SHOULD BE OUT SOON.

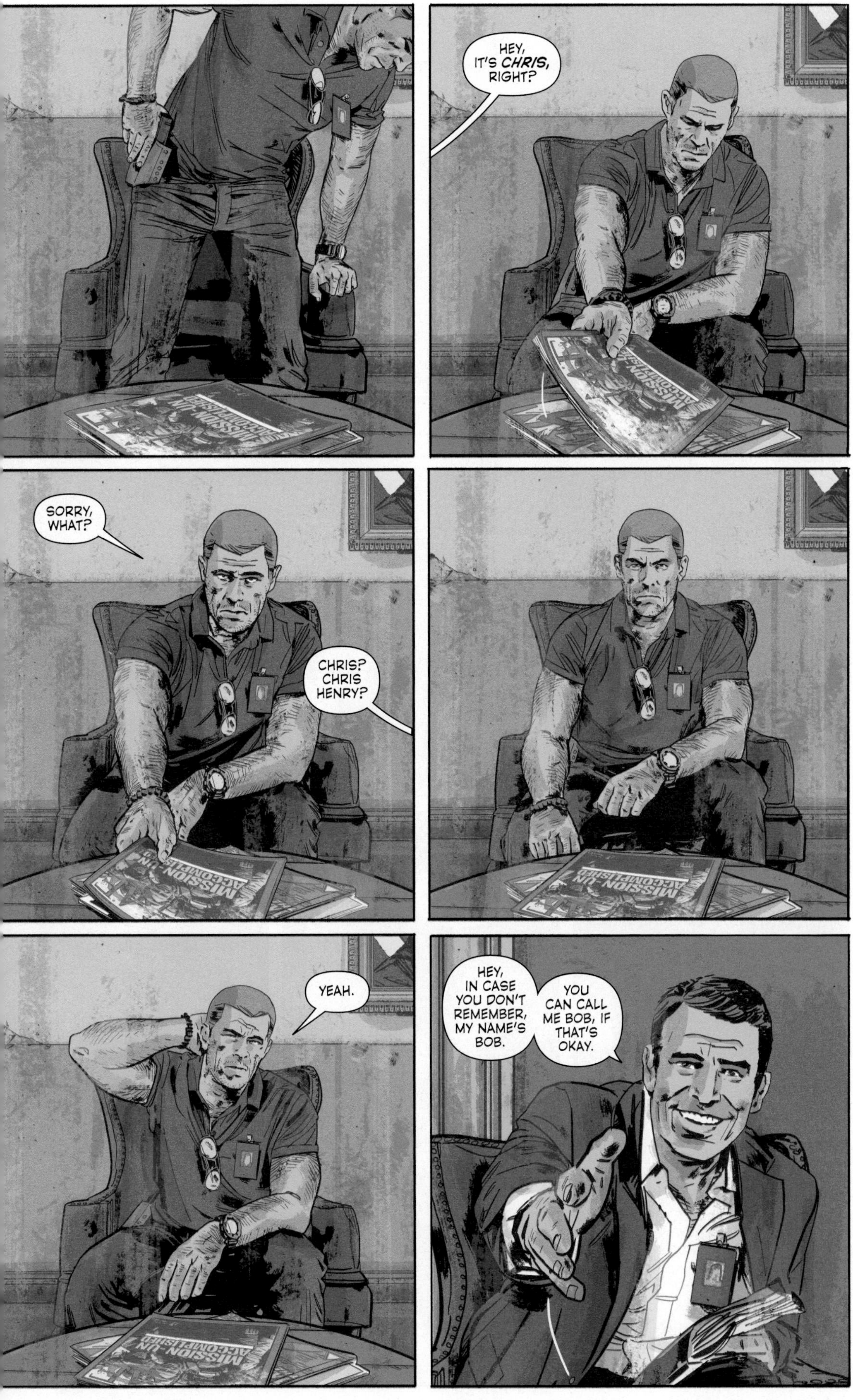

HEY, IT'S *CHRIS,* RIGHT?
MISSION-UN-ACCOMPLISHED
SORRY, WHAT?
CHRIS? CHRIS HENRY?
YEAH.
HEY, IN CASE YOU DON'T REMEMBER, MY NAME'S BOB.
YOU CAN CALL ME BOB, IF THAT'S OKAY.

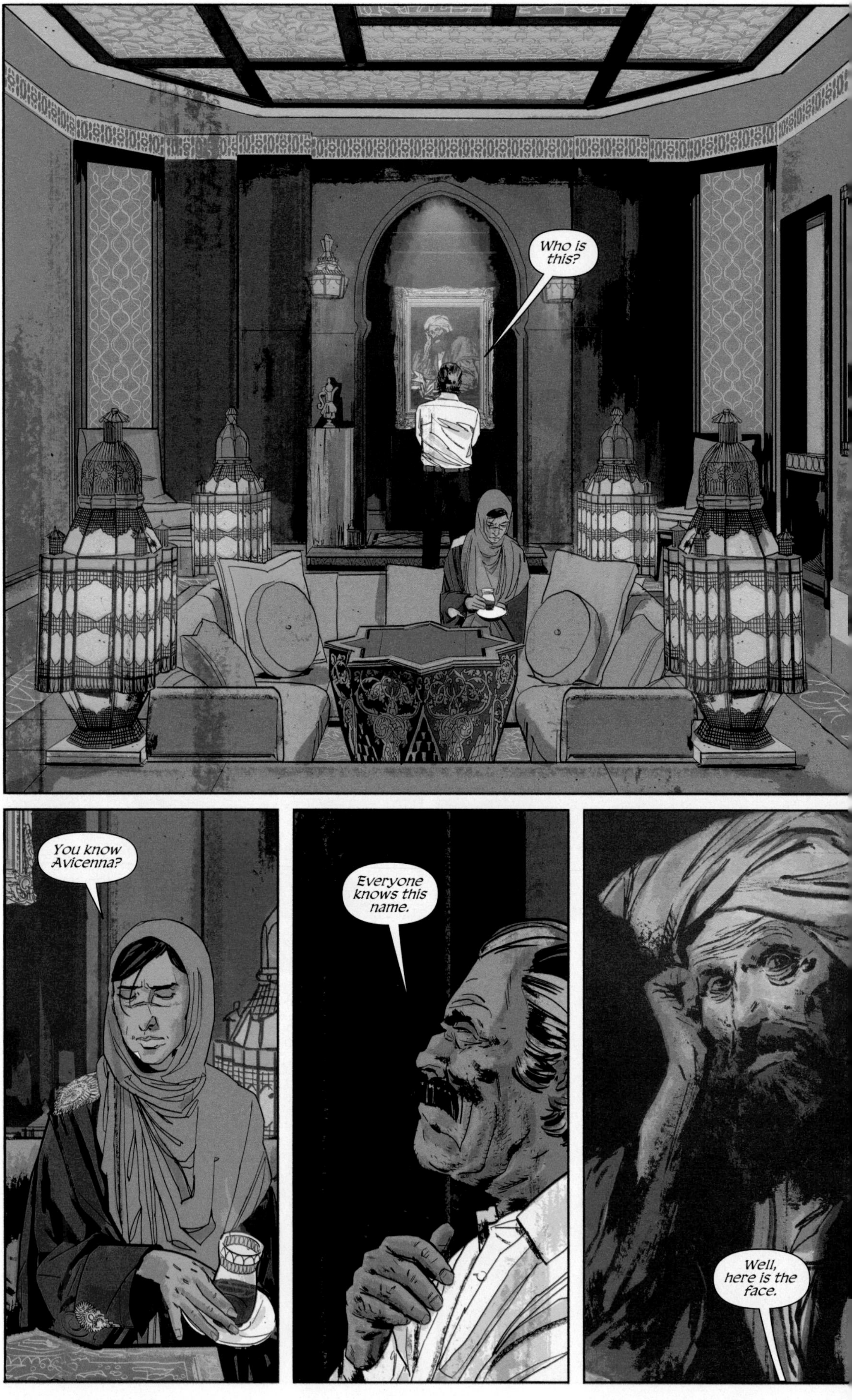
Who is this?
You know Avicenna?
Everyone knows this name.
Well, here is the face.

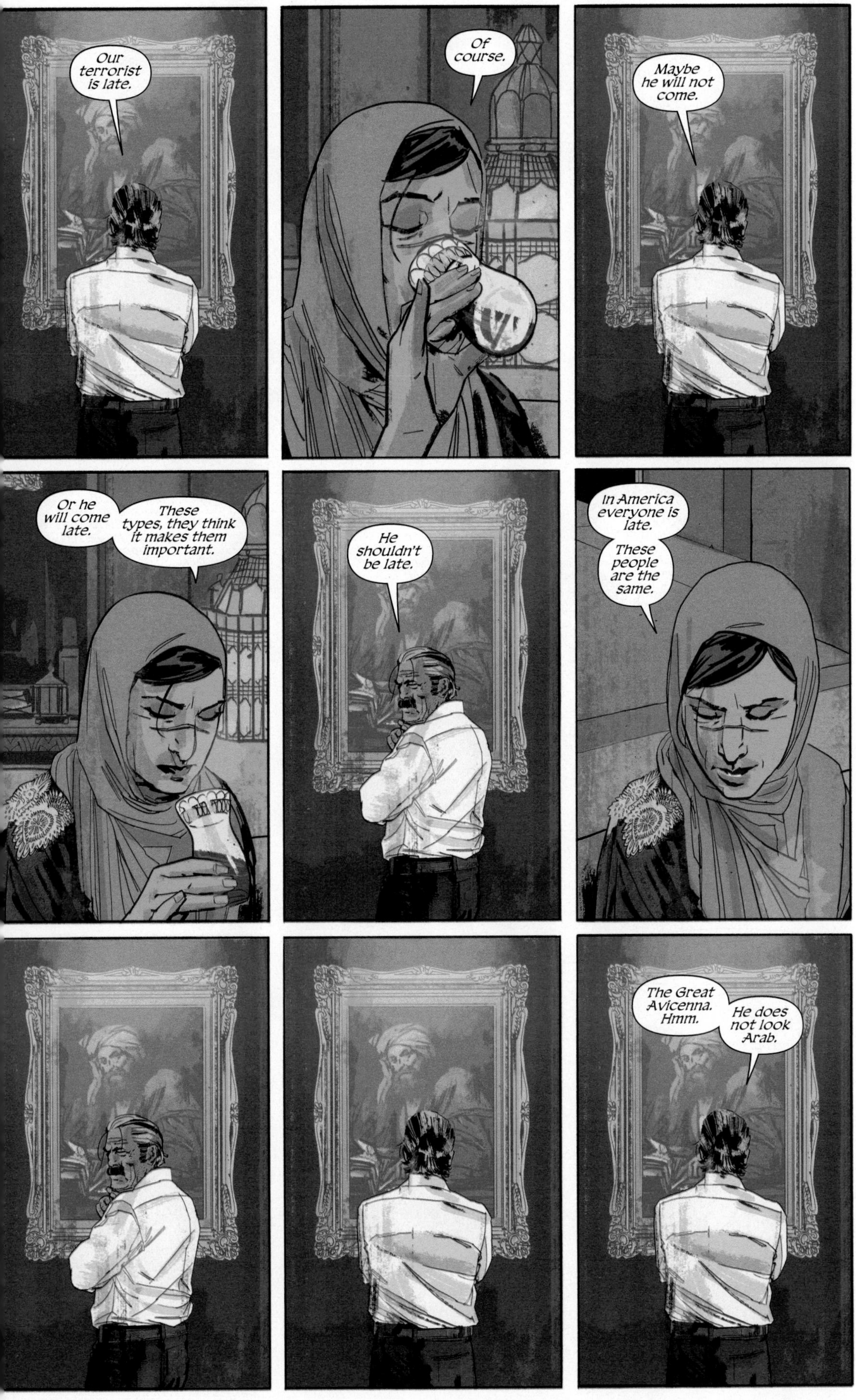
Our terrorist is late.
Of course.
Maybe he will not come.
Or he will come late.
These types, they think it makes them important.
He shouldn't be late.
In America everyone is late.
These people are the same.
The Great Avicenna. Hmm.
He does not look Arab.

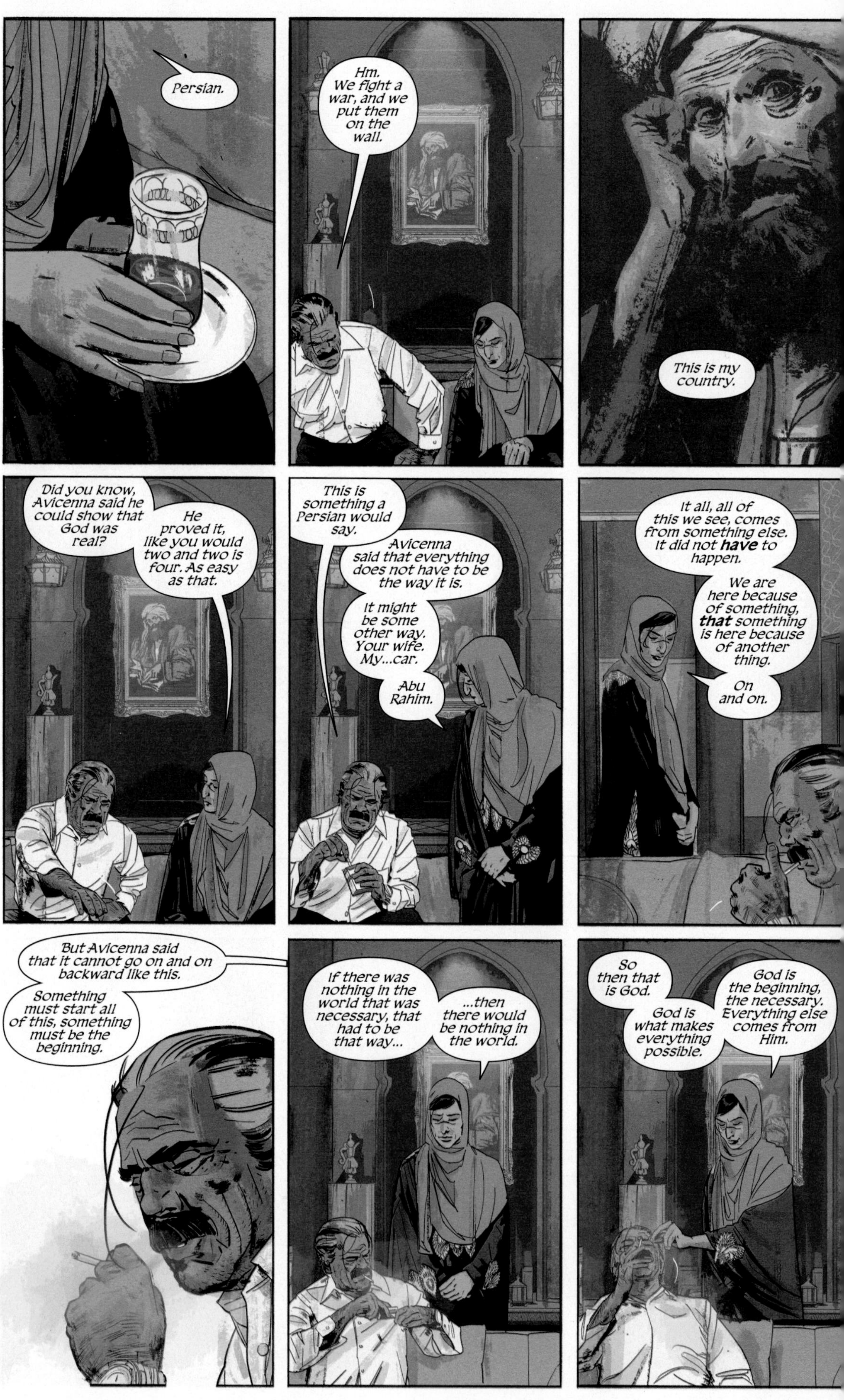
Persian.
Hm. We fight a war, and we put them on the wall.
This is my country.
Did you know, Avicenna said he could show that God was real?
He proved it, like you would two and two is four. As easy as that.
This is something a Persian would say.
Avicenna said that everything does not have to be the way it is.
It might be some other way. Your wife. My...car.
Abu Rahim.
It all, all of this we see, comes from something else. It did not **have** to happen.
We are here because of something, **that** something is here because of another thing.
On and on.
But Avicenna said that it cannot go on and on backward like this.
Something must start all of this, something must be the beginning.
If there was nothing in the world that was necessary, that had to be that way...
...then there would be nothing in the world.
So then that is God.
God is what makes everything possible.
God is the beginning, the necessary. Everything else comes from Him.

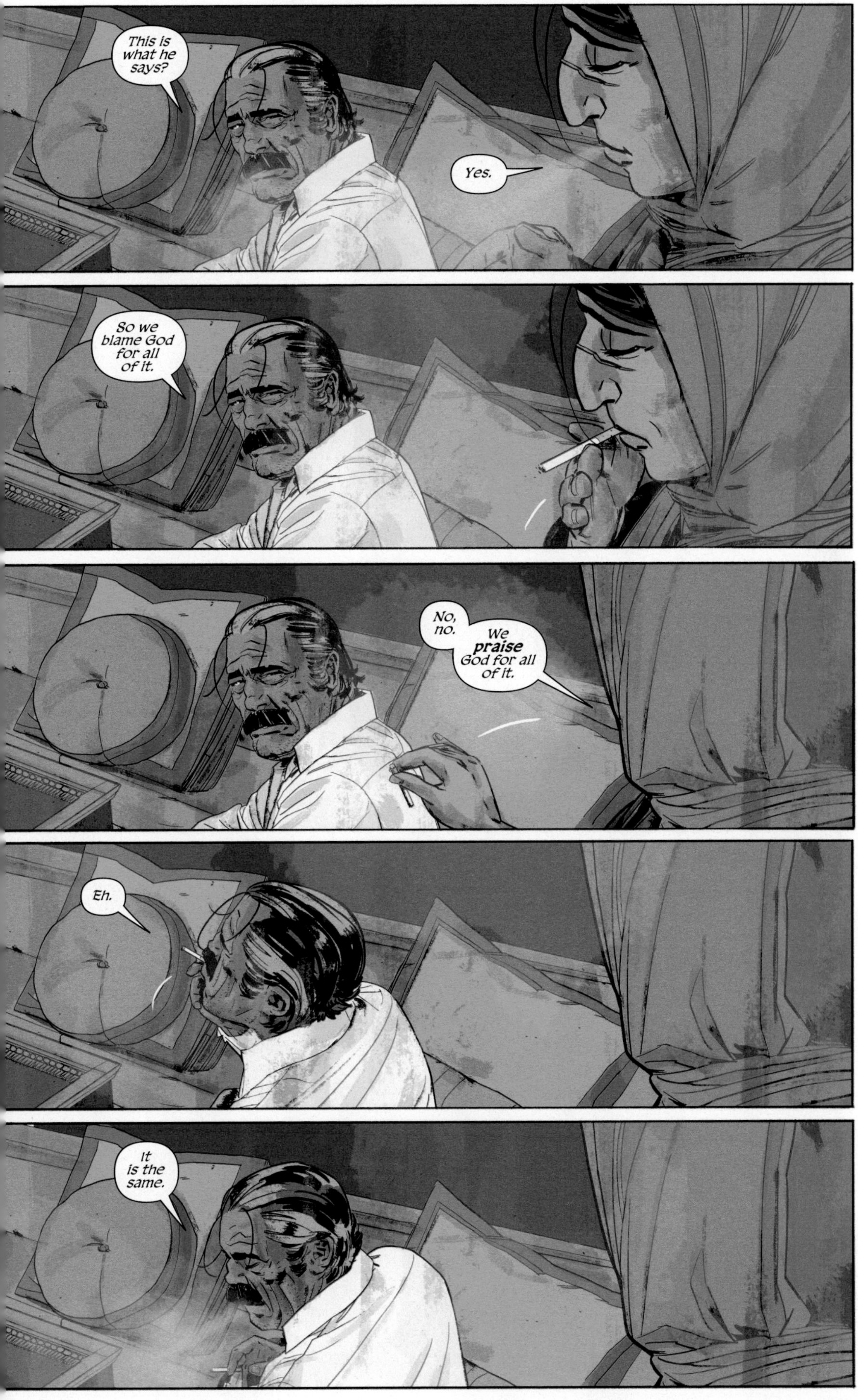
This is what he says?
Yes.
So we blame God for all of it.
No, no.
We **praise** God for all of it.
Eh.
It is the same.

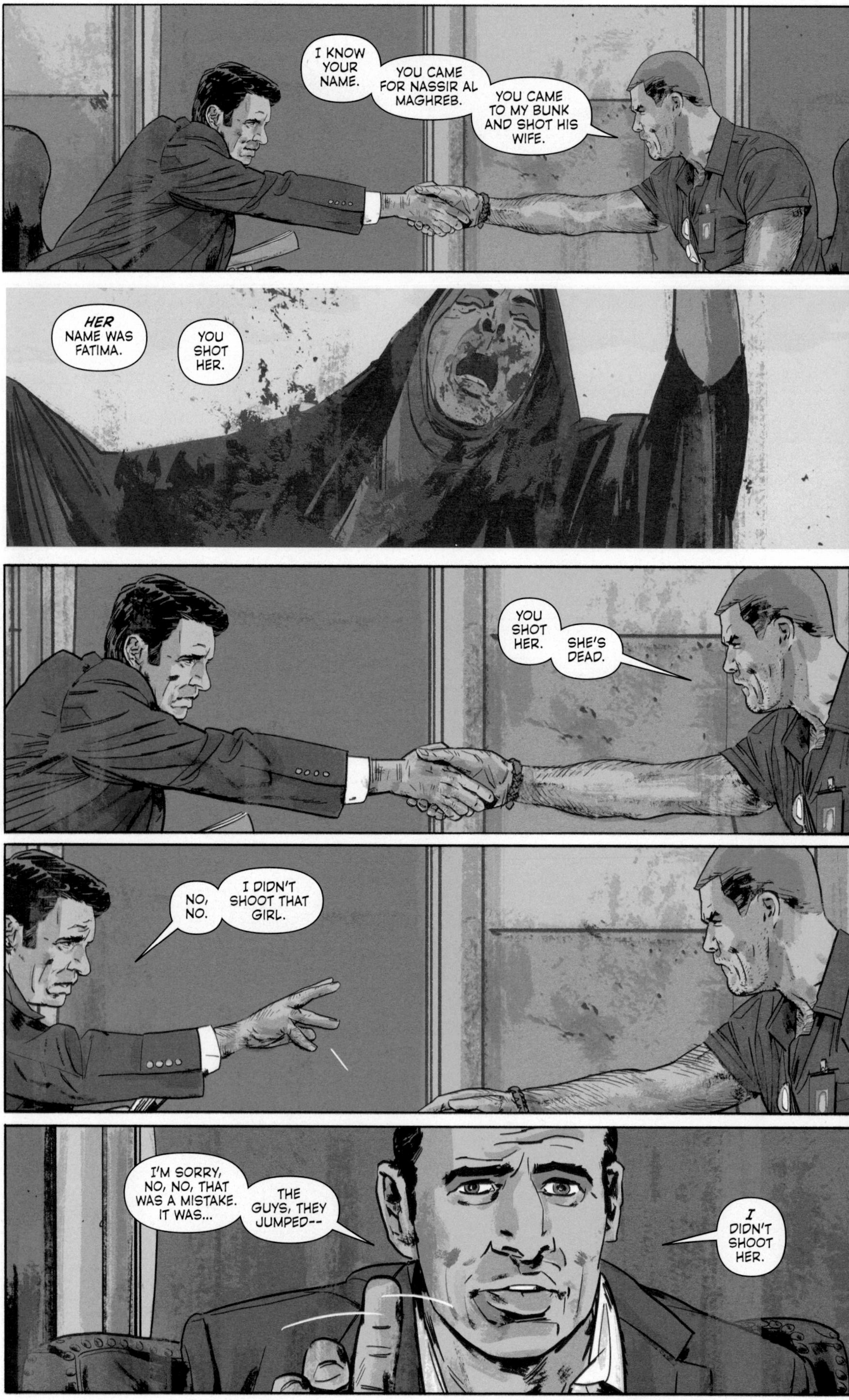
I KNOW YOUR NAME.
YOU CAME FOR NASSIR AL MAGHREB.
YOU CAME TO MY BUNK AND SHOT HIS WIFE.
HER NAME WAS FATIMA.
YOU SHOT HER.
YOU SHOT HER.
SHE'S DEAD.
NO, NO.
I DIDN'T SHOOT THAT GIRL.
I'M SORRY, NO, NO, THAT WAS A MISTAKE. IT WAS...
THE GUYS, THEY JUMPED--
I DIDN'T SHOOT HER.

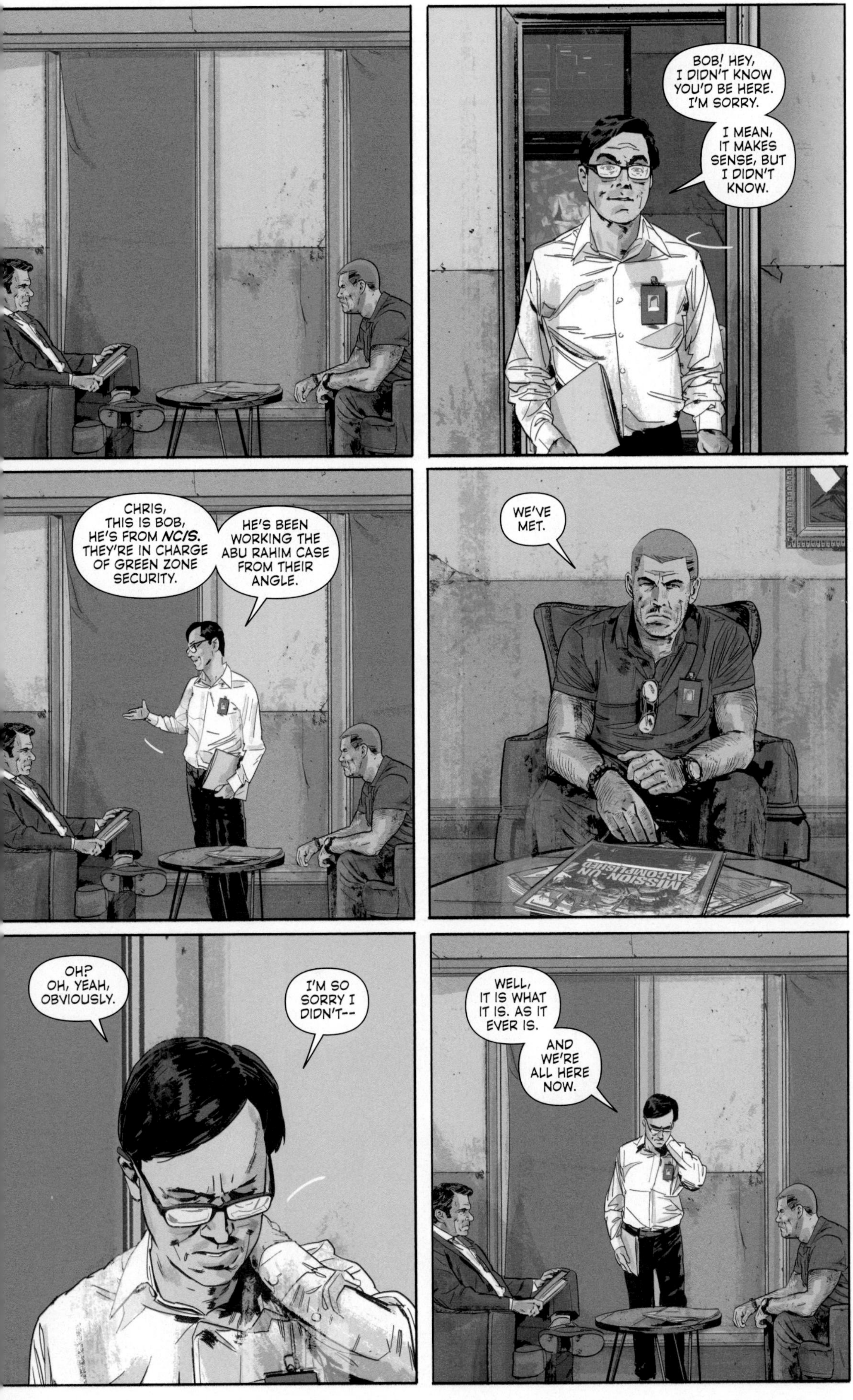
BOB! HEY, I DIDN'T KNOW YOU'D BE HERE. I'M SORRY.
I MEAN, IT MAKES SENSE, BUT I DIDN'T KNOW.
CHRIS, THIS IS BOB, HE'S FROM *NCIS*. THEY'RE IN CHARGE OF GREEN ZONE SECURITY.
HE'S BEEN WORKING THE ABU RAHIM CASE FROM THEIR ANGLE.
WE'VE MET.
MISSION-UN ACCOMPLISHED
OH? OH, YEAH, OBVIOUSLY.
I'M SO SORRY I DIDN'T--
WELL, IT IS WHAT IT IS. AS IT EVER IS.
AND WE'RE ALL HERE NOW.

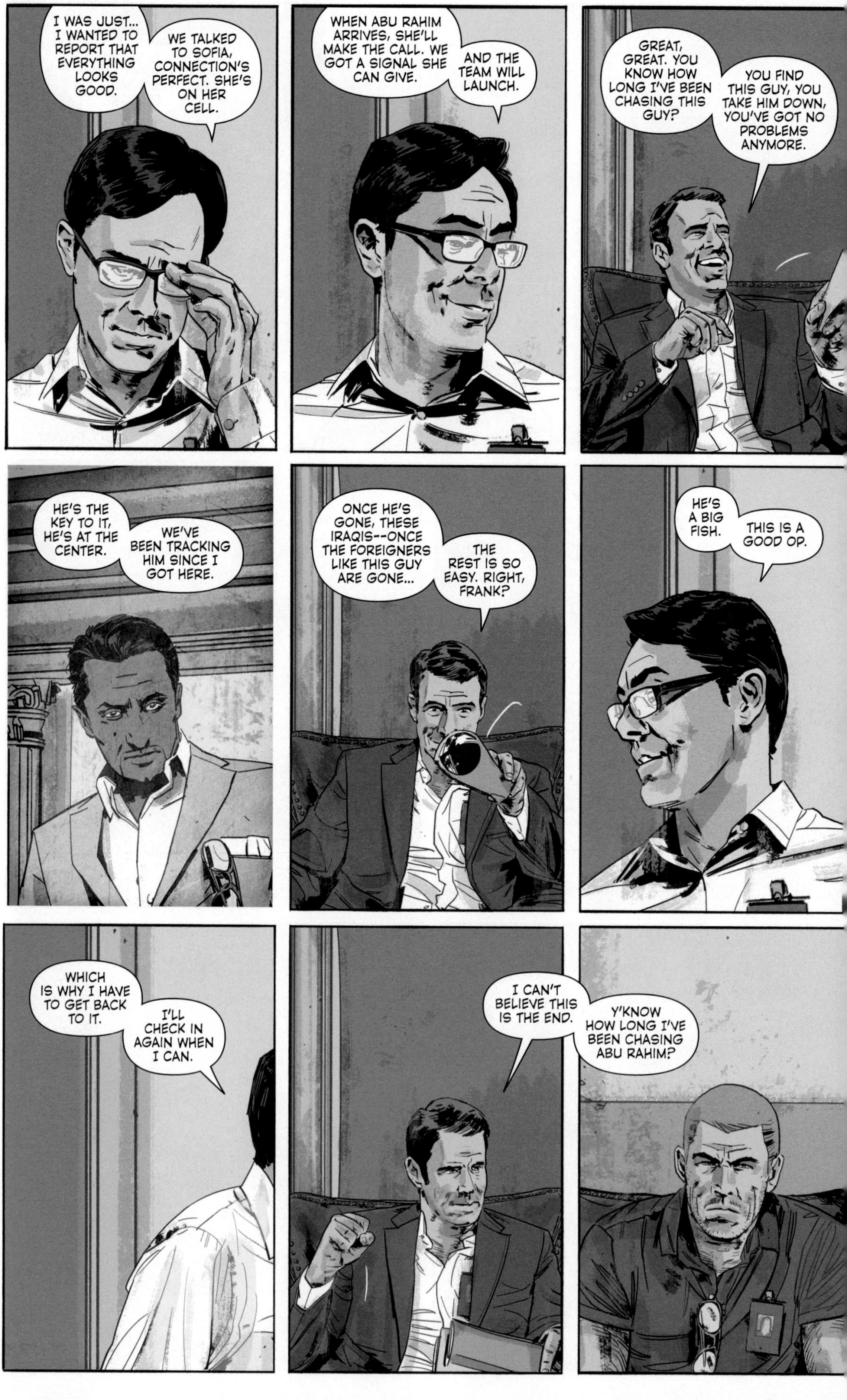
I WAS JUST... I WANTED TO REPORT THAT EVERYTHING LOOKS GOOD.
WE TALKED TO SOFIA, CONNECTION'S PERFECT. SHE'S ON HER CELL.
WHEN ABU RAHIM ARRIVES, SHE'LL MAKE THE CALL. WE GOT A SIGNAL SHE CAN GIVE.
AND THE TEAM WILL LAUNCH.
GREAT, GREAT. YOU KNOW HOW LONG I'VE BEEN CHASING THIS GUY?
YOU FIND THIS GUY, YOU TAKE HIM DOWN, YOU'VE GOT NO PROBLEMS ANYMORE.
HE'S THE KEY TO IT, HE'S AT THE CENTER.
WE'VE BEEN TRACKING HIM SINCE I GOT HERE.
ONCE HE'S GONE, THESE IRAQIS--ONCE THE FOREIGNERS LIKE THIS GUY ARE GONE...
THE REST IS SO EASY. RIGHT, FRANK?
HE'S A BIG FISH.
THIS IS A GOOD OP.
WHICH IS WHY I HAVE TO GET BACK TO IT.
I'LL CHECK IN AGAIN WHEN I CAN.
I CAN'T BELIEVE THIS IS THE END.
Y'KNOW HOW LONG I'VE BEEN CHASING ABU RAHIM?

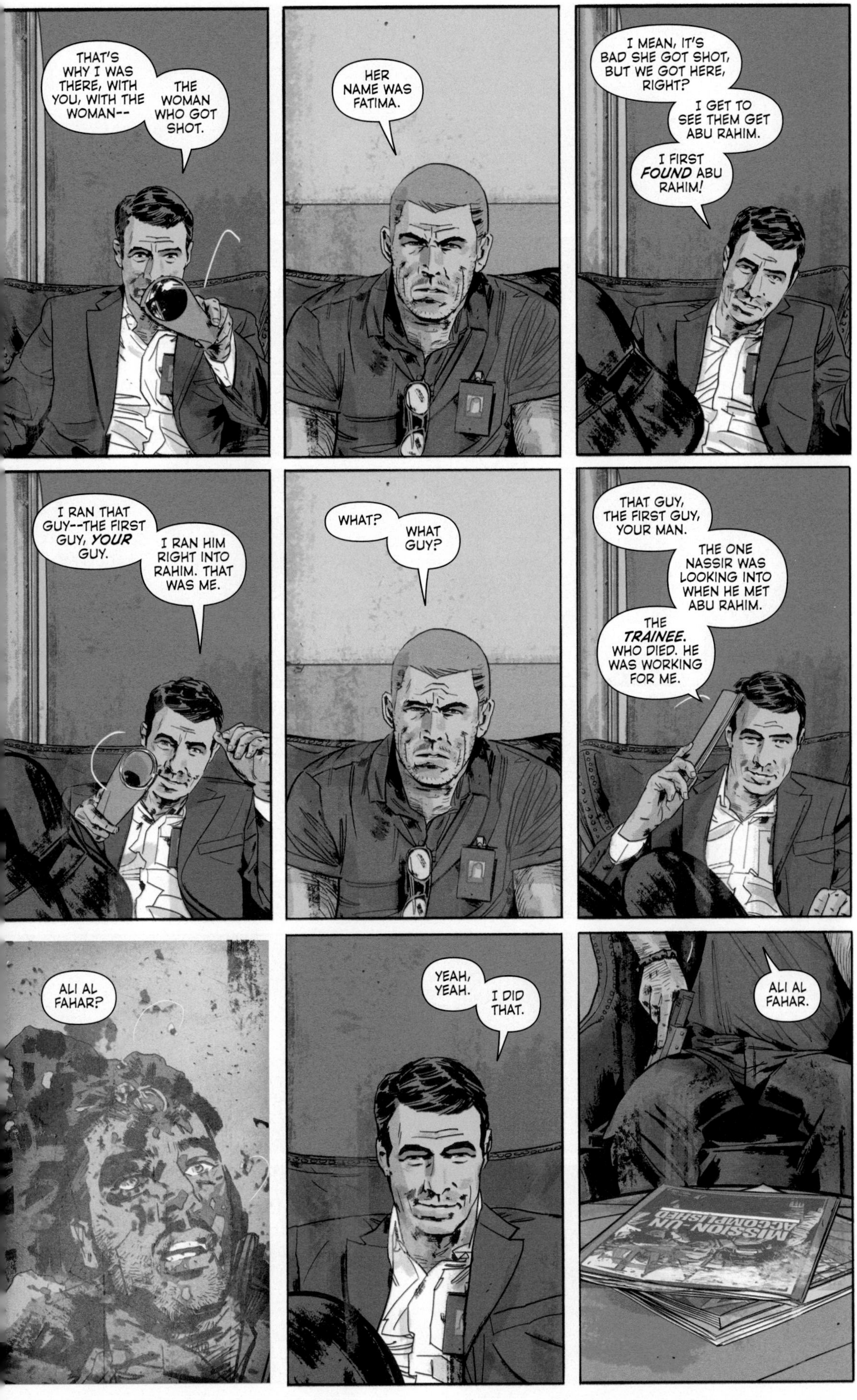
THAT'S WHY I WAS THERE, WITH YOU, WITH THE WOMAN--
THE WOMAN WHO GOT SHOT.
HER NAME WAS FATIMA.
I MEAN, IT'S BAD SHE GOT SHOT, BUT WE GOT HERE, RIGHT?
I GET TO SEE THEM GET ABU RAHIM.
I FIRST FOUND ABU RAHIM!
I RAN THAT GUY--THE FIRST GUY, YOUR GUY.
I RAN HIM RIGHT INTO RAHIM. THAT WAS ME.
WHAT?
WHAT GUY?
THAT GUY, THE FIRST GUY, YOUR MAN.
THE ONE NASSIR WAS LOOKING INTO WHEN HE MET ABU RAHIM.
THE TRAINEE. WHO DIED. HE WAS WORKING FOR ME.
ALI AL FAHAR?
YEAH, YEAH.
I DID THAT.
ALI AL FAHAR.
MISSION-UN-ACCOMPLISHED

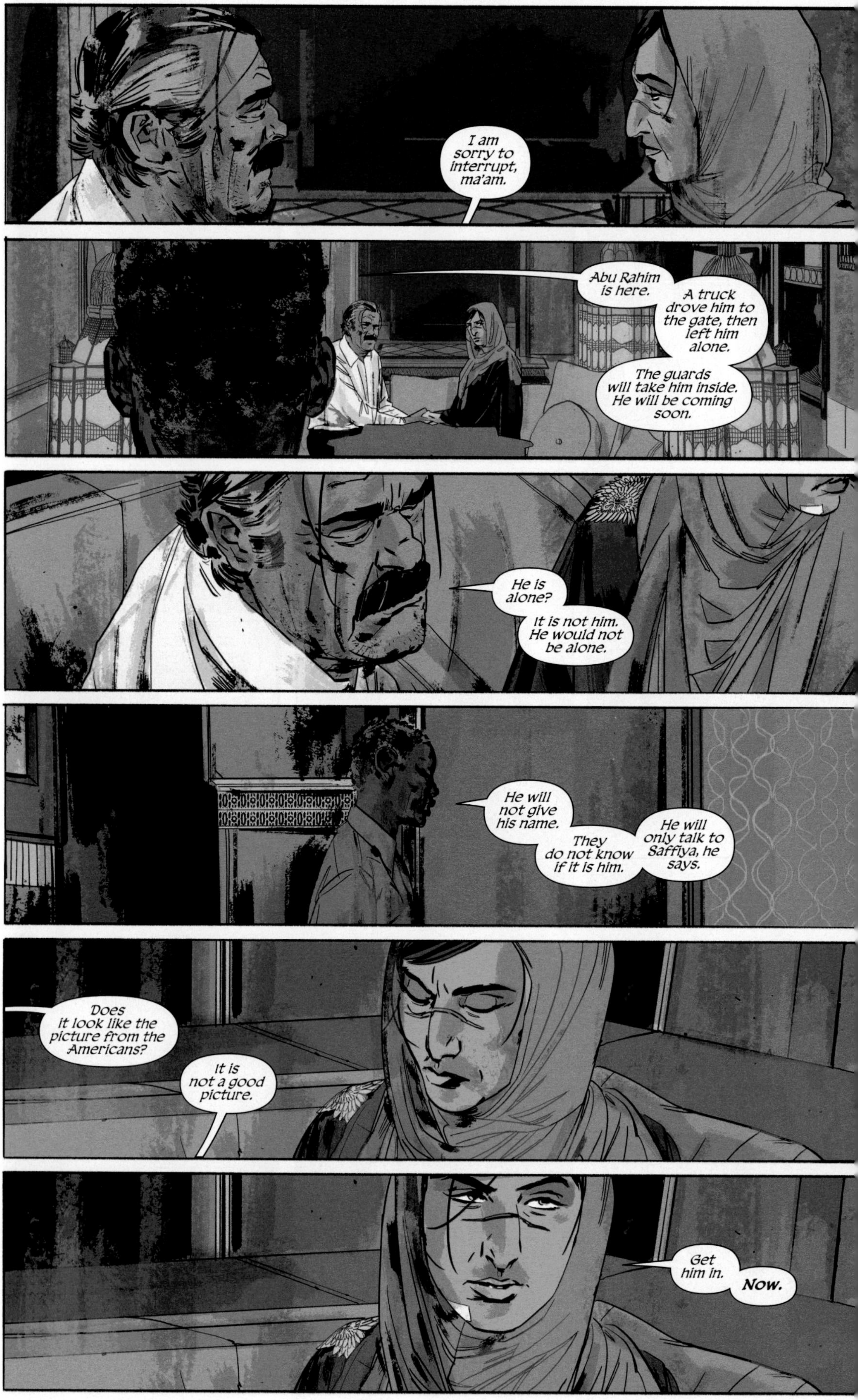
I am sorry to interrupt, ma'am.
Abu Rahim is here.
A truck drove him to the gate, then left him alone.
The guards will take him inside. He will be coming soon.
He is alone?
It is not him. He would not be alone.
He will not give his name.
They do not know if it is him.
He will only talk to Saffiya, he says.
Does it look like the picture from the Americans?
It is not a good picture.
Get him in.
Now.

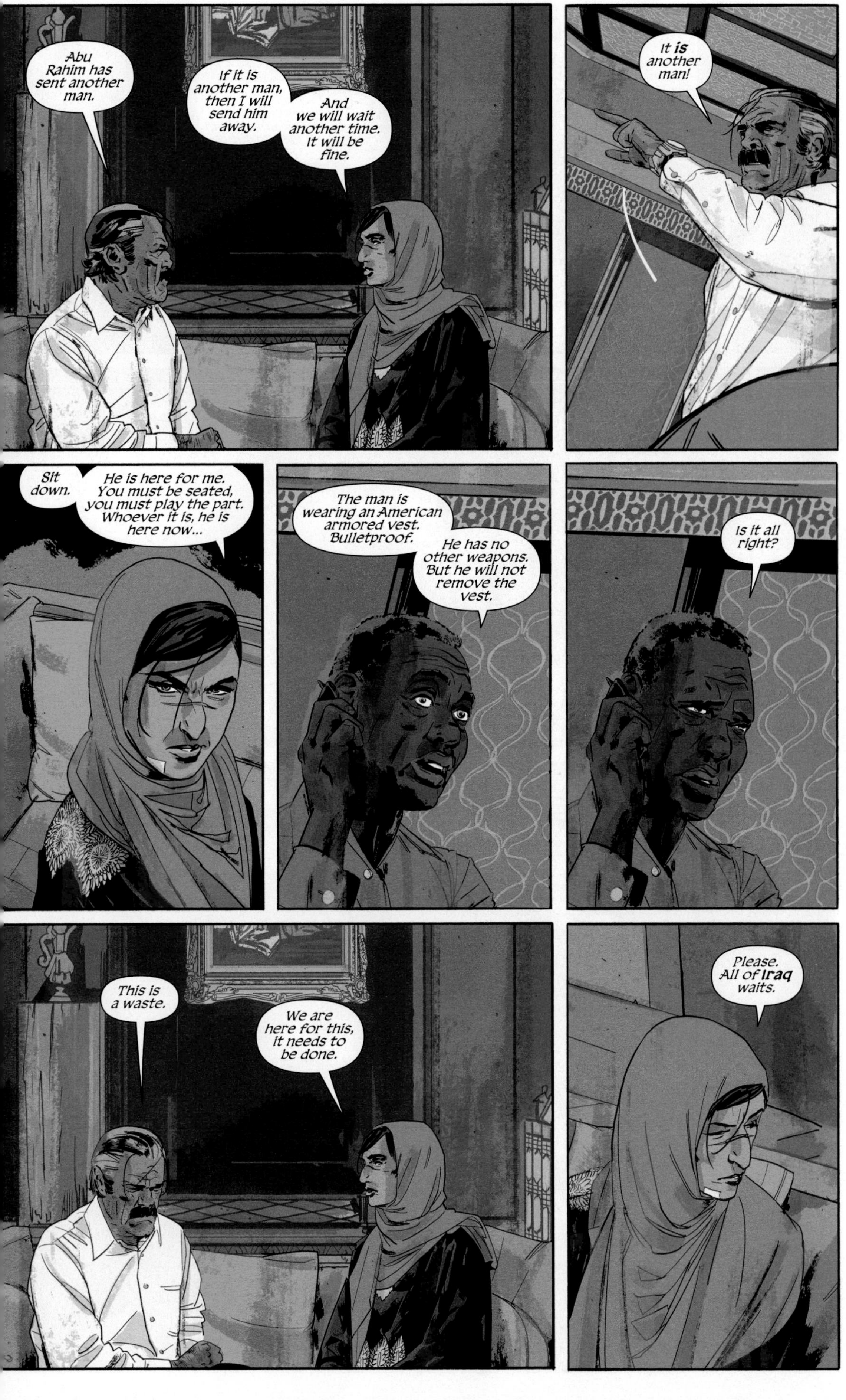
Abu Rahim has sent another man.
If it is another man, then I will send him away.
And we will wait another time. It will be fine.
It is another man!
Sit down.
He is here for me. You must be seated, you must play the part. Whoever it is, he is here now...
The man is wearing an American armored vest. Bulletproof.
He has no other weapons. But he will not remove the vest.
Is it all right?
This is a waste.
We are here for this, it needs to be done.
Please. All of Iraq waits.

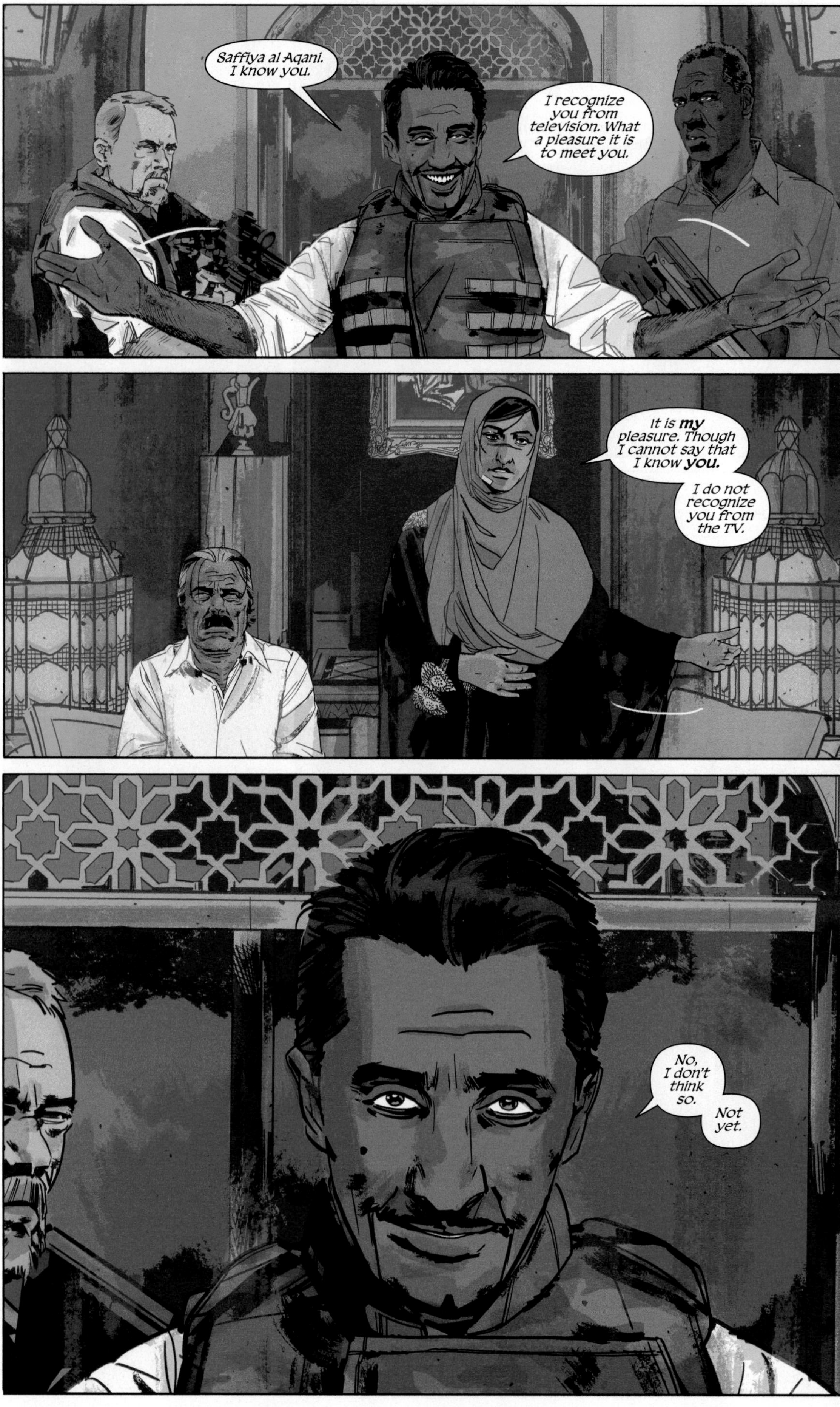
Saffiya al Aqani. I know you.
I recognize you from television. What a pleasure it is to meet you.
It is **my** pleasure. Though I cannot say that I know **you.**
I do not recognize you from the TV.
No, I don't think so.
Not yet.

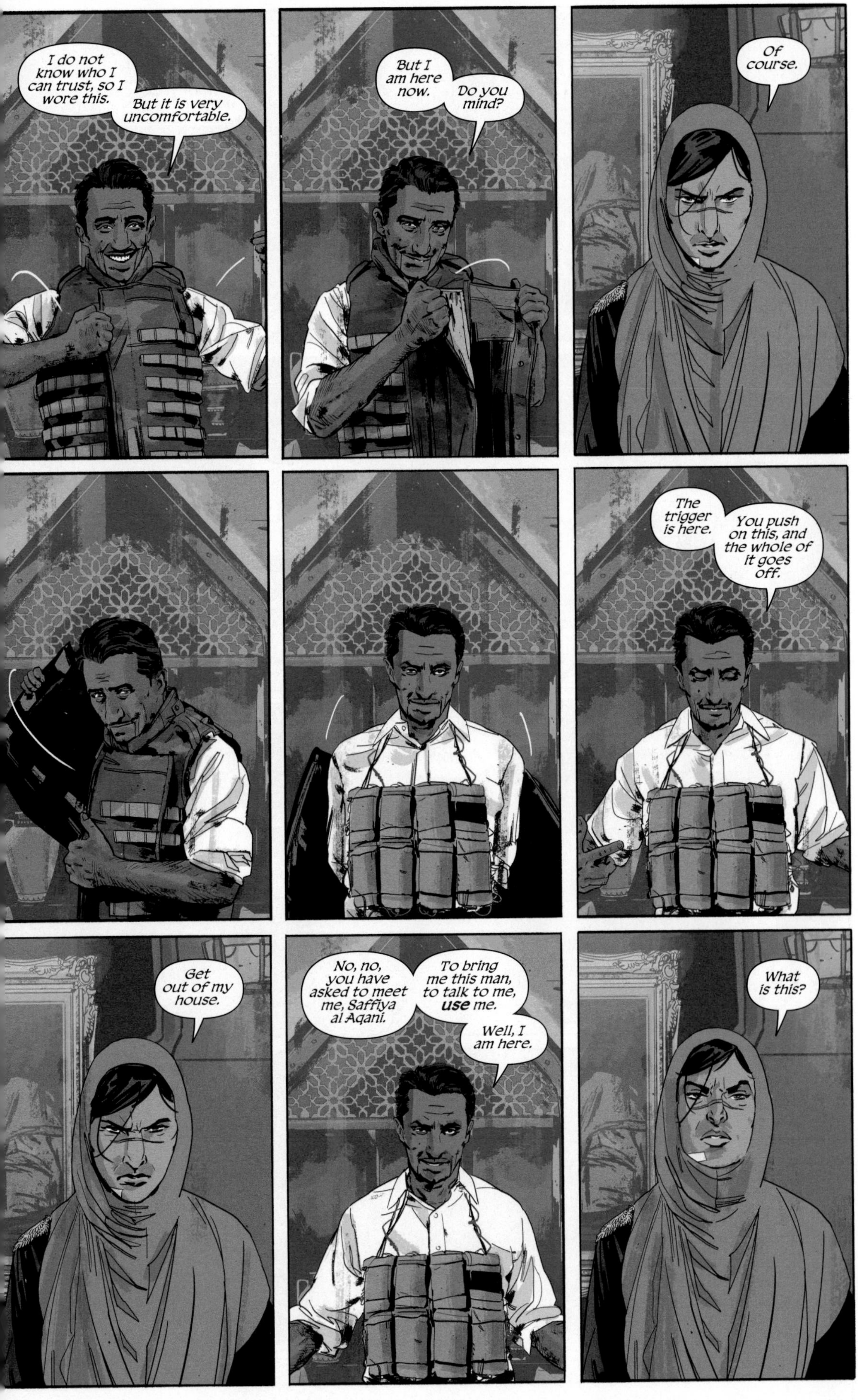
I do not know who I can trust, so I wore this.
But it is very uncomfortable.
But I am here now.
Do you mind?
Of course.
The trigger is here.
You push on this, and the whole of it goes off.
Get out of my house.
No, no, you have asked to meet me, Saffiya al Aqani.
To bring me this man, to talk to me, **use** me.
Well, I am here.
What is this?

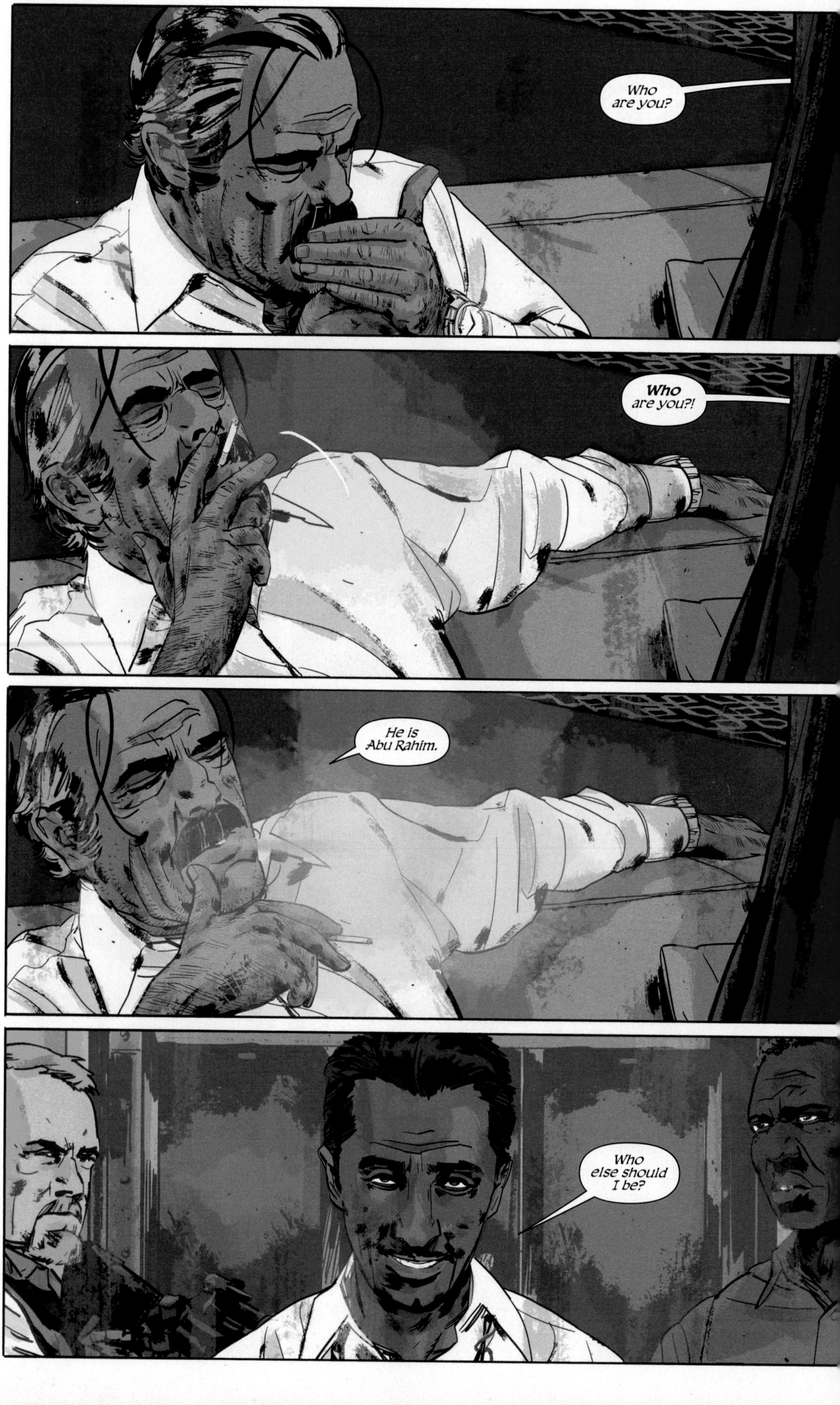
Who are you?
Who are you?!
He is Abu Rahim.
Who else should I be?

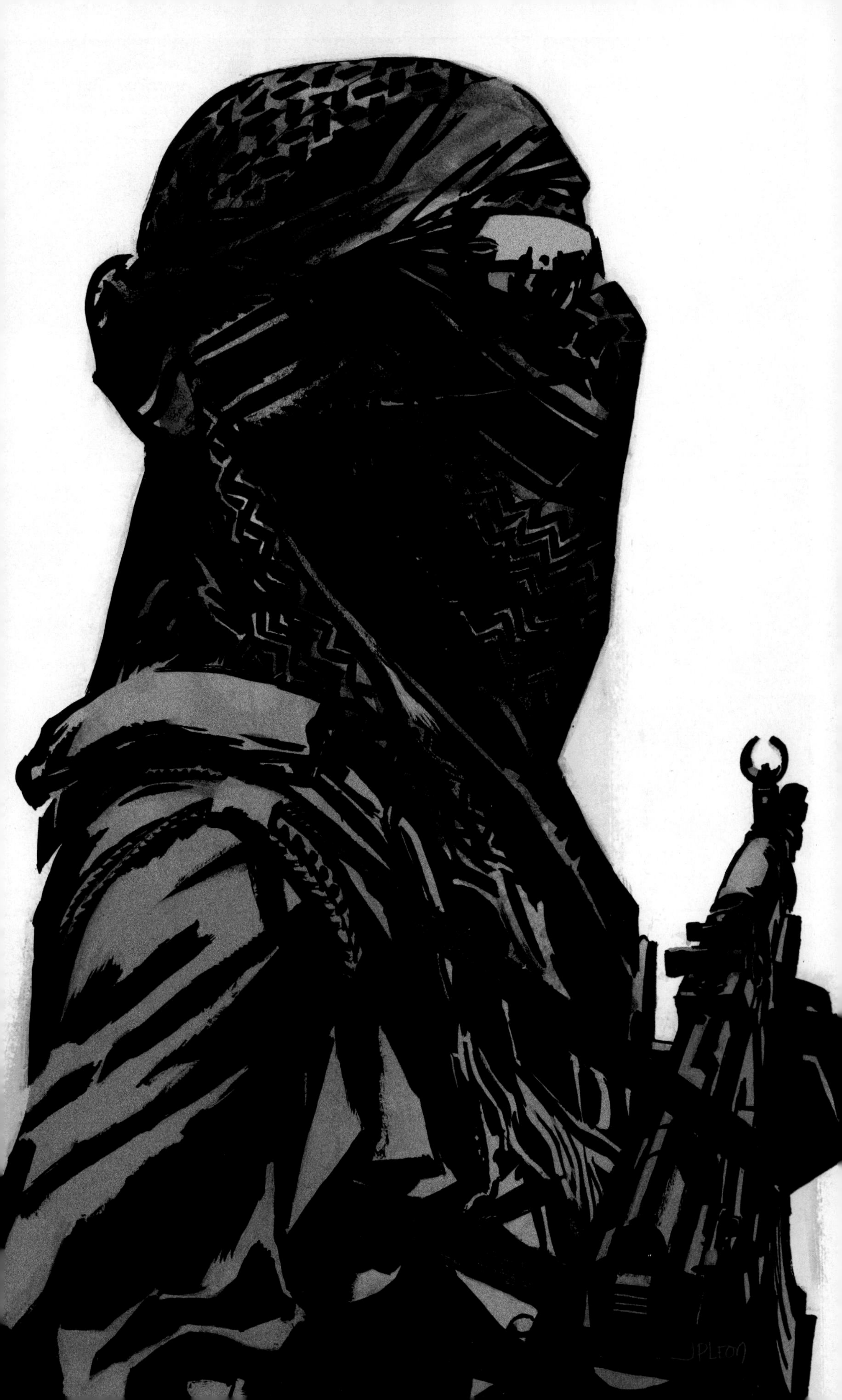
JPLEON

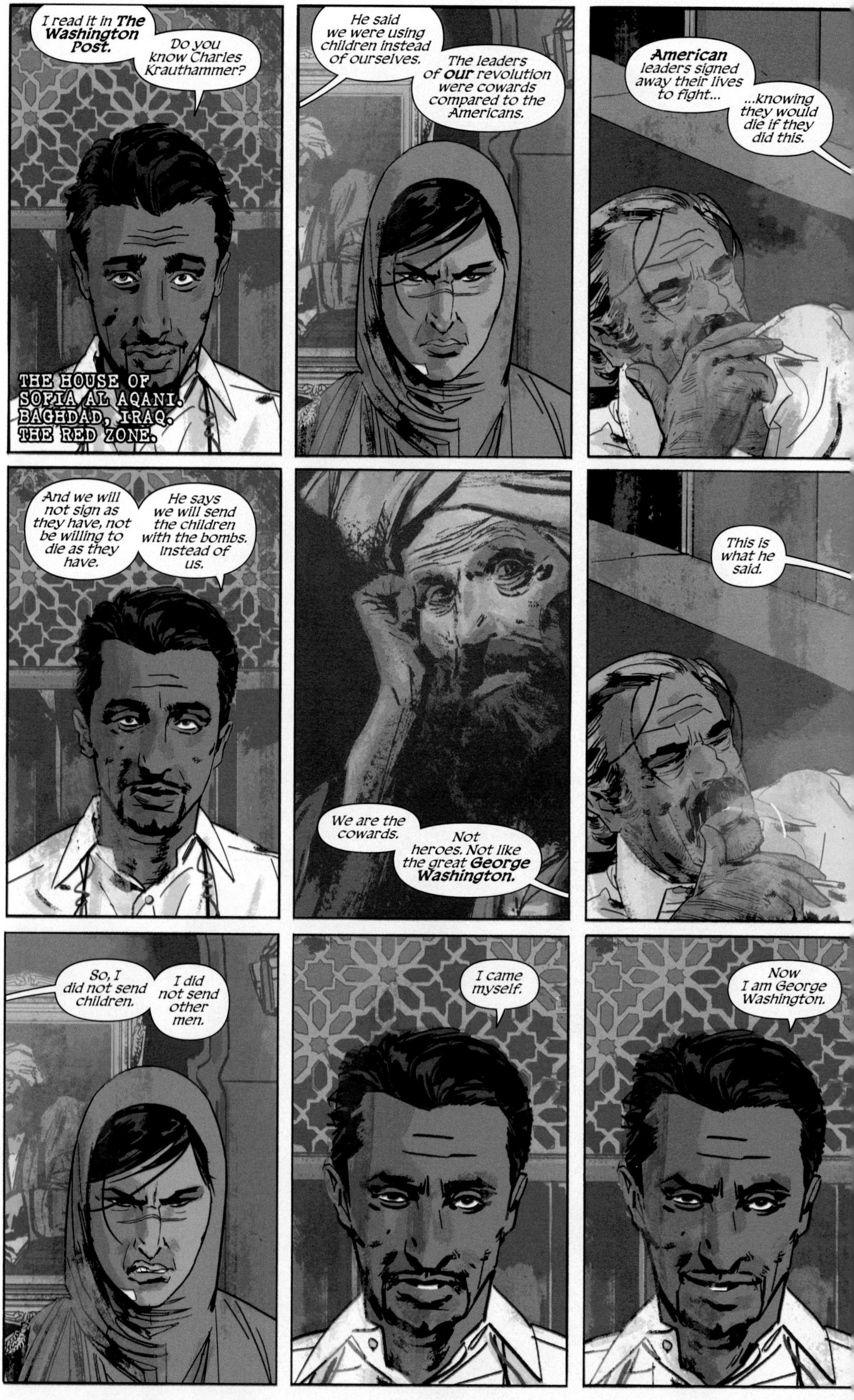
I read it in The Washington Post.
Do you know Charles Krauthammer?
THE HOUSE OF SOFIA AL AQANI. BAGHDAD, IRAQ. THE RED ZONE.
He said we were using children instead of ourselves.
The leaders of our revolution were cowards compared to the Americans.
American leaders signed away their lives to fight...
...knowing they would die if they did this.
And we will not sign as they have, not be willing to die as they have.
He says we will send the children with the bombs. Instead of us.
We are the cowards.
Not heroes. Not like the great George Washington.
This is what he said.
So, I did not send children.
I did not send other men.
I came myself.
Now I am George Washington.

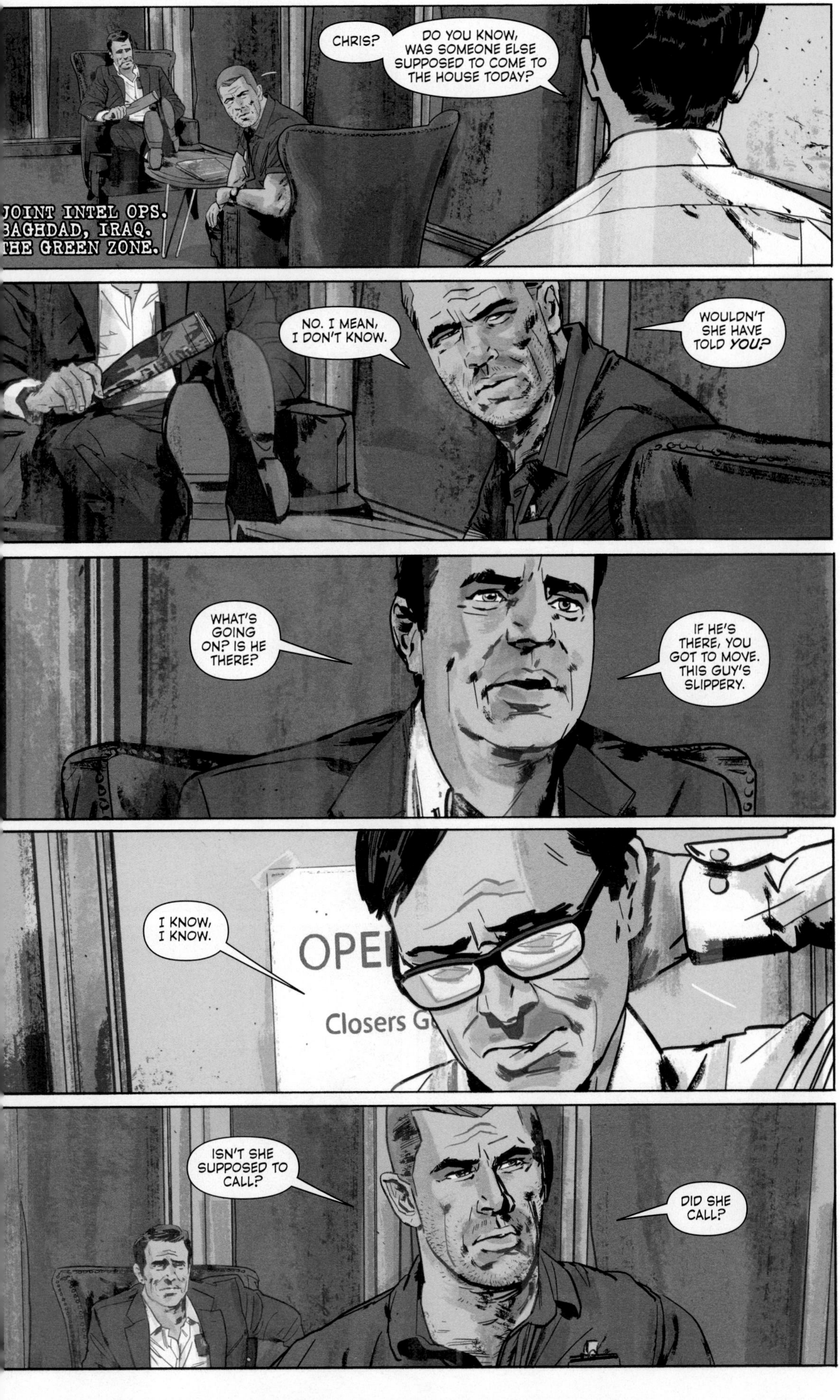
JOINT INTEL OPS.
BAGHDAD, IRAQ.
THE GREEN ZONE.
CHRIS?
DO YOU KNOW, WAS SOMEONE ELSE SUPPOSED TO COME TO THE HOUSE TODAY?
NO. I MEAN, I DON'T KNOW.
WOULDN'T SHE HAVE TOLD *YOU?*
WHAT'S GOING ON? IS HE THERE?
IF HE'S THERE, YOU GOT TO MOVE. THIS GUY'S SLIPPERY.
I KNOW, I KNOW.
OPE
Closers G
ISN'T SHE SUPPOSED TO CALL?
DID SHE CALL?

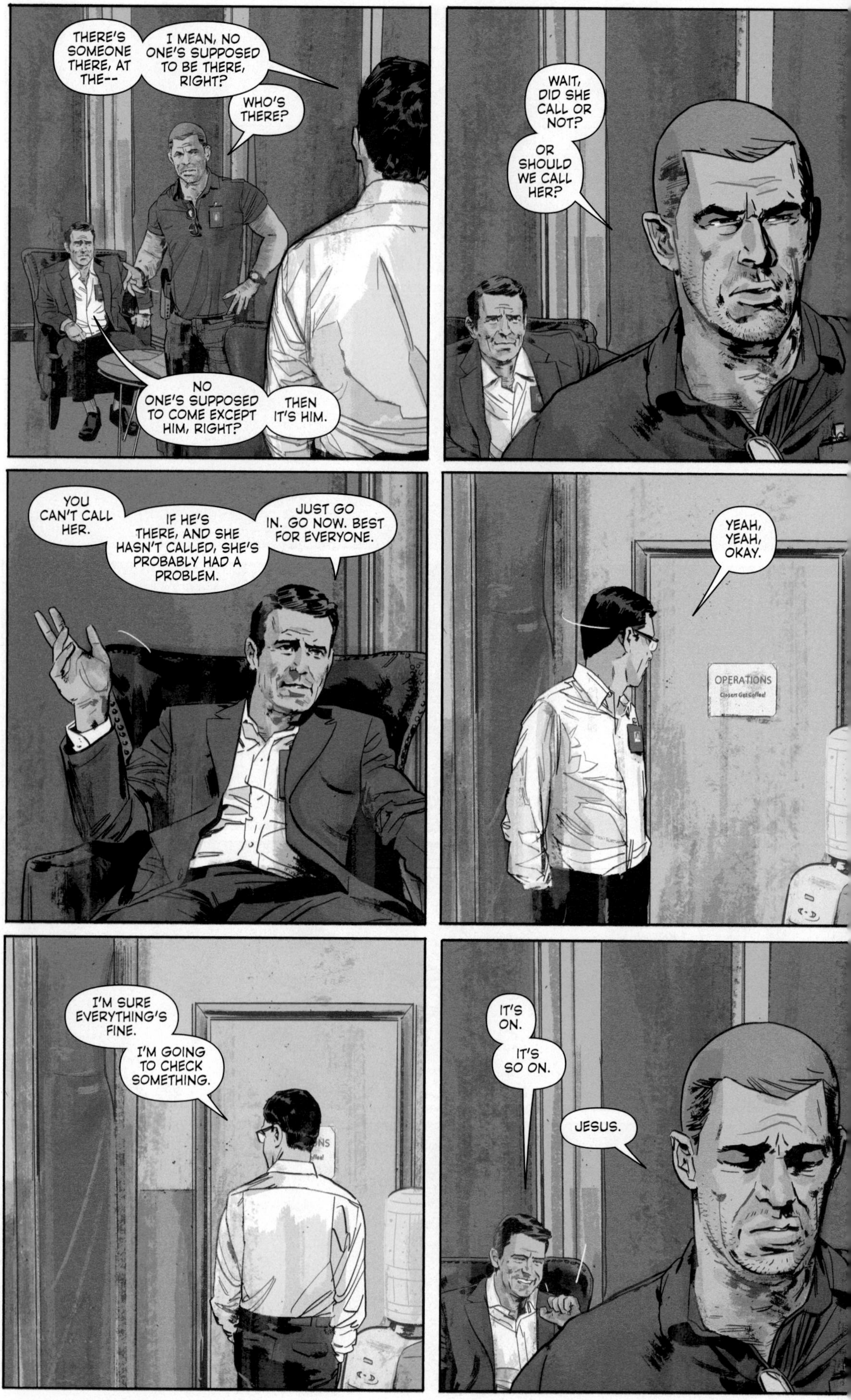
THERE'S SOMEONE THERE, AT THE--
I MEAN, NO ONE'S SUPPOSED TO BE THERE, RIGHT?
WHO'S THERE?
NO ONE'S SUPPOSED TO COME EXCEPT HIM, RIGHT?
THEN IT'S HIM.
WAIT, DID SHE CALL OR NOT?
OR SHOULD WE CALL HER?
YOU CAN'T CALL HER.
IF HE'S THERE, AND SHE HASN'T CALLED, SHE'S PROBABLY HAD A PROBLEM.
JUST GO IN. GO NOW. BEST FOR EVERYONE.
YEAH, YEAH, OKAY.
OPERATIONS
I'M SURE EVERYTHING'S FINE.
I'M GOING TO CHECK SOMETHING.
IT'S ON.
IT'S SO ON.
JESUS.

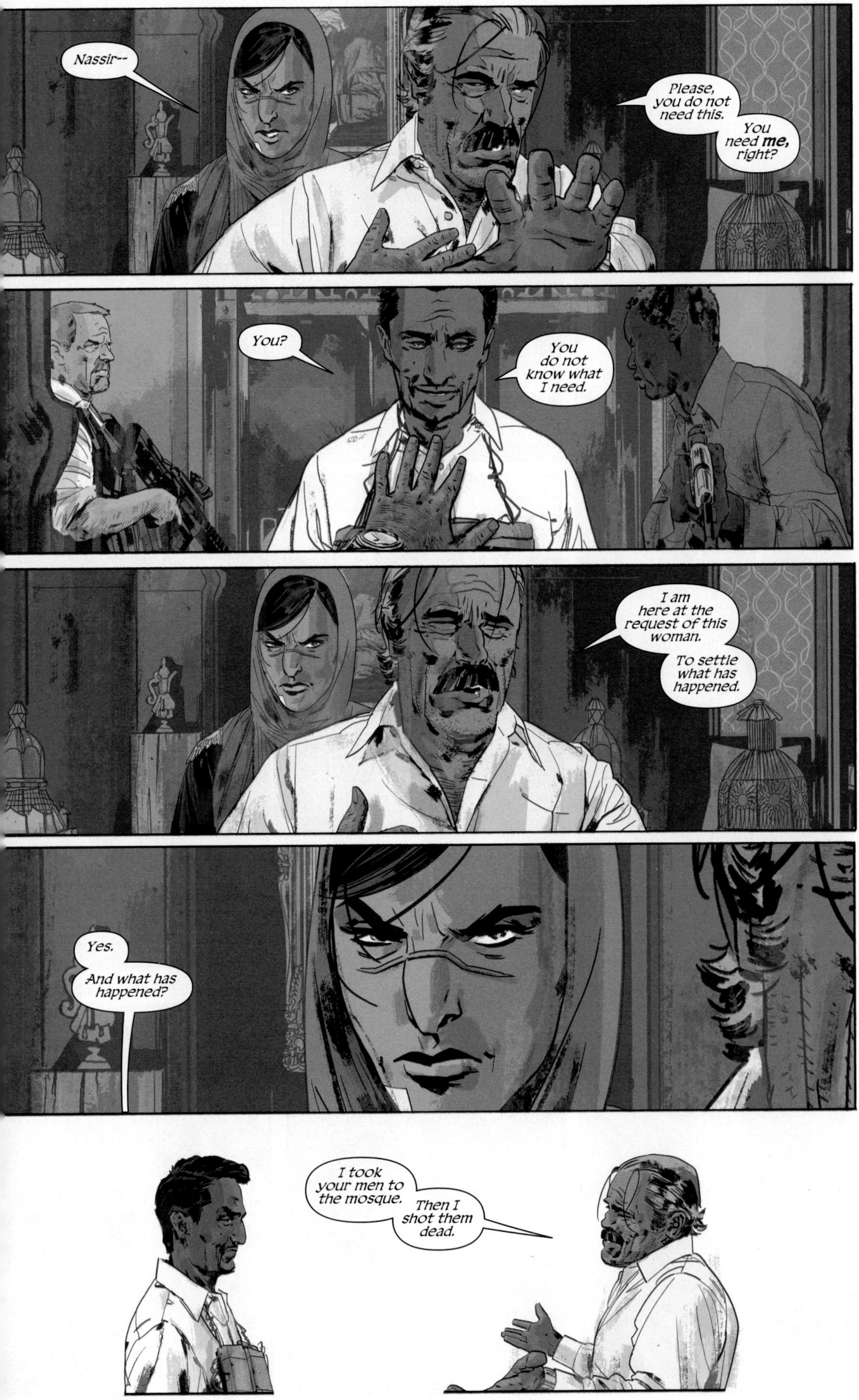
Nassir--
Please, you do not need this.
You need **me,** right?
You?
You do not know what I need.
I am here at the request of this woman.
To settle what has happened.
Yes.
And what has happened?
I took your men to the mosque.
Then I shot them dead.

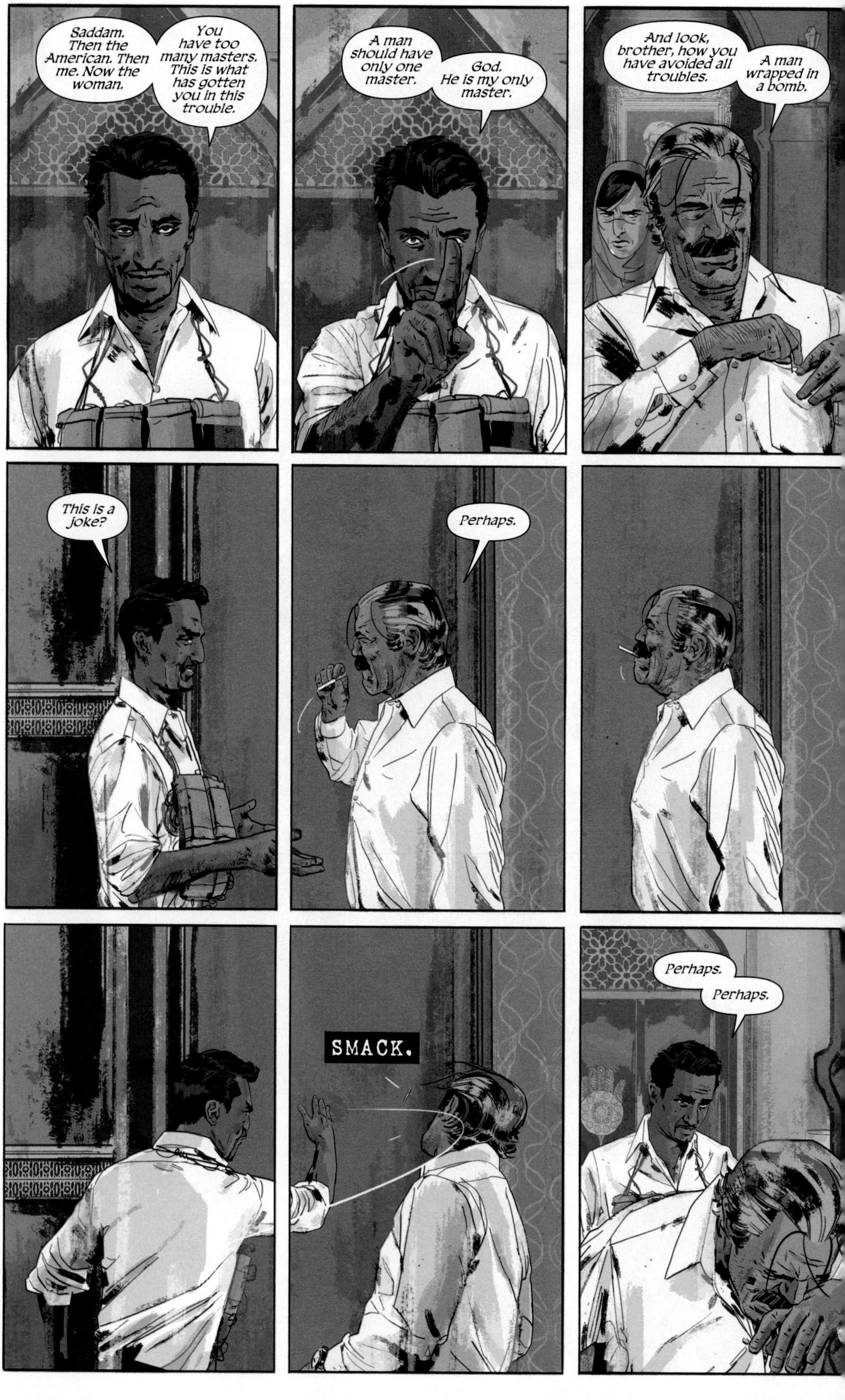
Saddam. Then the American. Then me. Now the woman.
You have too many masters. This is what has gotten you in this trouble.
A man should have only one master.
God. He is my only master.
And look, brother, how you have avoided all troubles.
A man wrapped in a bomb.
This is a joke?
Perhaps.
SMACK.
Perhaps.
Perhaps.

HE IS SLIPPERY. ABU RAHIM, MAN.

YOU THINK YOU'VE GOT IT ALL FIGURED OUT, AND WHEW, IT'S JUST GONE, HE'S ALL GONE.

I HAD THE CLOSEST OP.

DID YOU HEAR ABOUT THAT, DID FRANKLIN TELL YOU?

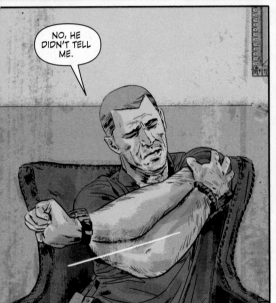

NO, HE DIDN'T TELL ME.

WE WERE SO CLOSE.

GODDAMN!

THIS IS WITH ALI. YOUR GUY.

THE ONE WE WERE RUNNING IN ON RAHIM.

WE WERE CLOSE, MAN.

WE WERE SO CLOSE IT WAS IN MY MOUTH, YOU KNOW?

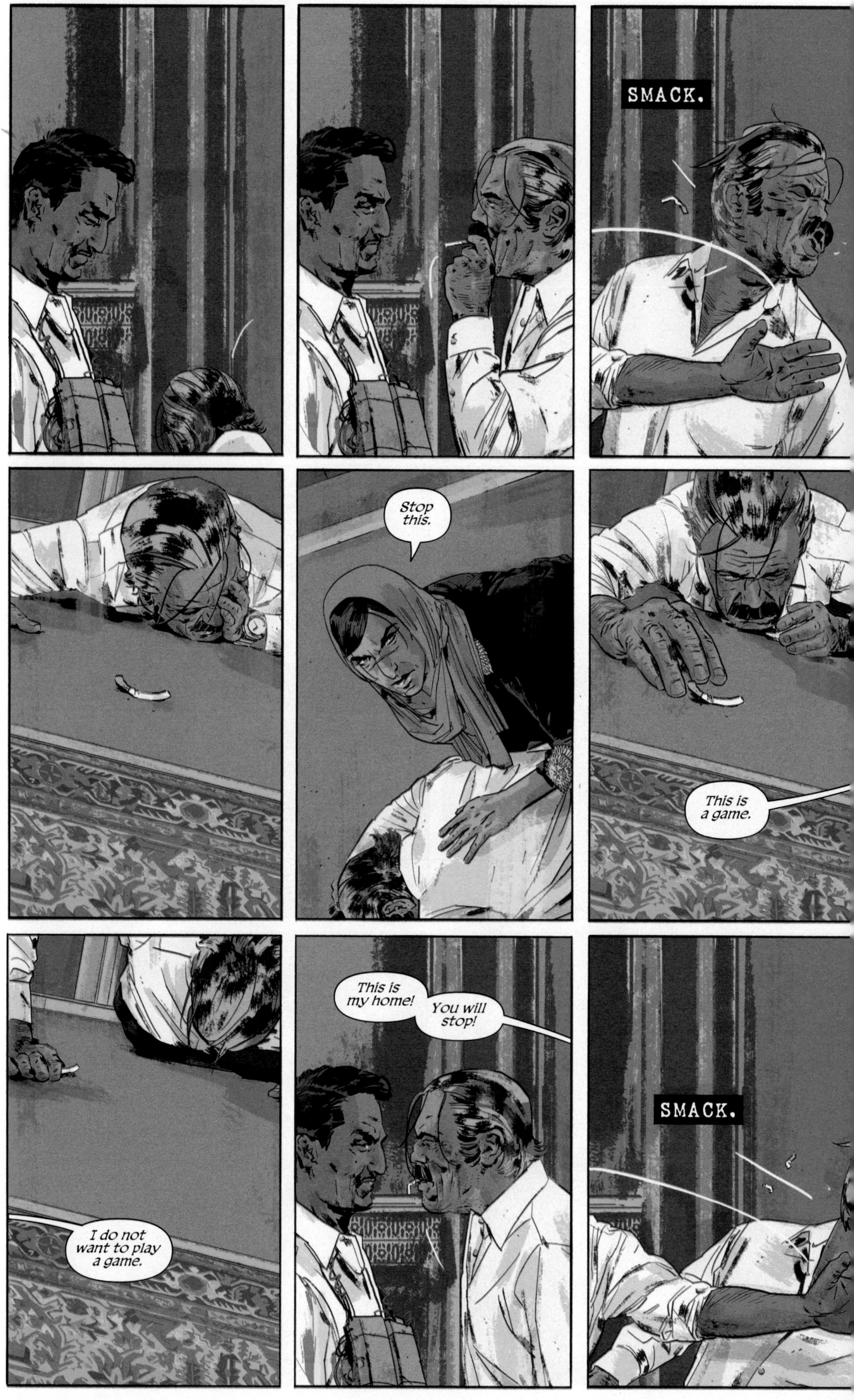
SMACK.
Stop this.
This is a game.
I do not want to play a game.
This is my home!
You will stop!
SMACK.

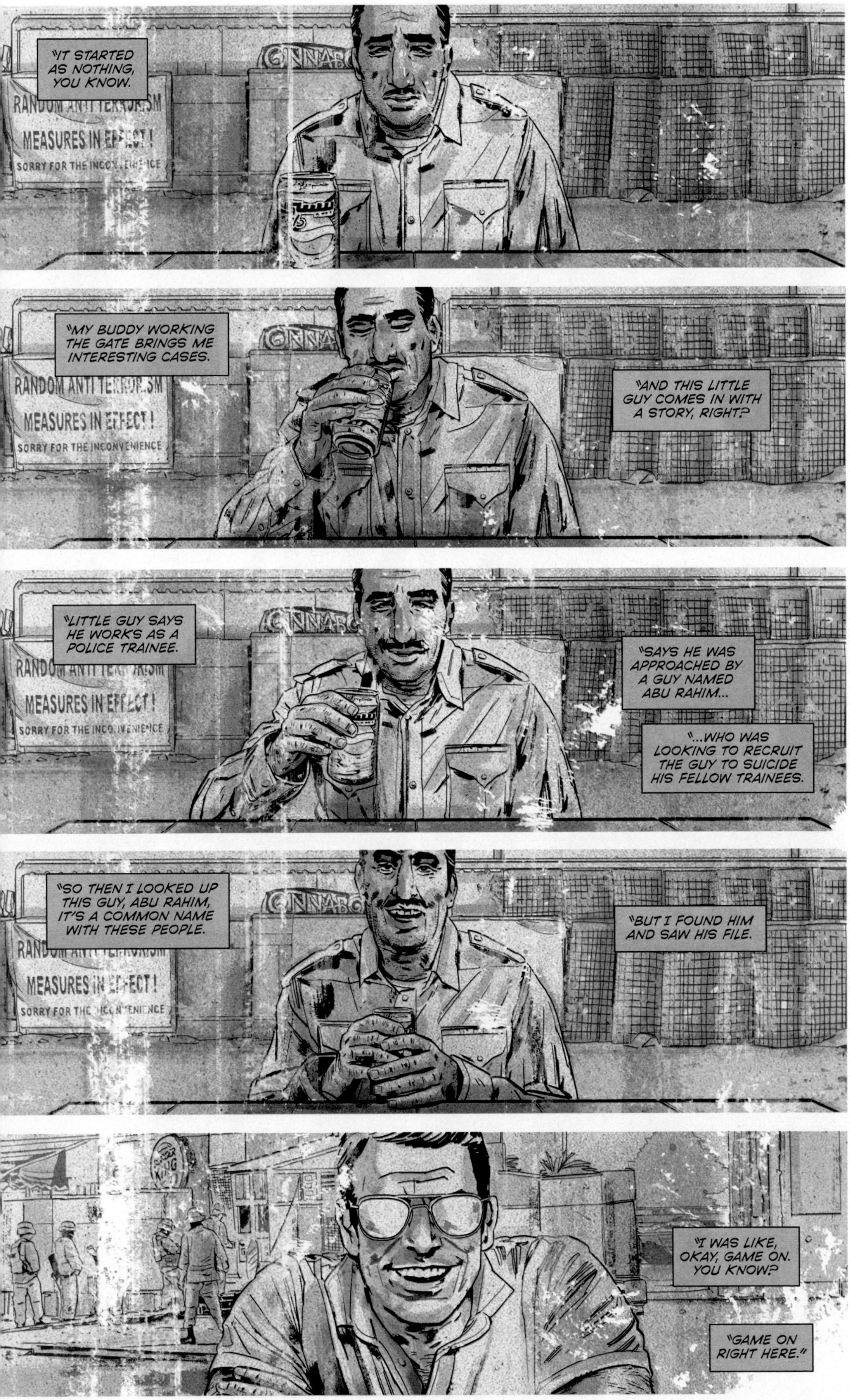
"IT STARTED AS NOTHING, YOU KNOW.
RANDOM ANTI TERRORISM MEASURES IN EFFECT! SORRY FOR THE INCONVENIENCE
"MY BUDDY WORKING THE GATE BRINGS ME INTERESTING CASES.
"AND THIS LITTLE GUY COMES IN WITH A STORY, RIGHT?
"LITTLE GUY SAYS HE WORKS AS A POLICE TRAINEE.
"SAYS HE WAS APPROACHED BY A GUY NAMED ABU RAHIM...
"...WHO WAS LOOKING TO RECRUIT THE GUY TO SUICIDE HIS FELLOW TRAINEES.
"SO THEN I LOOKED UP THIS GUY, ABU RAHIM, IT'S A COMMON NAME WITH THESE PEOPLE.
"BUT I FOUND HIM AND SAW HIS FILE.
"I WAS LIKE, OKAY, GAME ON. YOU KNOW?
"GAME ON RIGHT HERE."

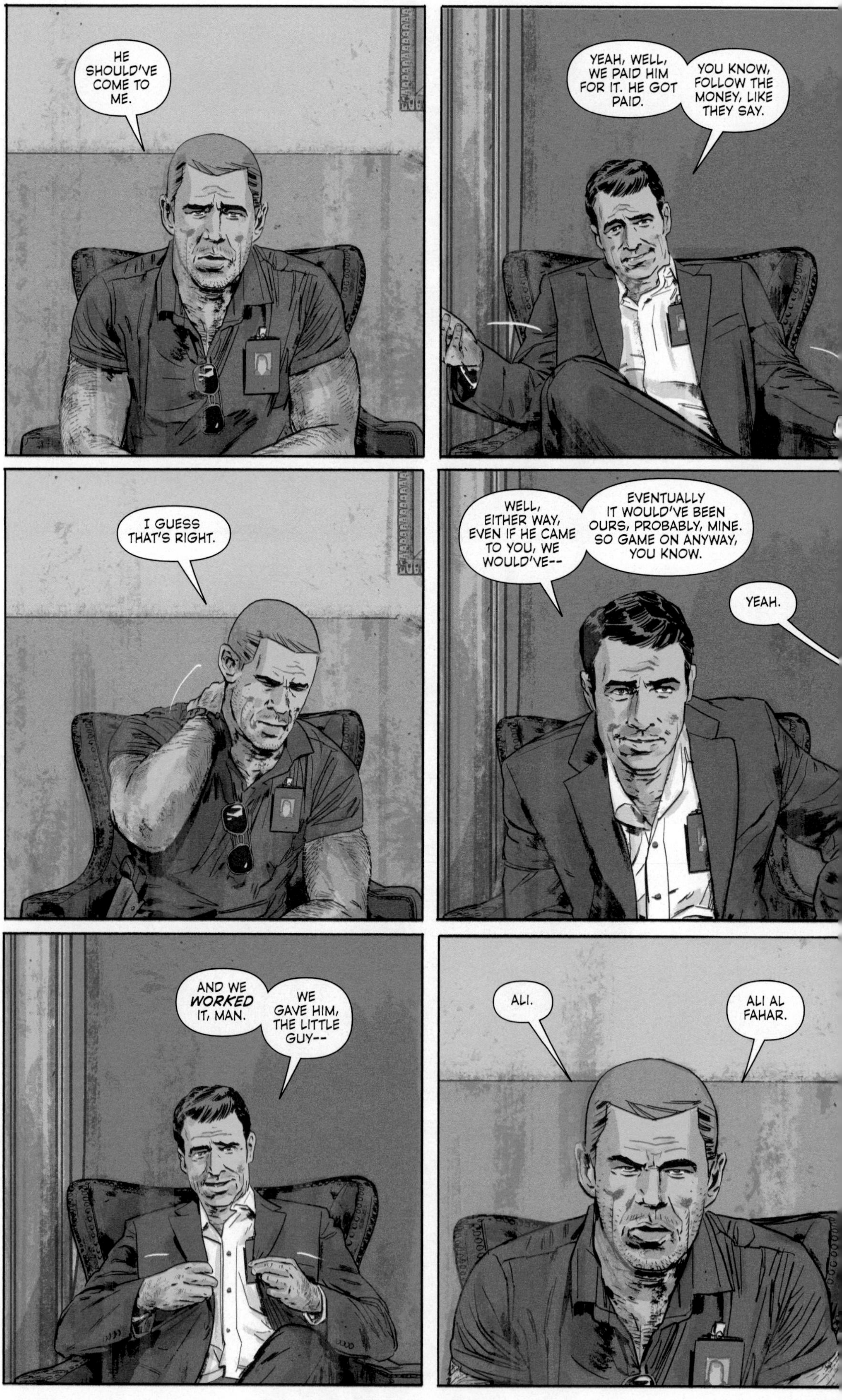
HE SHOULD'VE COME TO ME.
YEAH, WELL, WE PAID HIM FOR IT. HE GOT PAID.
YOU KNOW, FOLLOW THE MONEY, LIKE THEY SAY.
I GUESS THAT'S RIGHT.
WELL, EITHER WAY, EVEN IF HE CAME TO YOU, WE WOULD'VE--
EVENTUALLY IT WOULD'VE BEEN OURS, PROBABLY, MINE. SO GAME ON ANYWAY, YOU KNOW.
YEAH.
AND WE *WORKED* IT, MAN.
WE GAVE HIM, THE LITTLE GUY--
ALI.
ALI AL FAHAR.

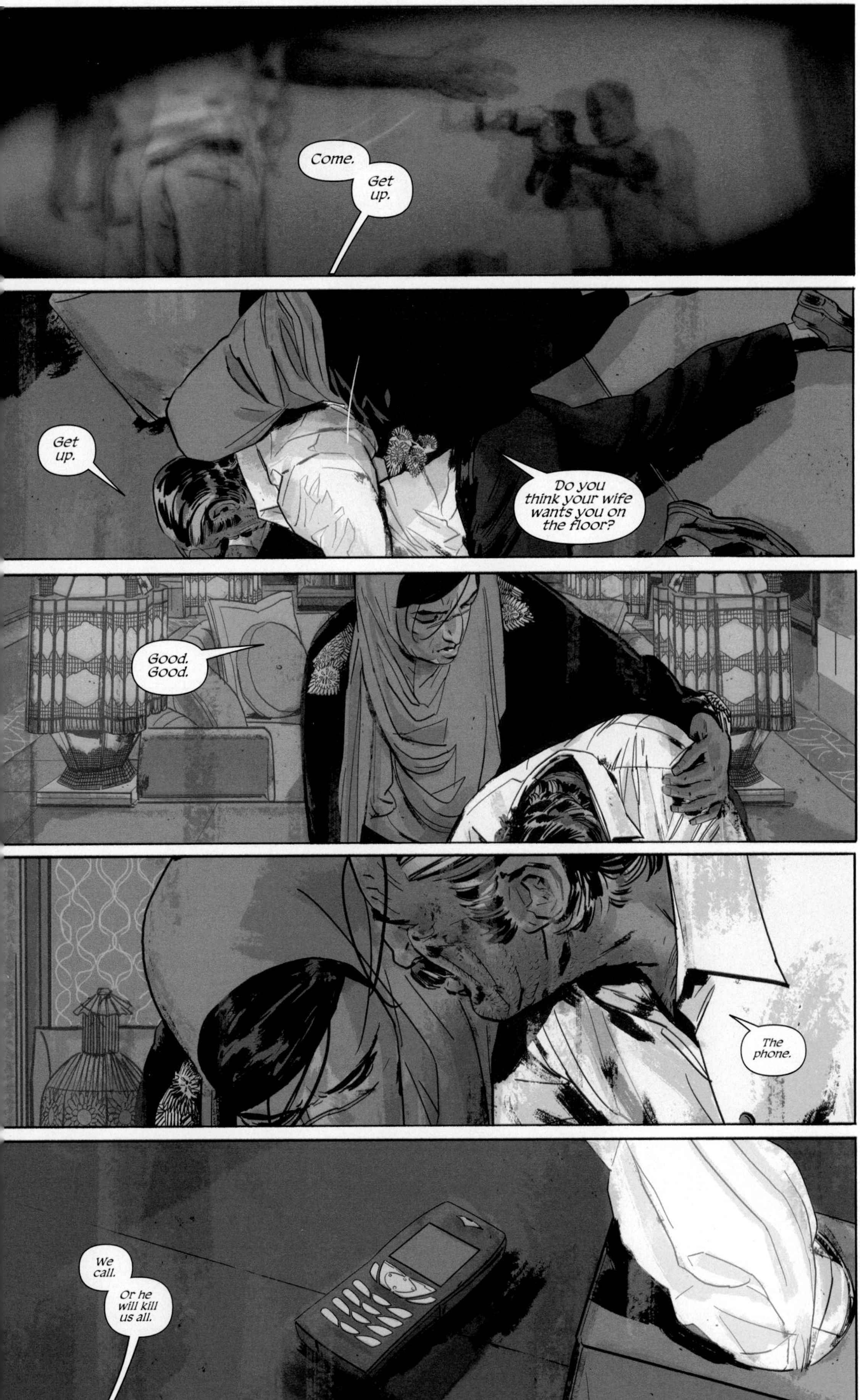
Come.
Get up.
Get up.
Do you think your wife wants you on the floor?
Good. Good.
The phone.
We call.
Or he will kill us all.

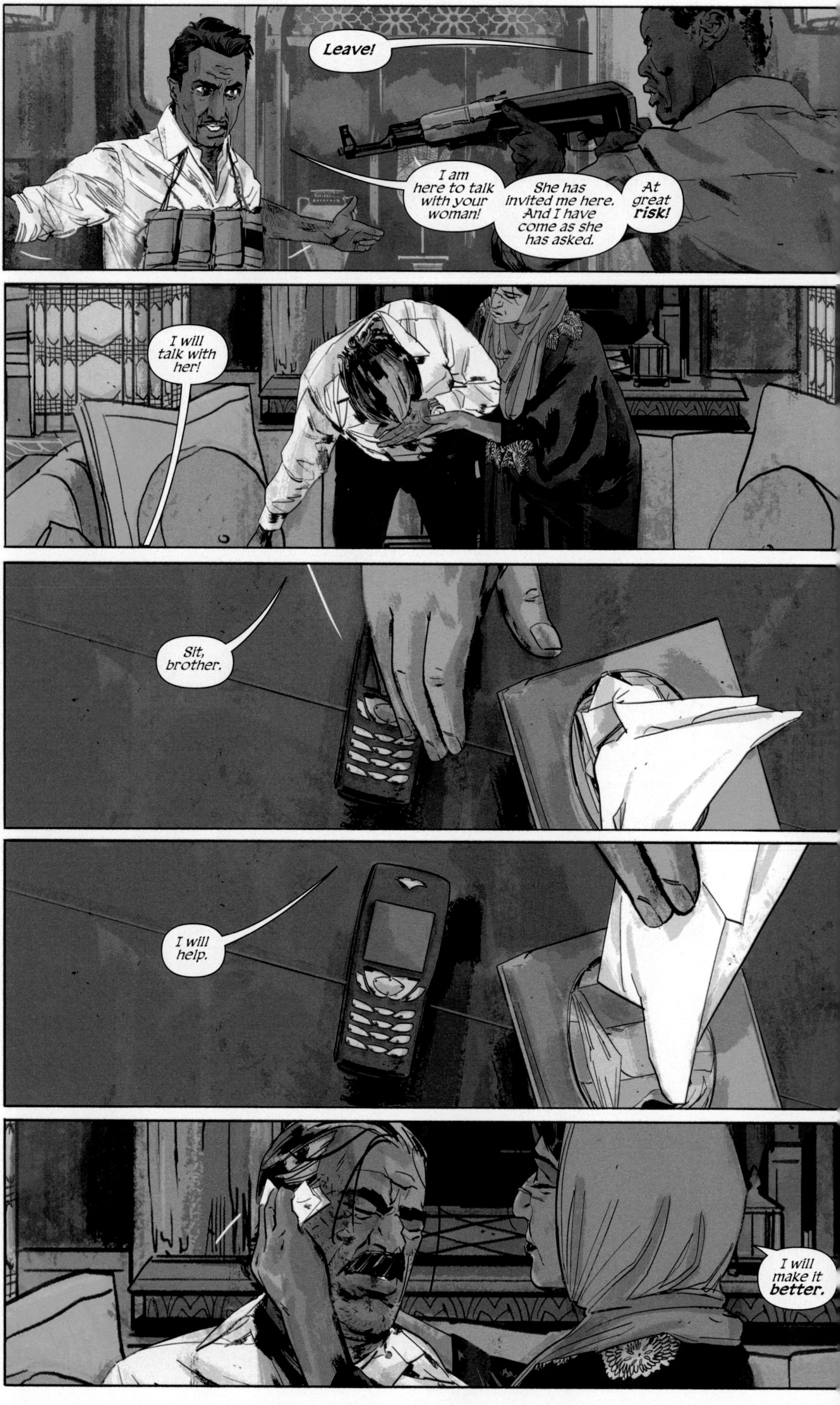
Leave!
I am here to talk with your woman!
She has invited me here. And I have come as she has asked.
At great risk!
I will talk with her!
Sit, brother.
I will help.
I will make it better.

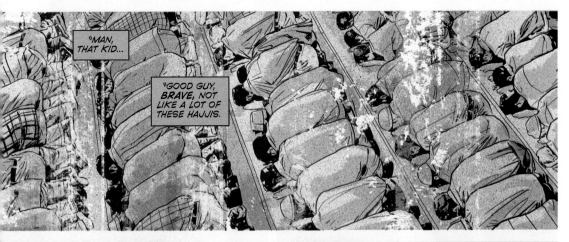

"MAN, THAT KID...

"GOOD GUY, *BRAVE*, NOT LIKE A LOT OF THESE HAJJIS.

"WAS REALLY WILLING TO PUT IT ALL OUT THERE, YOU KNOW?

"THEY GOT A HISTORY OF IT, IF YOU READ WHAT THEY DID.

"AND HE HAD THAT IN HIM.

"IF YOU KNOW THESE PEOPLE...

"...THEY'RE NOT LIKE HOW THEY ARE ALL THE TIME."

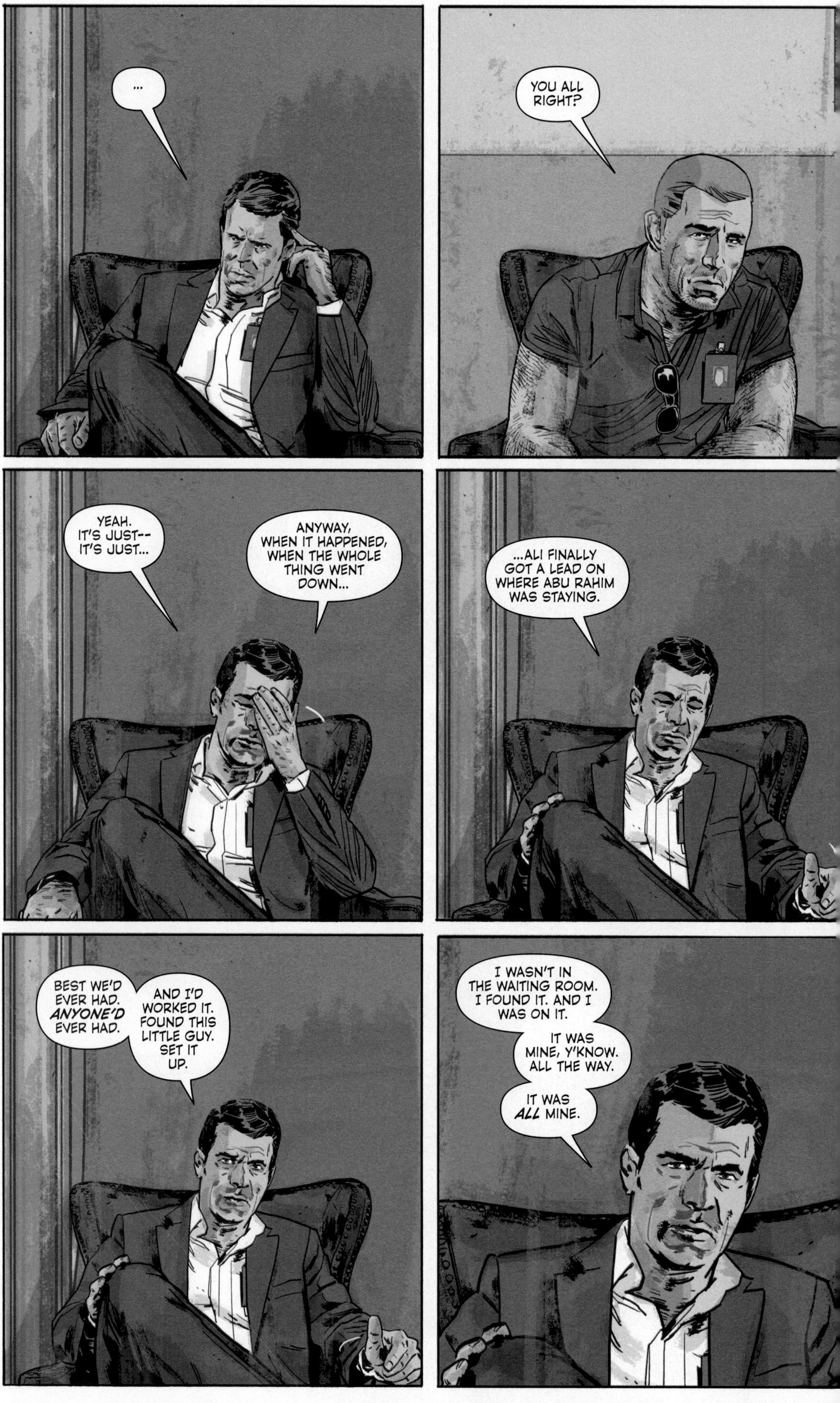
...
YOU ALL RIGHT?
YEAH. IT'S JUST-- IT'S JUST...
ANYWAY, WHEN IT HAPPENED, WHEN THE WHOLE THING WENT DOWN...
...ALI FINALLY GOT A LEAD ON WHERE ABU RAHIM WAS STAYING.
BEST WE'D EVER HAD. ***ANYONE'D*** EVER HAD.
AND I'D WORKED IT. FOUND THIS LITTLE GUY. SET IT UP.
I WASN'T IN THE WAITING ROOM. I FOUND IT. AND I WAS ON IT.
IT WAS MINE, Y'KNOW. ALL THE WAY.
IT WAS ***ALL*** MINE.

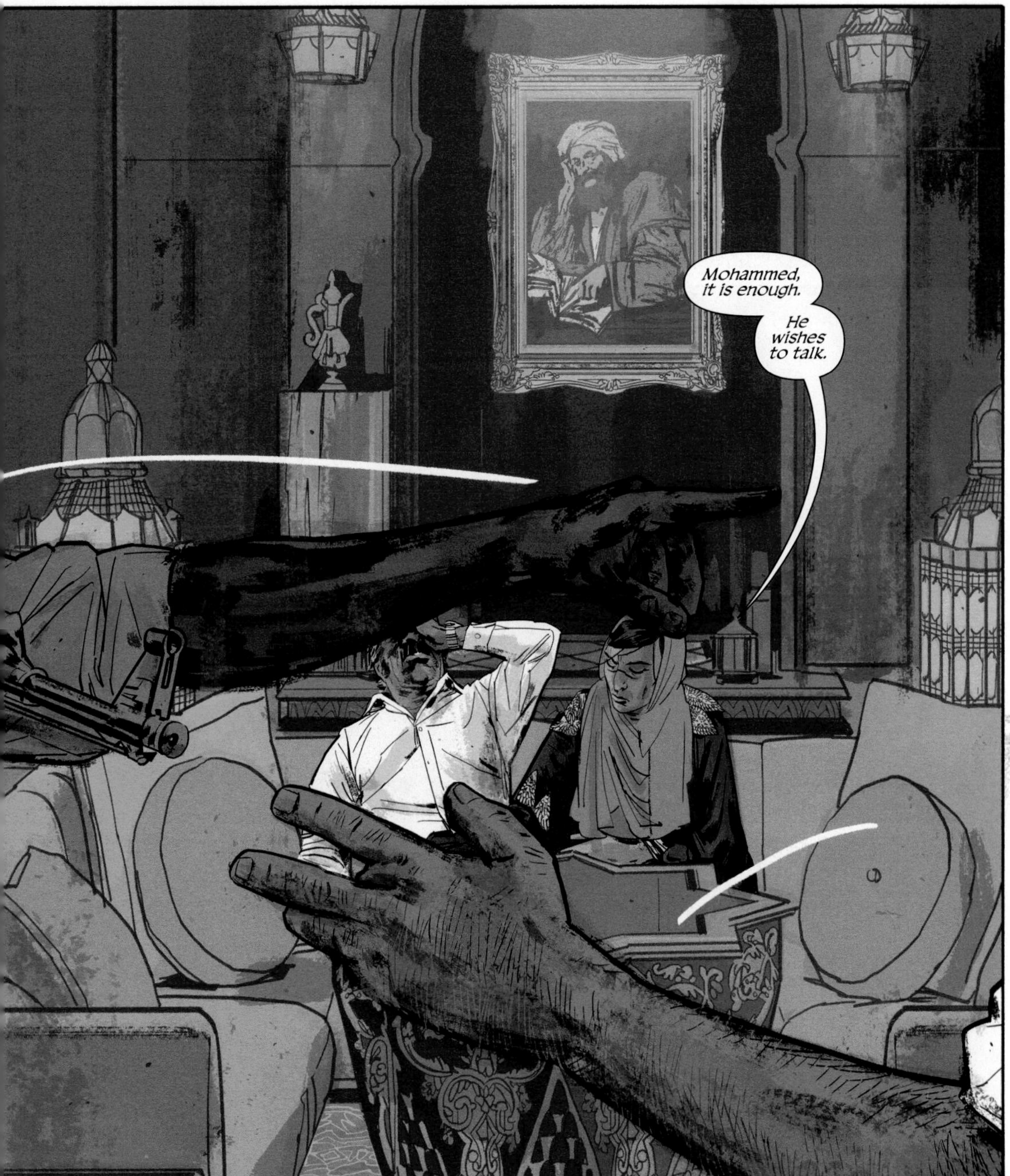
Mohammed, it is enough.
He wishes to talk.

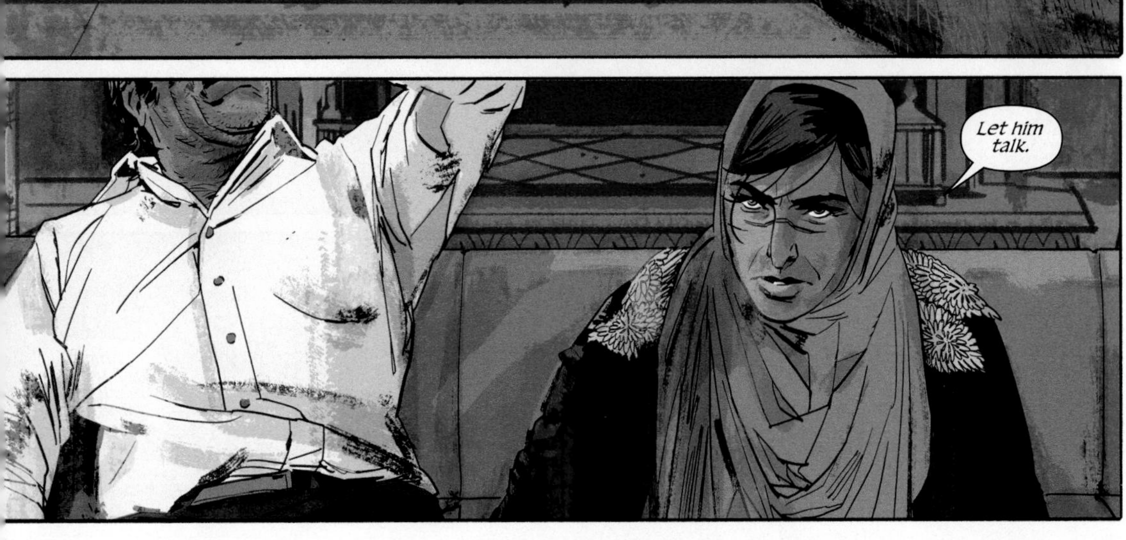
Let him talk.

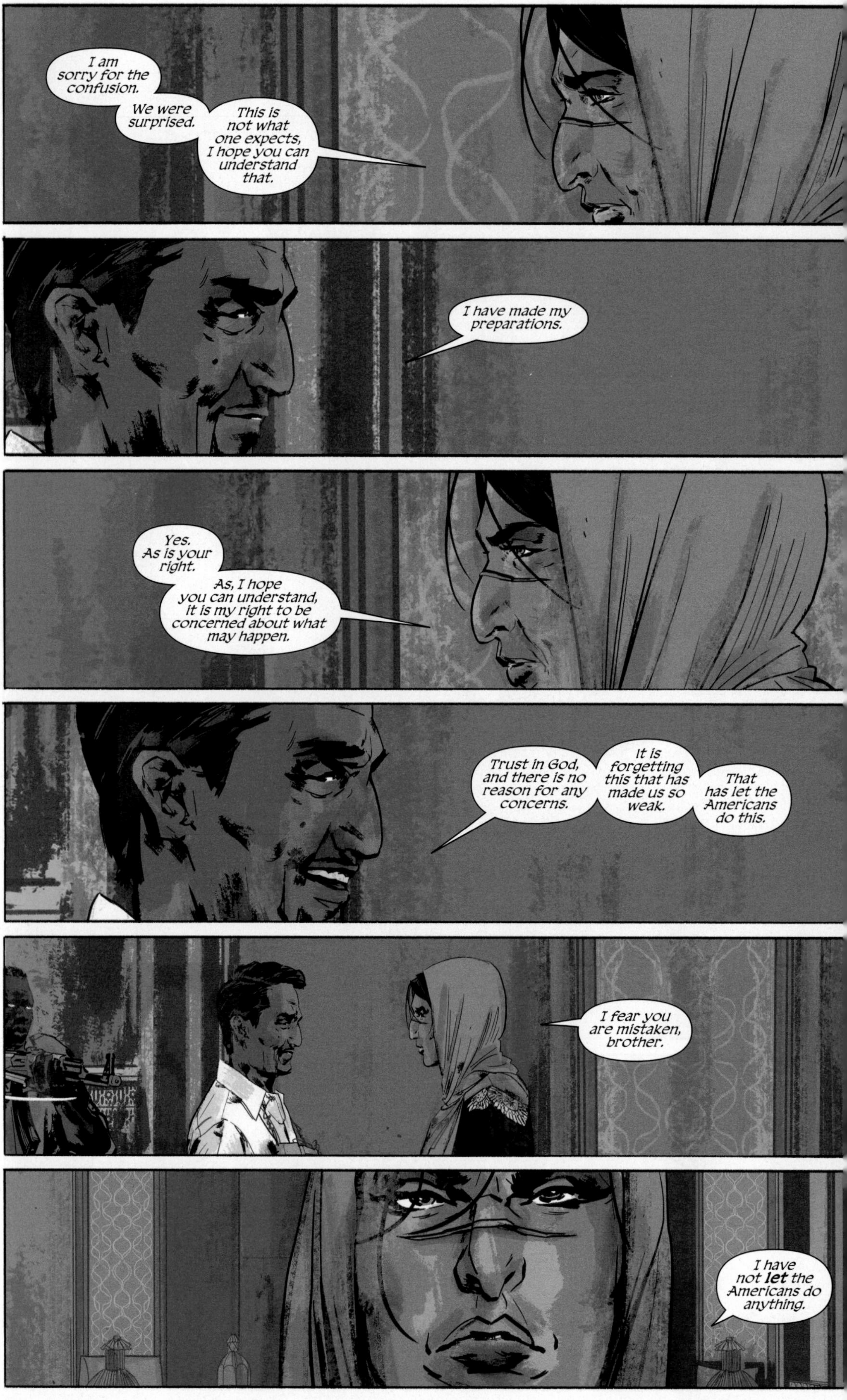
I am sorry for the confusion.
We were surprised.
This is not what one expects, I hope you can understand that.
I have made my preparations.
Yes. As is your right.
As, I hope you can understand, it is my right to be concerned about what may happen.
Trust in God, and there is no reason for any concerns.
It is forgetting this that has made us so weak.
That has let the Americans do this.
I fear you are mistaken, brother.
I have not **let** the Americans do anything.

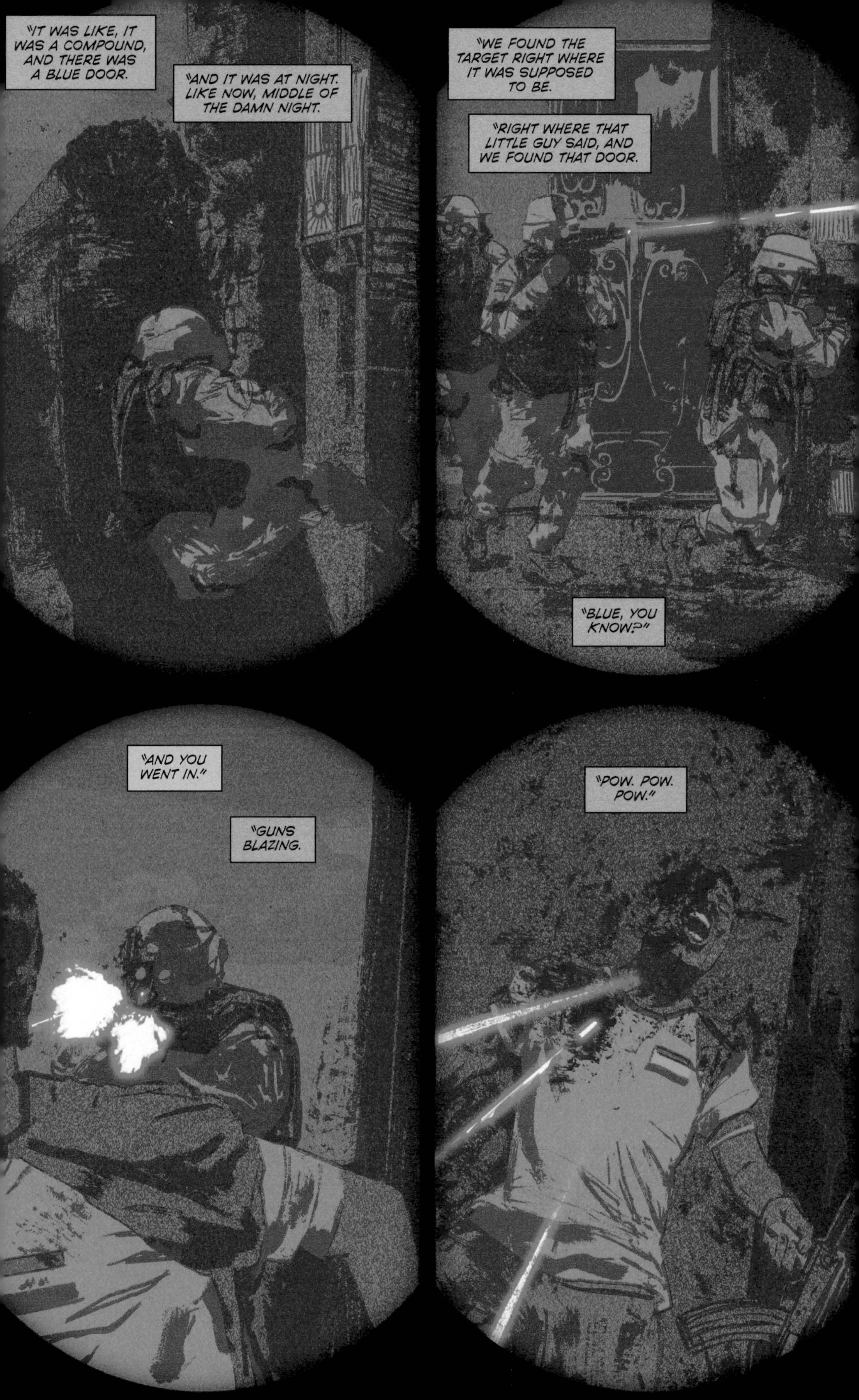
"IT WAS LIKE, IT WAS A COMPOUND, AND THERE WAS A BLUE DOOR.
"AND IT WAS AT NIGHT. LIKE NOW, MIDDLE OF THE DAMN NIGHT.
"WE FOUND THE TARGET RIGHT WHERE IT WAS SUPPOSED TO BE.
"RIGHT WHERE THAT LITTLE GUY SAID, AND WE FOUND THAT DOOR.
"BLUE, YOU KNOW?"
"AND YOU WENT IN."
"GUNS BLAZING.
"POW. POW. POW."

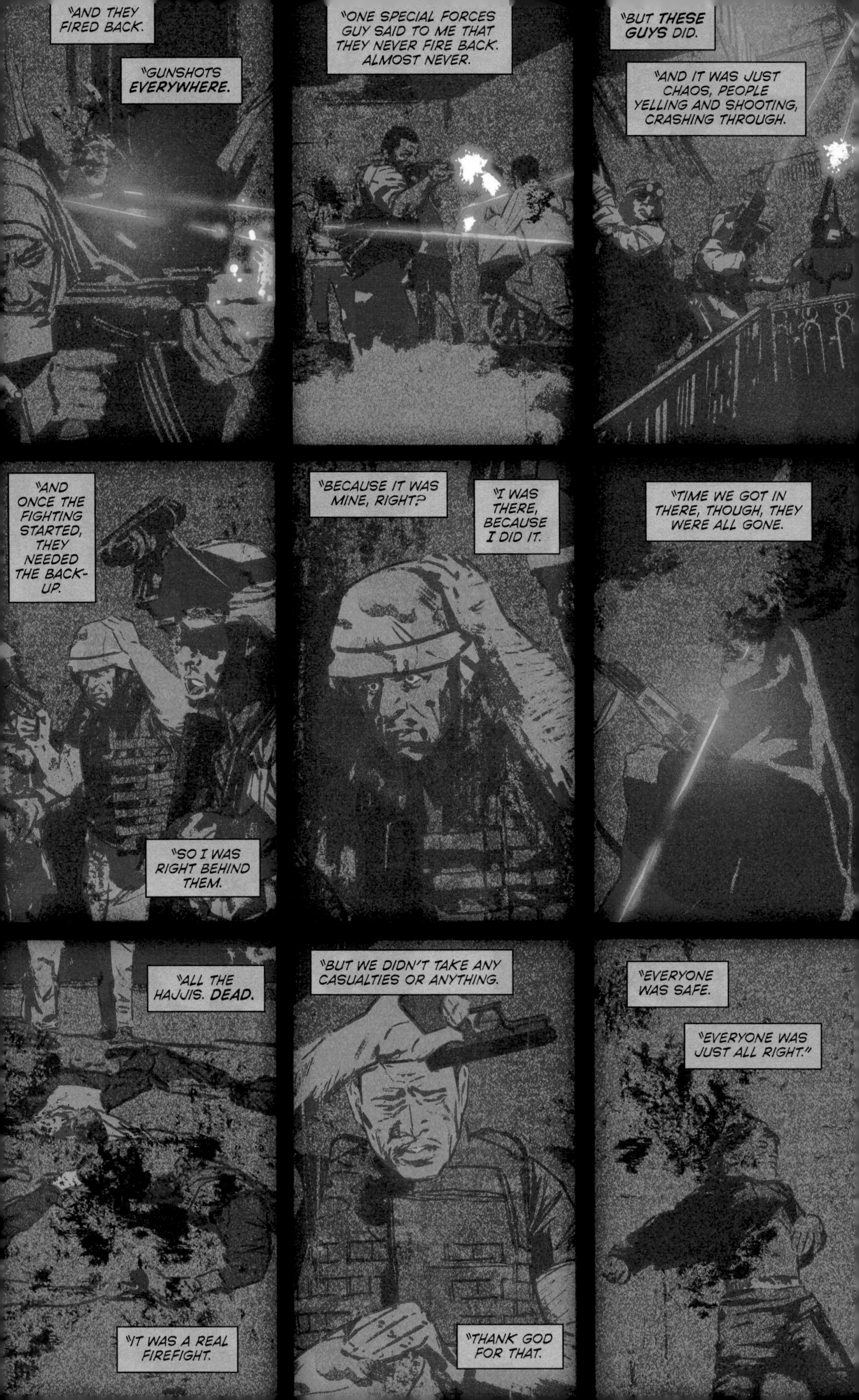
"AND THEY FIRED BACK.
"GUNSHOTS EVERYWHERE.
"ONE SPECIAL FORCES GUY SAID TO ME THAT THEY NEVER FIRE BACK. ALMOST NEVER.
"BUT THESE GUYS DID.
"AND IT WAS JUST CHAOS, PEOPLE YELLING AND SHOOTING, CRASHING THROUGH.
"AND ONCE THE FIGHTING STARTED, THEY NEEDED THE BACK-UP.
"SO I WAS RIGHT BEHIND THEM.
"BECAUSE IT WAS MINE, RIGHT?
"I WAS THERE, BECAUSE I DID IT.
"TIME WE GOT IN THERE, THOUGH, THEY WERE ALL GONE.
"ALL THE HAJJIS. DEAD.
"IT WAS A REAL FIREFIGHT.
"BUT WE DIDN'T TAKE ANY CASUALTIES OR ANYTHING.
"THANK GOD FOR THAT.
"EVERYONE WAS SAFE.
"EVERYONE WAS JUST ALL RIGHT."

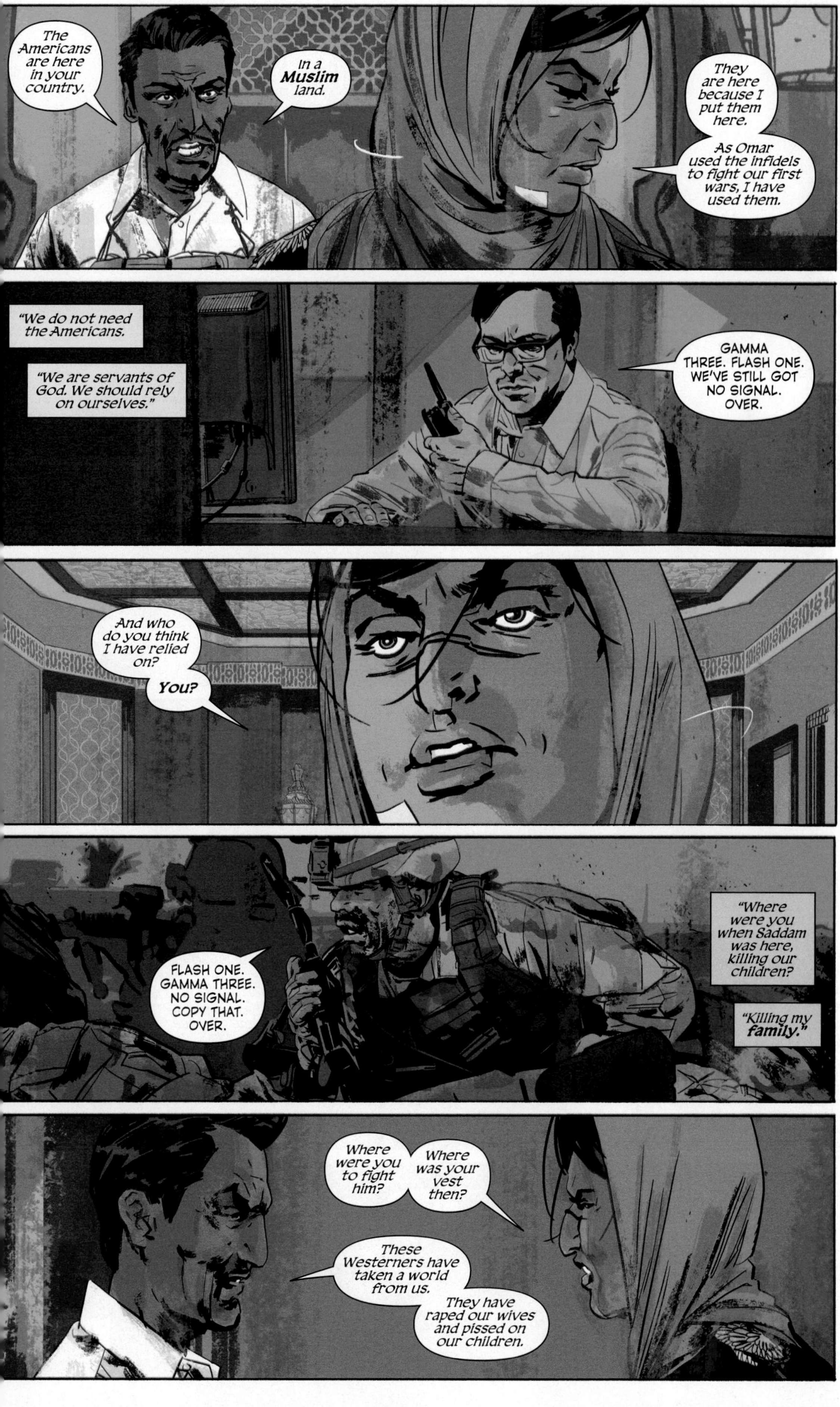

The Americans are here in your country.
In a **Muslim** land.
They are here because I put them here.
As Omar used the infidels to fight our first wars, I have used them.
"We do not need the Americans.
"We are servants of God. We should rely on ourselves."
GAMMA THREE. FLASH ONE. WE'VE STILL GOT NO SIGNAL. OVER.
And who do you think I have relied on?
You?
FLASH ONE. GAMMA THREE. NO SIGNAL. COPY THAT. OVER.
"Where were you when Saddam was here, killing our children?
"Killing my **family.**"
Where were you to fight him?
Where was your vest then?
These Westerners have taken a world from us.
They have raped our wives and pissed on our children.

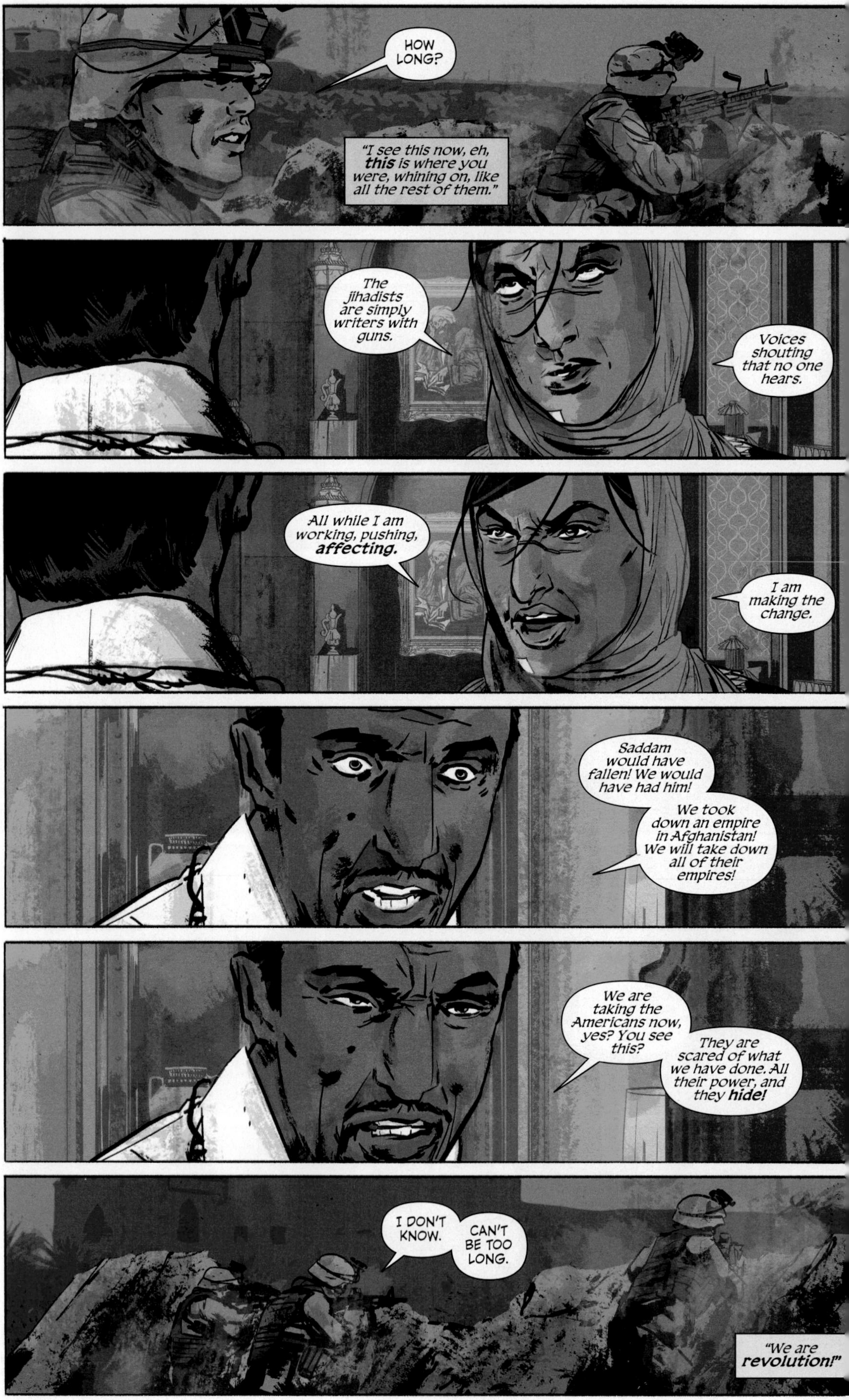
HOW LONG?
"I see this now, eh, this is where you were, whining on, like all the rest of them."
The jihadists are simply writers with guns.
Voices shouting that no one hears.
All while I am working, pushing, affecting.
I am making the change.
Saddam would have fallen! We would have had him!
We took down an empire in Afghanistan! We will take down all of their empires!
We are taking the Americans now, yes? You see this?
They are scared of what we have done. All their power, and they hide!
I DON'T KNOW.
CAN'T BE TOO LONG.
"We are revolution!"

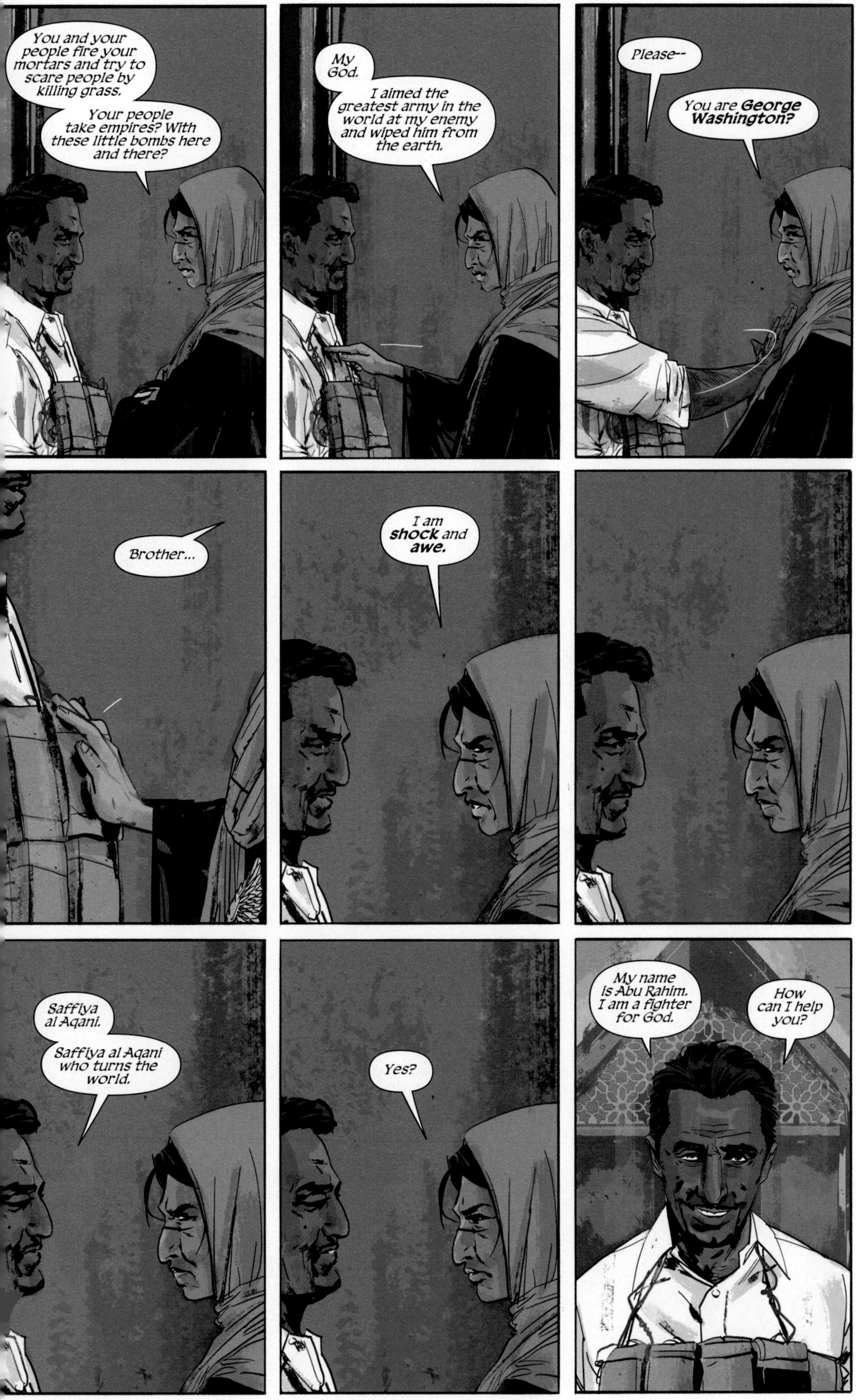
You and your people fire your mortars and try to scare people by killing grass.
Your people take empires? With these little bombs here and there?
My God.
I aimed the greatest army in the world at my enemy and wiped him from the earth.
Please--
You are George Washington?
Brother...
I am shock and awe.
Saffiya al Aqani.
Saffiya al Aqani who turns the world.
Yes?
My name is Abu Rahim. I am a fighter for God.
How can I help you?

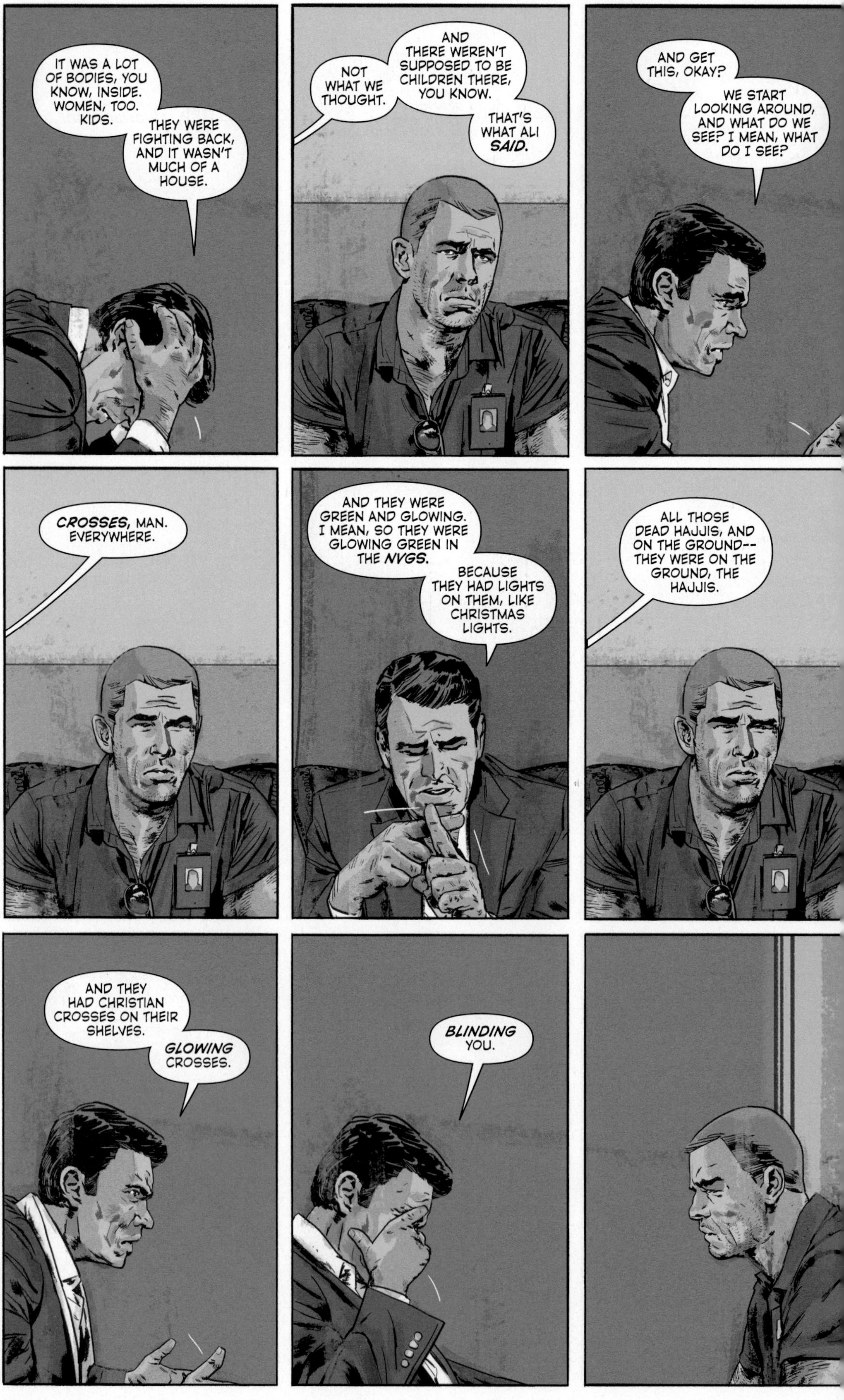
IT WAS A LOT OF BODIES, YOU KNOW, INSIDE. WOMEN, TOO. KIDS.
THEY WERE FIGHTING BACK, AND IT WASN'T MUCH OF A HOUSE.
NOT WHAT WE THOUGHT.
AND THERE WEREN'T SUPPOSED TO BE CHILDREN THERE, YOU KNOW.
THAT'S WHAT ALI SAID.
AND GET THIS, OKAY?
WE START LOOKING AROUND, AND WHAT DO WE SEE? I MEAN, WHAT DO I SEE?
CROSSES, MAN. EVERYWHERE.
AND THEY WERE GREEN AND GLOWING. I MEAN, SO THEY WERE GLOWING GREEN IN THE NVGS.
BECAUSE THEY HAD LIGHTS ON THEM, LIKE CHRISTMAS LIGHTS.
ALL THOSE DEAD HAJJIS, AND ON THE GROUND-- THEY WERE ON THE GROUND, THE HAJJIS.
AND THEY HAD CHRISTIAN CROSSES ON THEIR SHELVES.
GLOWING CROSSES.
BLINDING YOU.

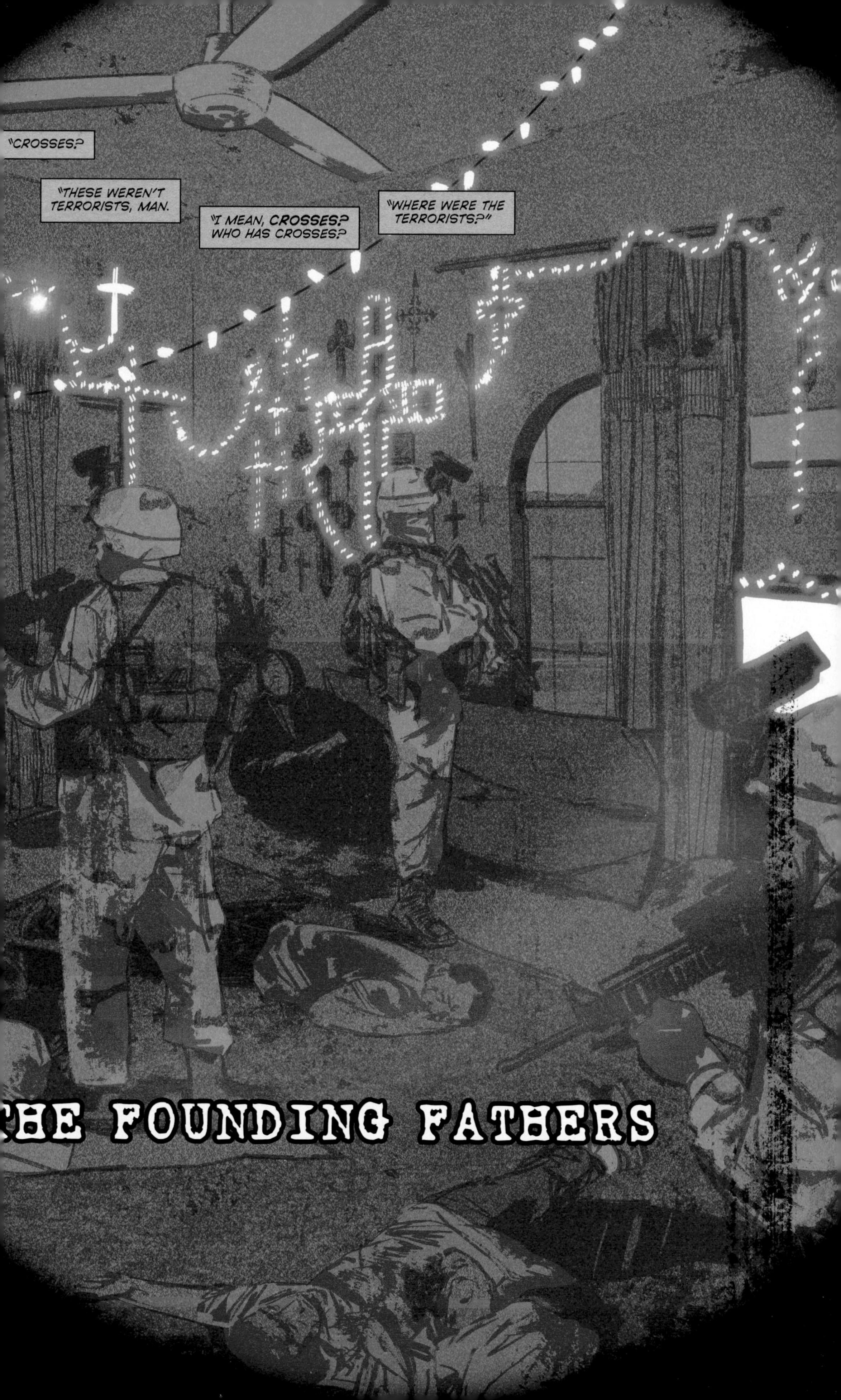
"CROSSES?
"THESE WEREN'T TERRORISTS, MAN.
"I MEAN, CROSSES? WHO HAS CROSSES?
"WHERE WERE THE TERRORISTS?"
THE FOUNDING FATHERS

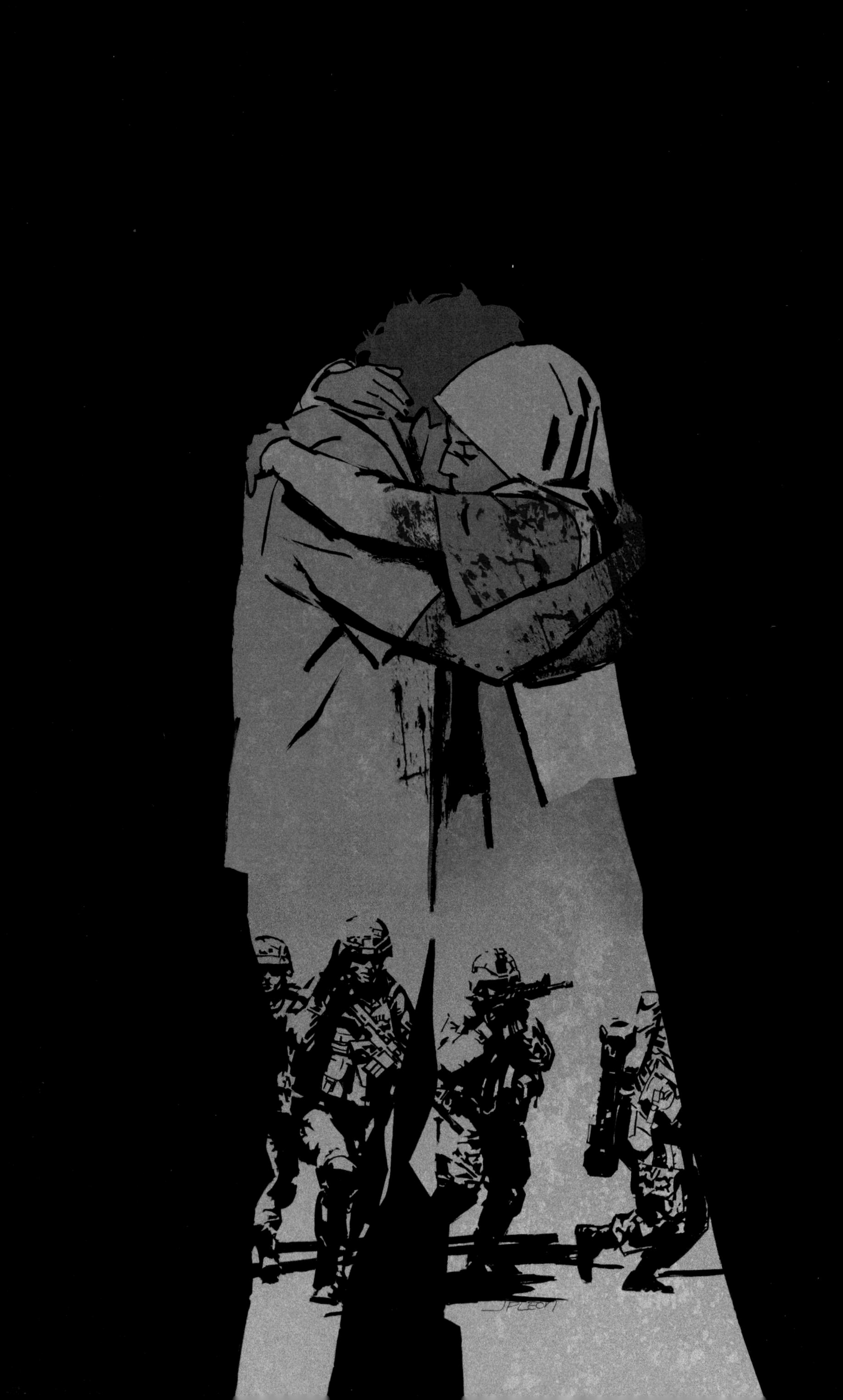

Chocolate.

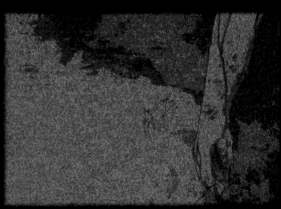

WHAT DID *ALI* SAY?

JOINT INTEL OPS. BAGHDAD, IRAQ. THE GREEN ZONE.

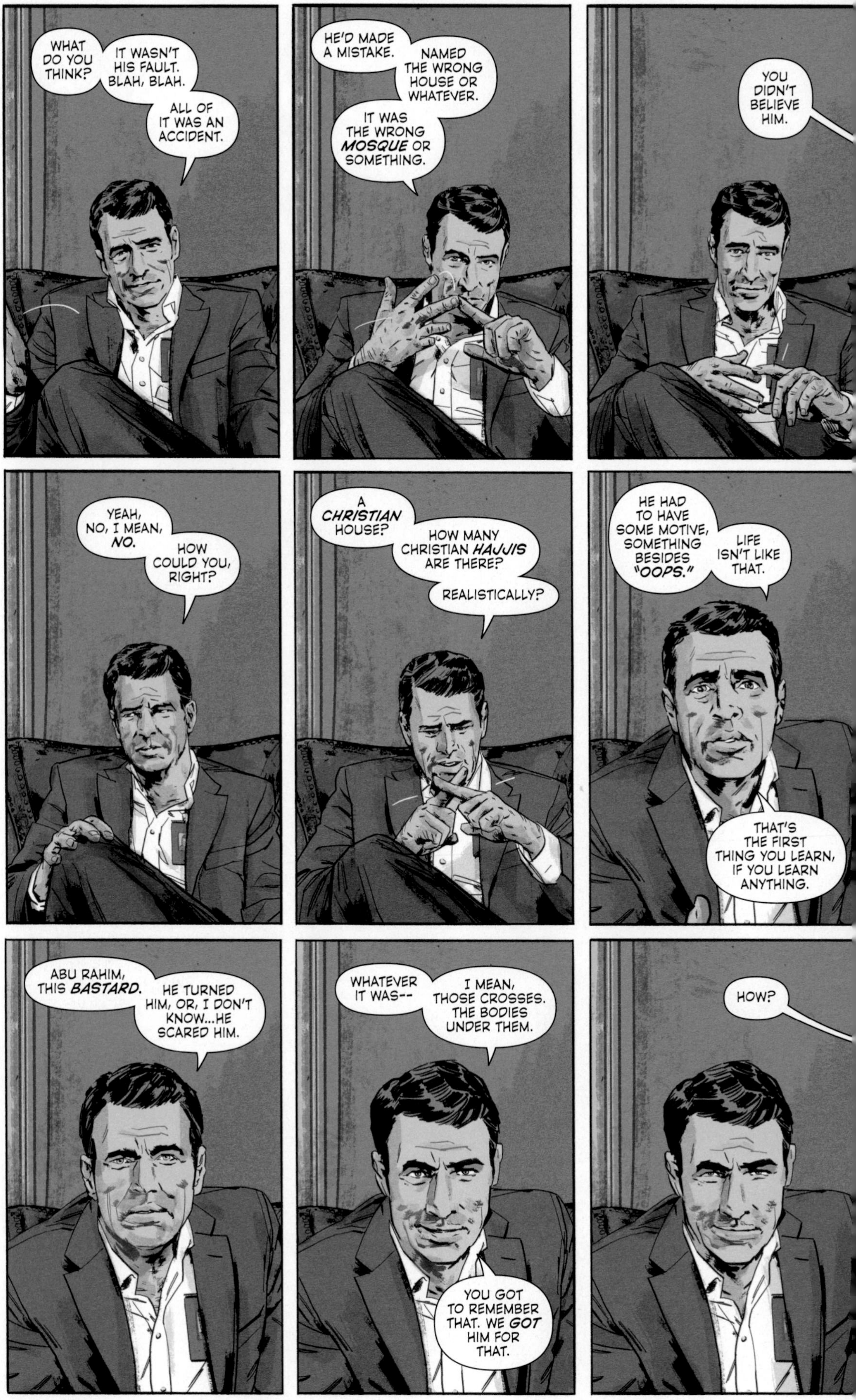
WHAT DO YOU THINK?
IT WASN'T HIS FAULT. BLAH, BLAH.
ALL OF IT WAS AN ACCIDENT.
HE'D MADE A MISTAKE.
NAMED THE WRONG HOUSE OR WHATEVER.
IT WAS THE WRONG *MOSQUE* OR SOMETHING.
YOU DIDN'T BELIEVE HIM.
YEAH, NO, I MEAN, *NO.*
HOW COULD YOU, RIGHT?
A *CHRISTIAN* HOUSE?
HOW MANY CHRISTIAN *HAJJIS* ARE THERE?
REALISTICALLY?
HE HAD TO HAVE SOME MOTIVE, SOMETHING BESIDES *"OOPS."*
LIFE ISN'T LIKE THAT.
THAT'S THE FIRST THING YOU LEARN, IF YOU LEARN ANYTHING.
ABU RAHIM, THIS *BASTARD.*
HE TURNED HIM, OR, I DON'T KNOW...HE SCARED HIM.
WHATEVER IT WAS--
I MEAN, THOSE CROSSES. THE BODIES UNDER THEM.
YOU GOT TO REMEMBER THAT. WE *GOT* HIM FOR THAT.
HOW?

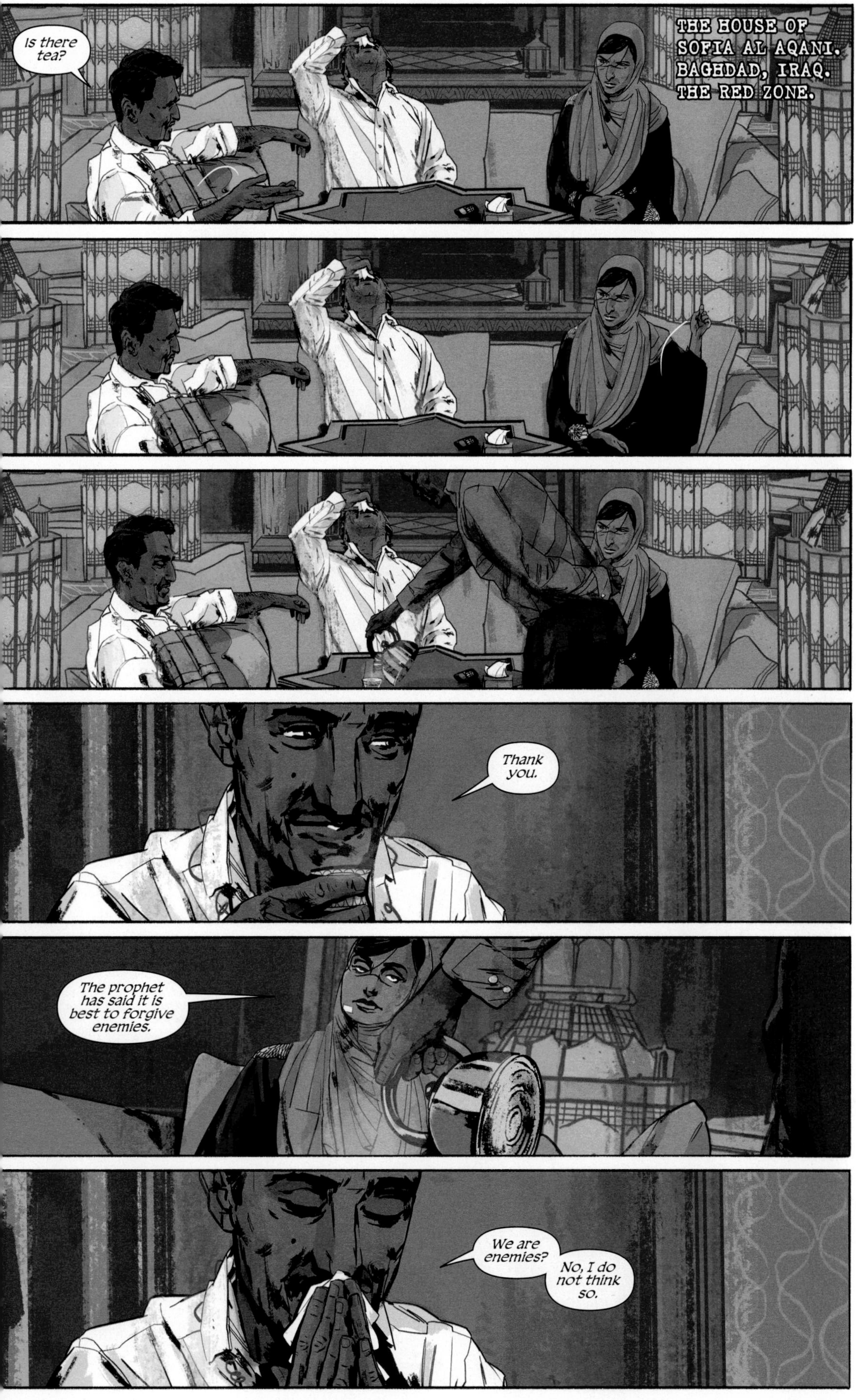
Is there tea?
THE HOUSE OF SOFIA AL AQANI. BAGHDAD, IRAQ. THE RED ZONE.
Thank you.
The prophet has said it is best to forgive enemies.
We are enemies?
No, I do not think so.

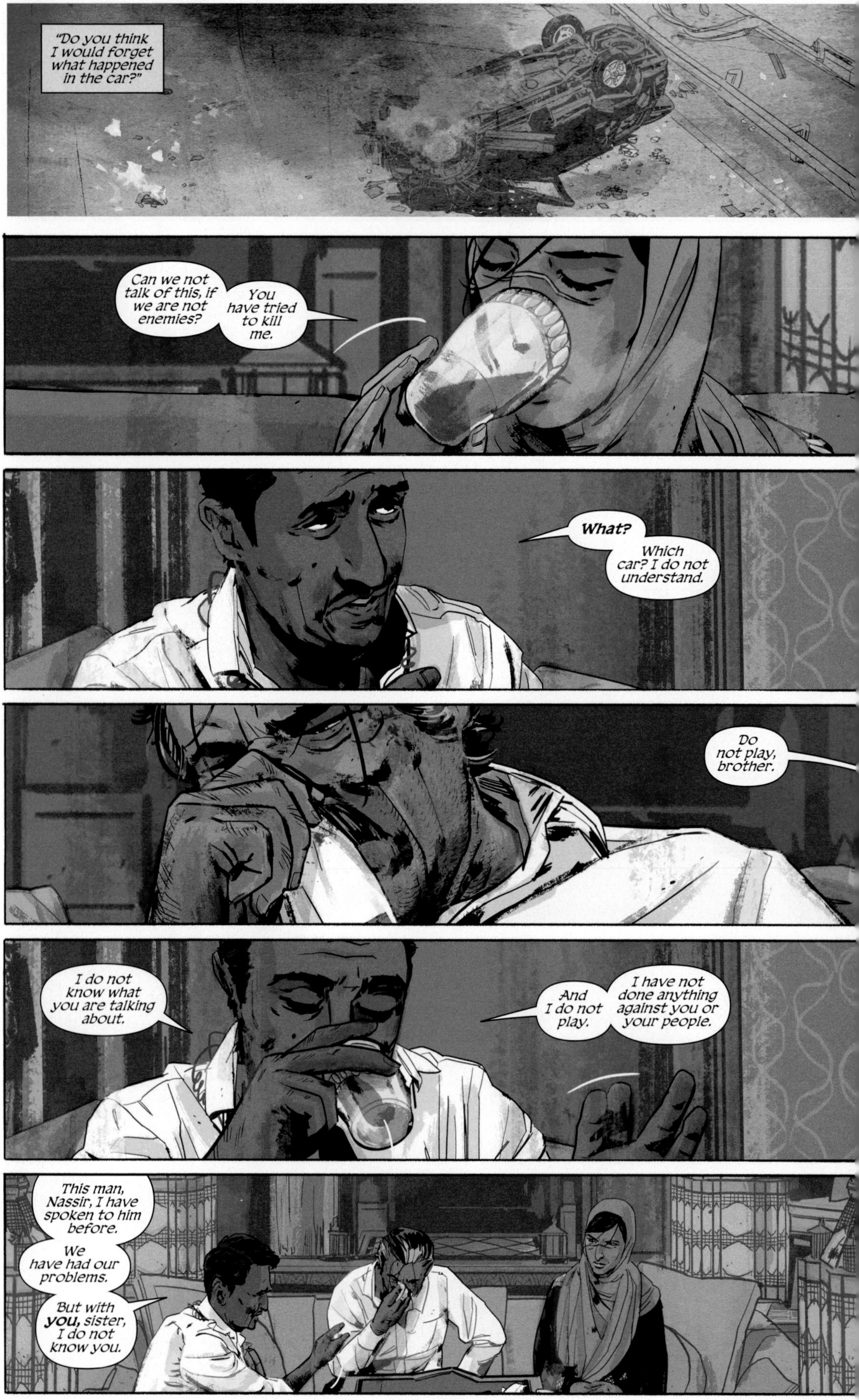
"Do you think I would forget what happened in the car?"
Can we not talk of this, if we are not enemies?
You have tried to kill me.
What?
Which car? I do not understand.
Do not play, brother.
I do not know what you are talking about.
And I do not play.
I have not done anything against you or your people.
This man, Nassir, I have spoken to him before.
We have had our problems.
But with you, sister, I do not know you.

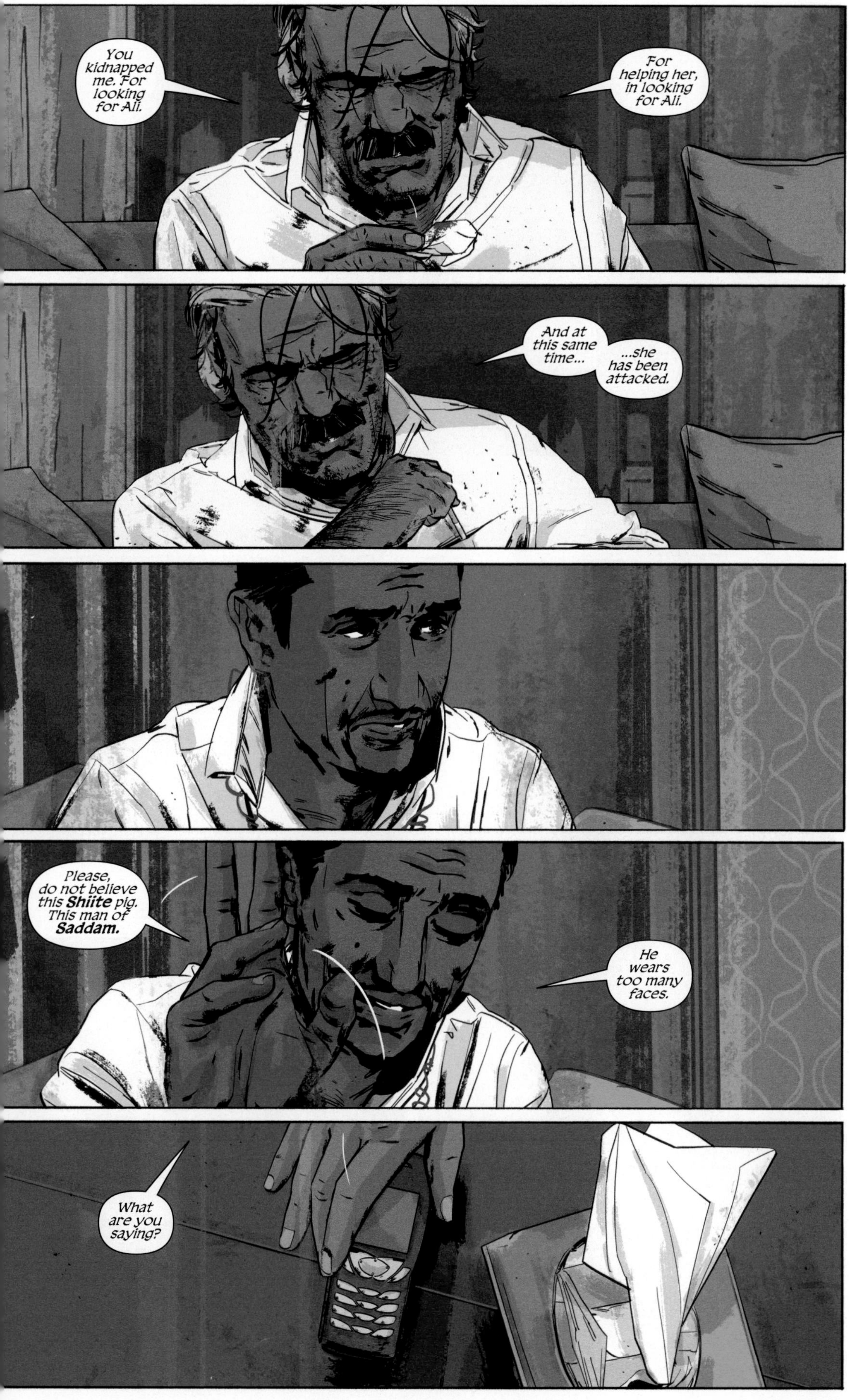
You kidnapped me. For looking for Ali.
For helping her, in looking for Ali.
And at this same time...
...she has been attacked.
Please, do not believe this **Shiite** pig. This man of **Saddam.**
He wears too many faces.
What are you saying?

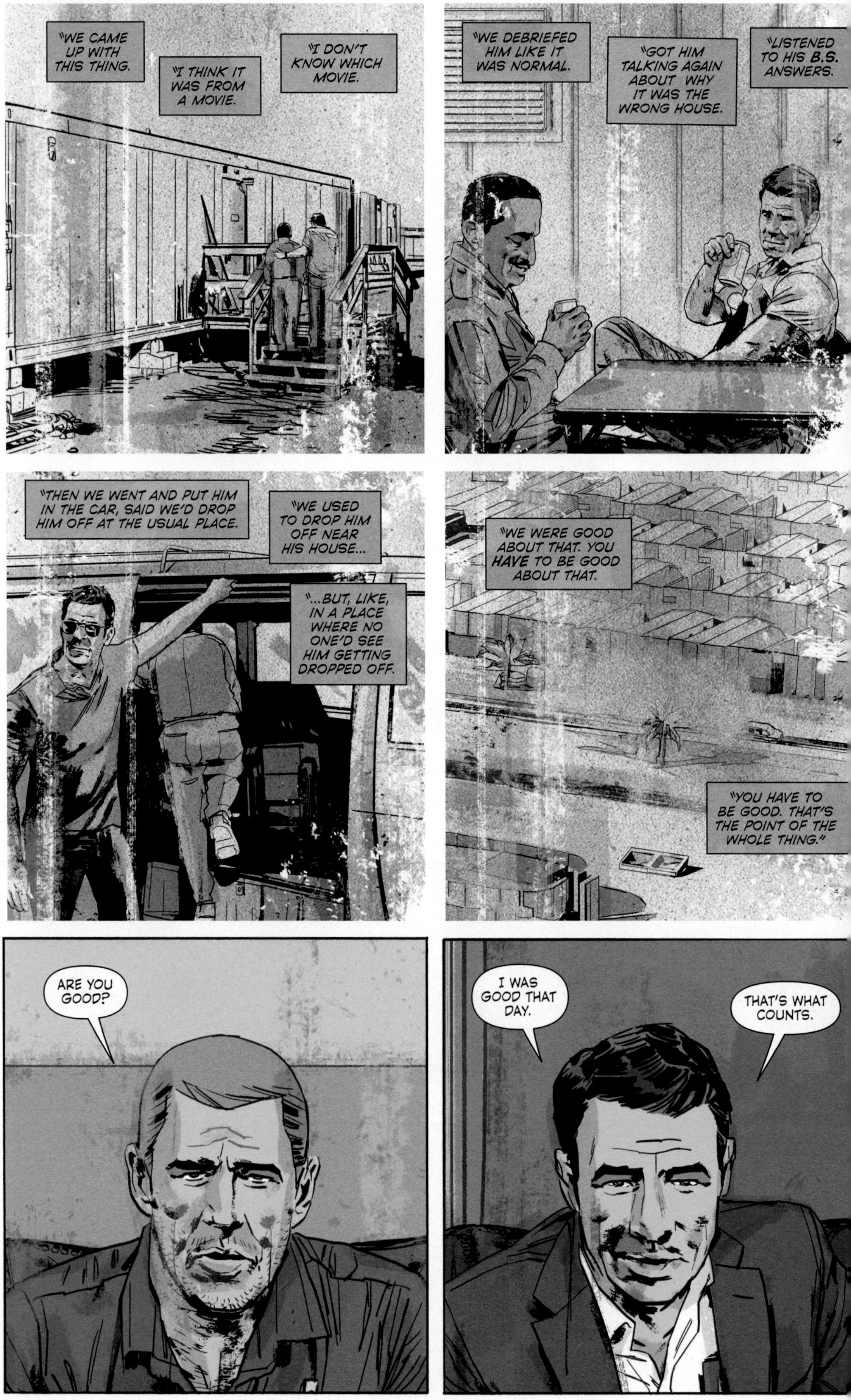

"WE CAME UP WITH THIS THING.
"I THINK IT WAS FROM A MOVIE.
"I DON'T KNOW WHICH MOVIE.
"WE DEBRIEFED HIM LIKE IT WAS NORMAL.
"GOT HIM TALKING AGAIN ABOUT WHY IT WAS THE WRONG HOUSE.
"LISTENED TO HIS B.S. ANSWERS.
"THEN WE WENT AND PUT HIM IN THE CAR, SAID WE'D DROP HIM OFF AT THE USUAL PLACE.
"WE USED TO DROP HIM OFF NEAR HIS HOUSE...
"...BUT, LIKE, IN A PLACE WHERE NO ONE'D SEE HIM GETTING DROPPED OFF.
"WE WERE GOOD ABOUT THAT. YOU HAVE TO BE GOOD ABOUT THAT.
"YOU HAVE TO BE GOOD. THAT'S THE POINT OF THE WHOLE THING."
ARE YOU GOOD?
I WAS GOOD THAT DAY.
THAT'S WHAT COUNTS.

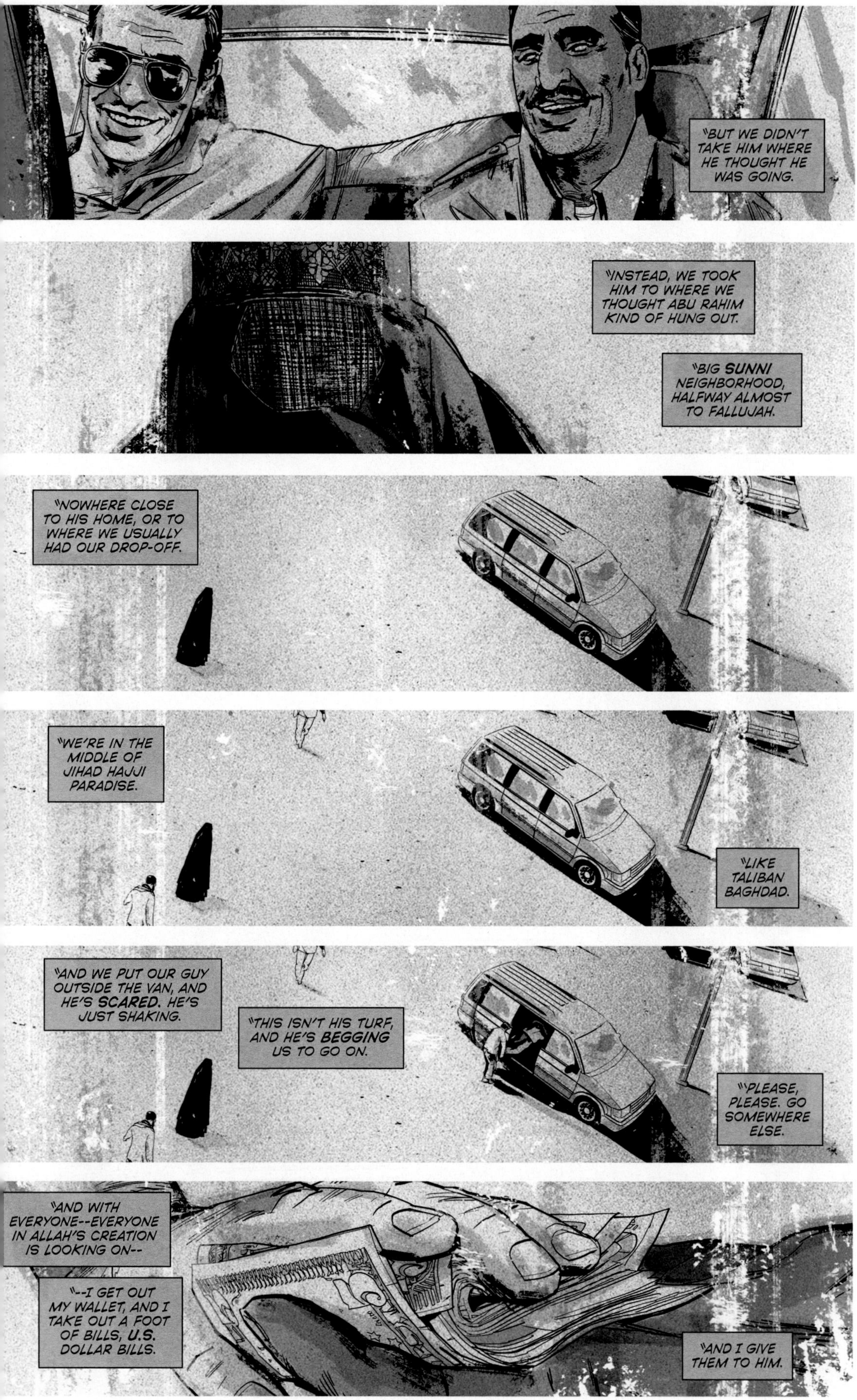
"BUT WE DIDN'T TAKE HIM WHERE HE THOUGHT HE WAS GOING.
"INSTEAD, WE TOOK HIM TO WHERE WE THOUGHT ABU RAHIM KIND OF HUNG OUT.
"BIG SUNNI NEIGHBORHOOD, HALFWAY ALMOST TO FALLUJAH.
"NOWHERE CLOSE TO HIS HOME, OR TO WHERE WE USUALLY HAD OUR DROP-OFF.
"WE'RE IN THE MIDDLE OF JIHAD HAJJI PARADISE.
"LIKE TALIBAN BAGHDAD.
"AND WE PUT OUR GUY OUTSIDE THE VAN, AND HE'S SCARED. HE'S JUST SHAKING.
"THIS ISN'T HIS TURF, AND HE'S BEGGING US TO GO ON.
"'PLEASE, PLEASE. GO SOMEWHERE ELSE.
"AND WITH EVERYONE--EVERYONE IN ALLAH'S CREATION IS LOOKING ON--
"--I GET OUT MY WALLET, AND I TAKE OUT A FOOT OF BILLS, U.S. DOLLAR BILLS.
"AND I GIVE THEM TO HIM.

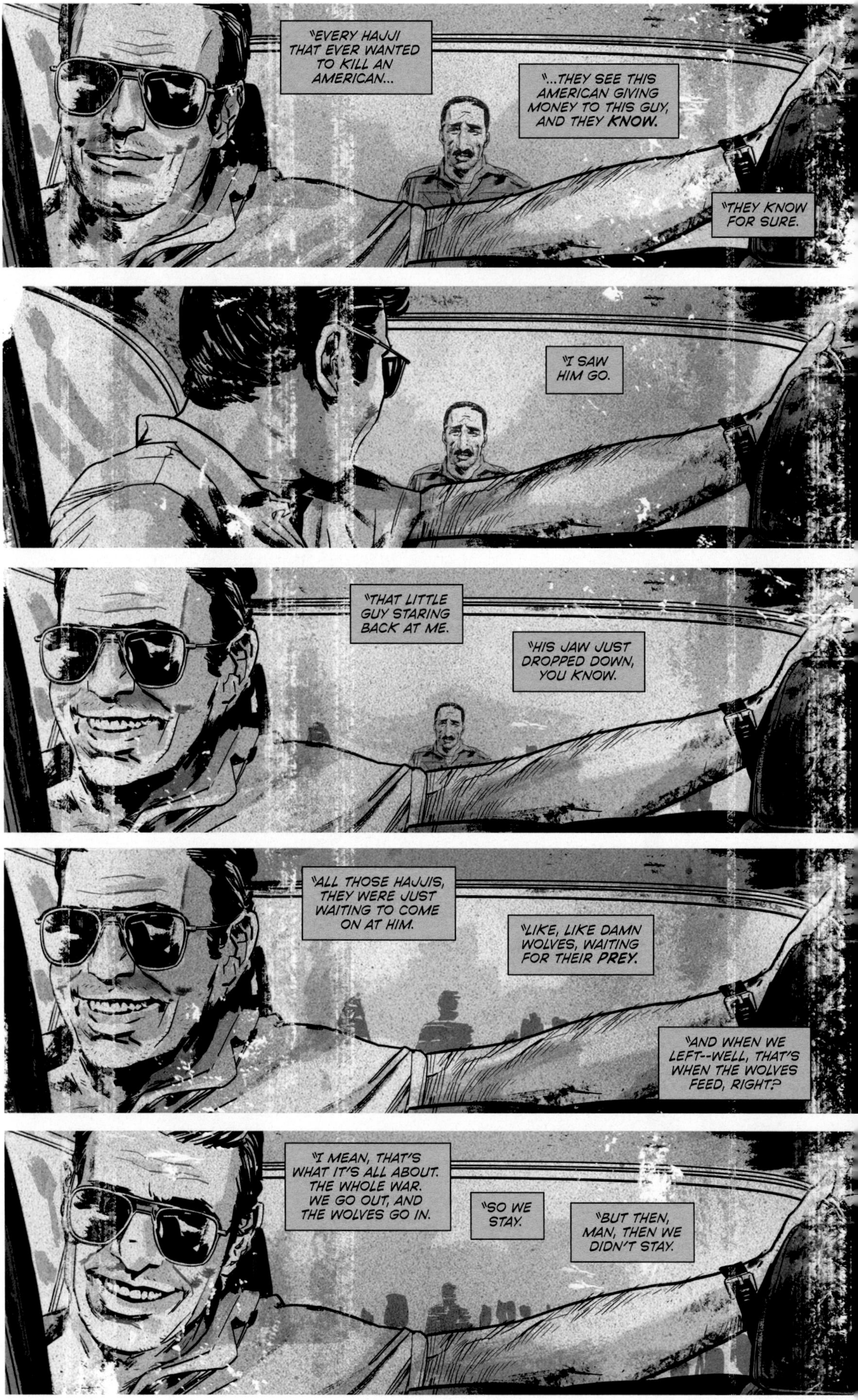
"EVERY HAJJI THAT EVER WANTED TO KILL AN AMERICAN...
"...THEY SEE THIS AMERICAN GIVING MONEY TO THIS GUY, AND THEY KNOW.
"THEY KNOW FOR SURE.
"I SAW HIM GO.
"THAT LITTLE GUY STARING BACK AT ME.
"HIS JAW JUST DROPPED DOWN, YOU KNOW.
"ALL THOSE HAJJIS, THEY WERE JUST WAITING TO COME ON AT HIM.
"LIKE, LIKE DAMN WOLVES, WAITING FOR THEIR PREY.
"AND WHEN WE LEFT--WELL, THAT'S WHEN THE WOLVES FEED, RIGHT?
"I MEAN, THAT'S WHAT IT'S ALL ABOUT. THE WHOLE WAR. WE GO OUT, AND THE WOLVES GO IN.
"SO WE STAY.
"BUT THEN, MAN, THEN WE DIDN'T STAY.

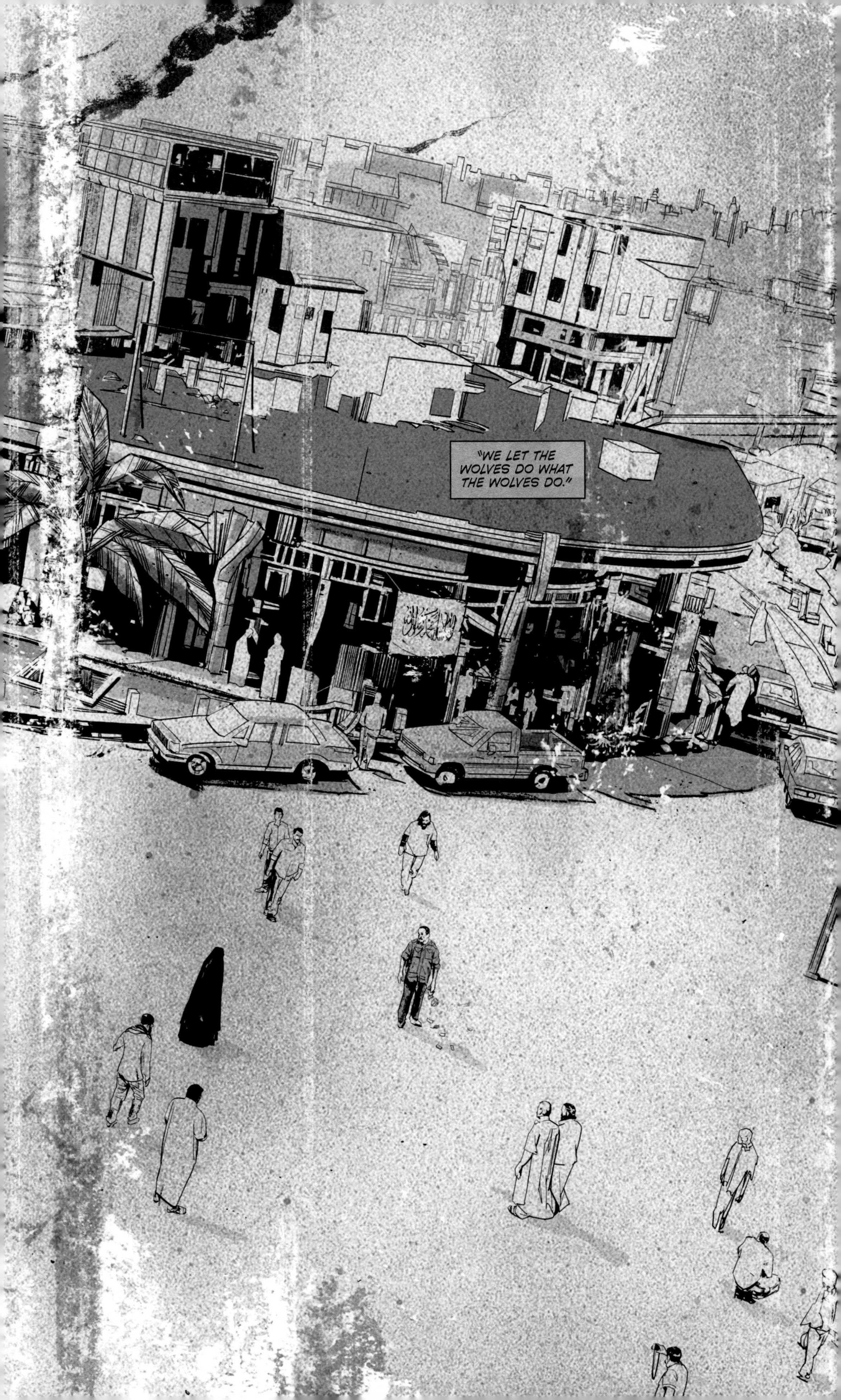
"WE LET THE WOLVES DO WHAT THE WOLVES DO."

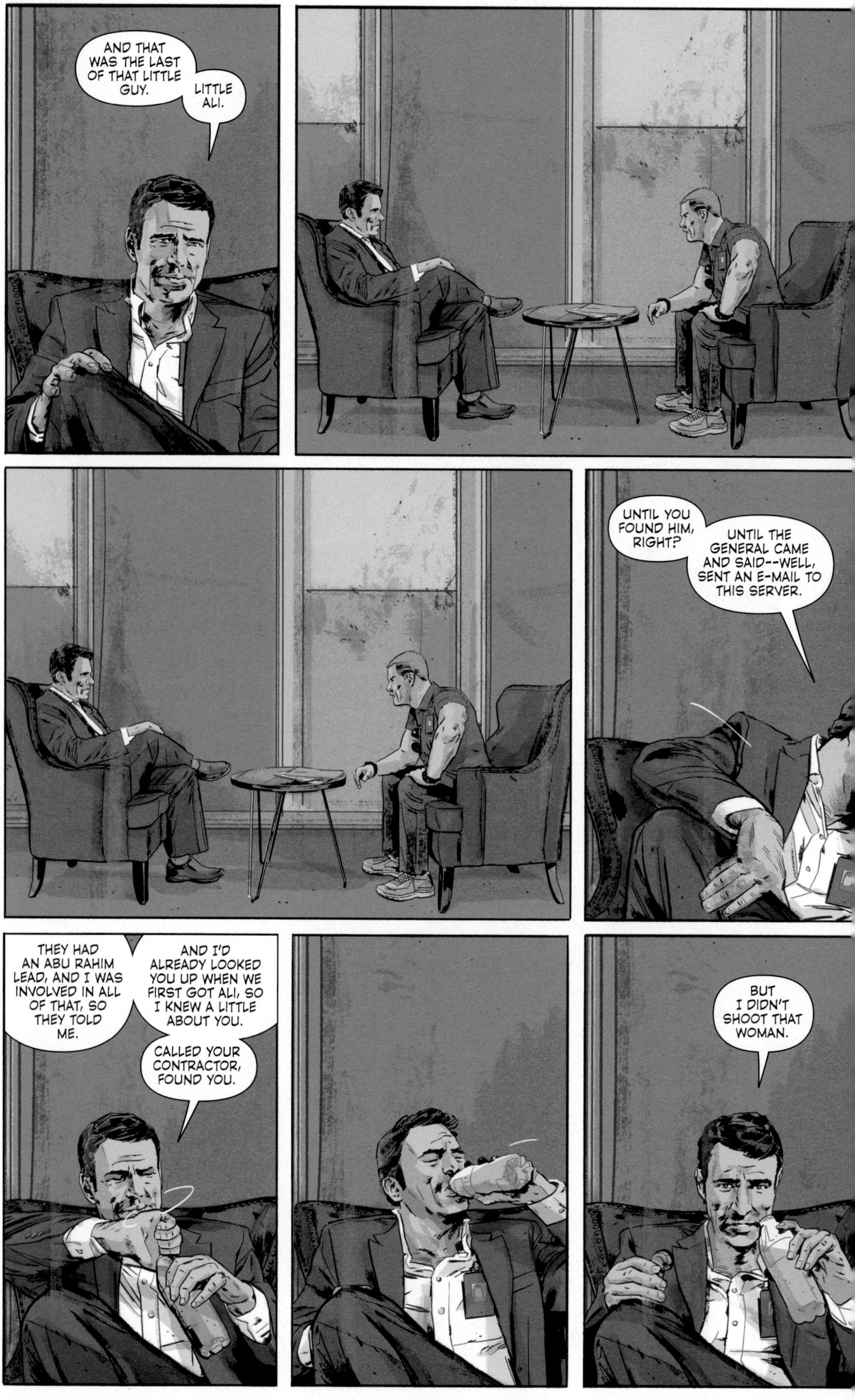

AND THAT WAS THE LAST OF THAT LITTLE GUY.
LITTLE ALI.
UNTIL YOU FOUND HIM, RIGHT?
UNTIL THE GENERAL CAME AND SAID--WELL, SENT AN E-MAIL TO THIS SERVER.
THEY HAD AN ABU RAHIM LEAD, AND I WAS INVOLVED IN ALL OF THAT, SO THEY TOLD ME.
AND I'D ALREADY LOOKED YOU UP WHEN WE FIRST GOT ALI, SO I KNEW A LITTLE ABOUT YOU.
CALLED YOUR CONTRACTOR, FOUND YOU.
BUT I DIDN'T SHOOT THAT WOMAN.

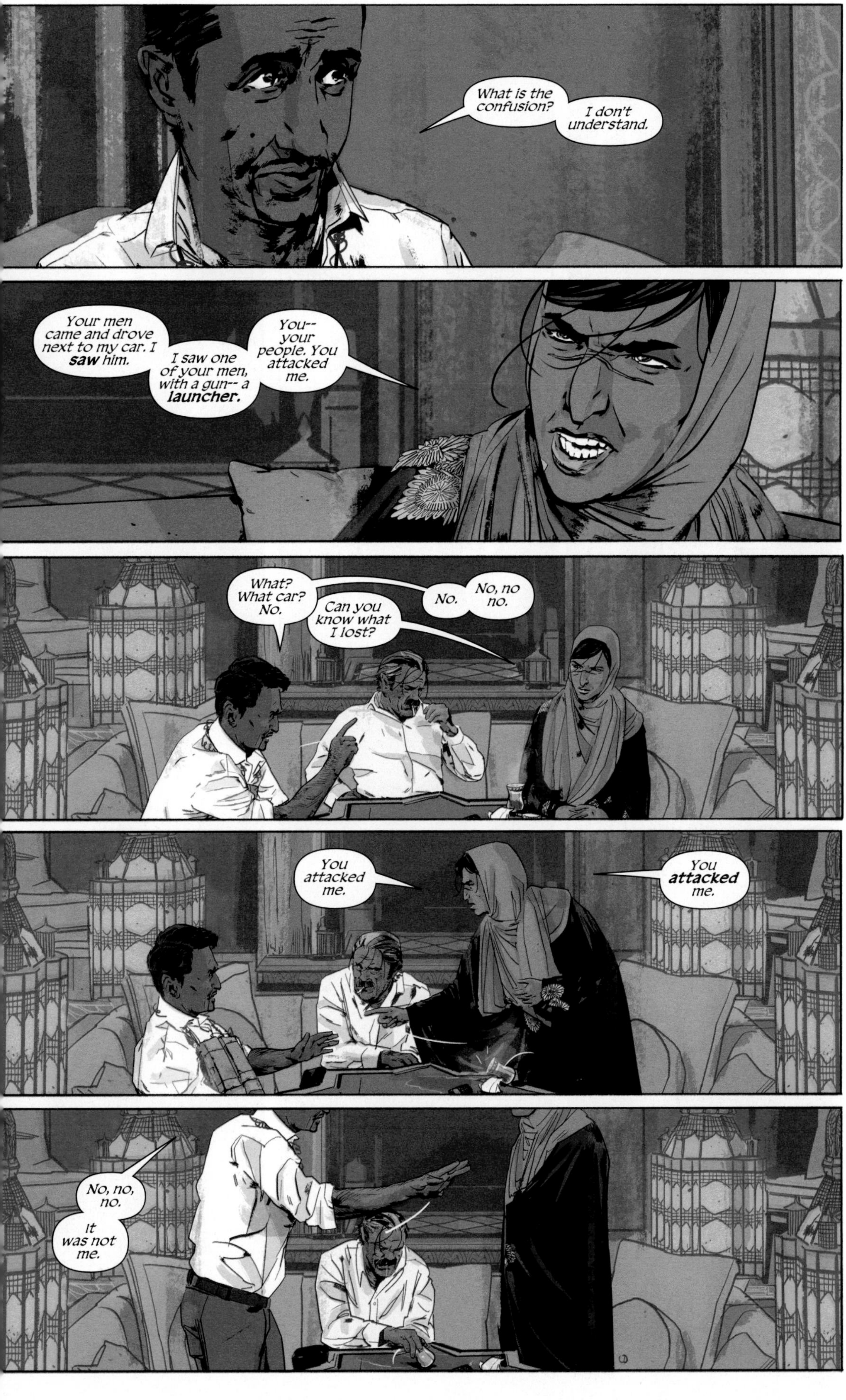
What is the confusion?
I don't understand.
Your men came and drove next to my car. I saw him.
I saw one of your men, with a gun-- a launcher.
You-- your people. You attacked me.
What? What car? No.
Can you know what I lost?
No.
No, no no.
You attacked me.
You attacked me.
No, no, no.
It was not me.

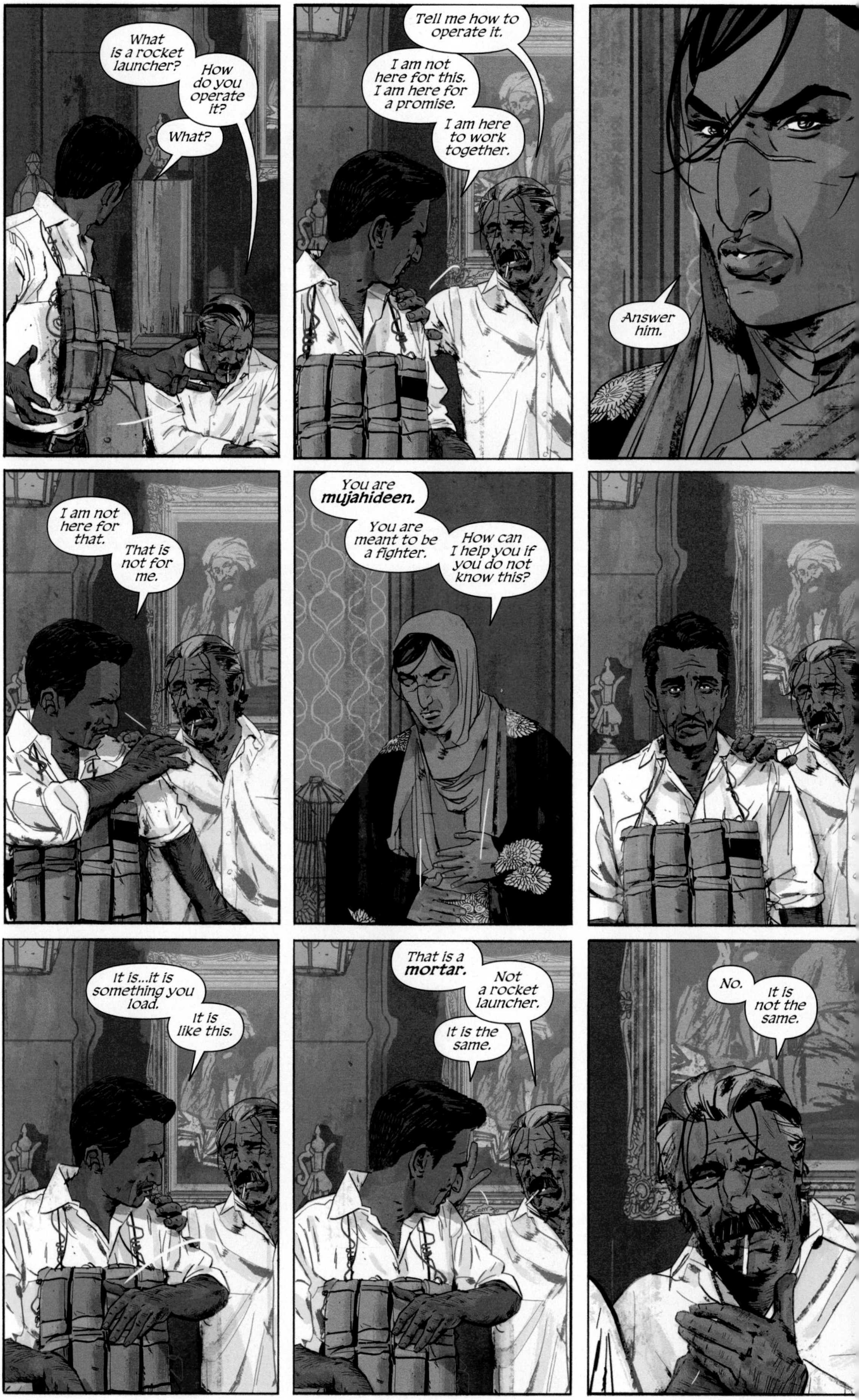
What is a rocket launcher?
How do you operate it?
What?
Tell me how to operate it.
I am not here for this. I am here for a promise.
I am here to work together.
Answer him.
I am not here for that.
That is not for me.
You are mujahideen.
You are meant to be a fighter.
How can I help you if you do not know this?
It is...it is something you load.
It is like this.
That is a mortar.
Not a rocket launcher.
It is the same.
No.
It is not the same.

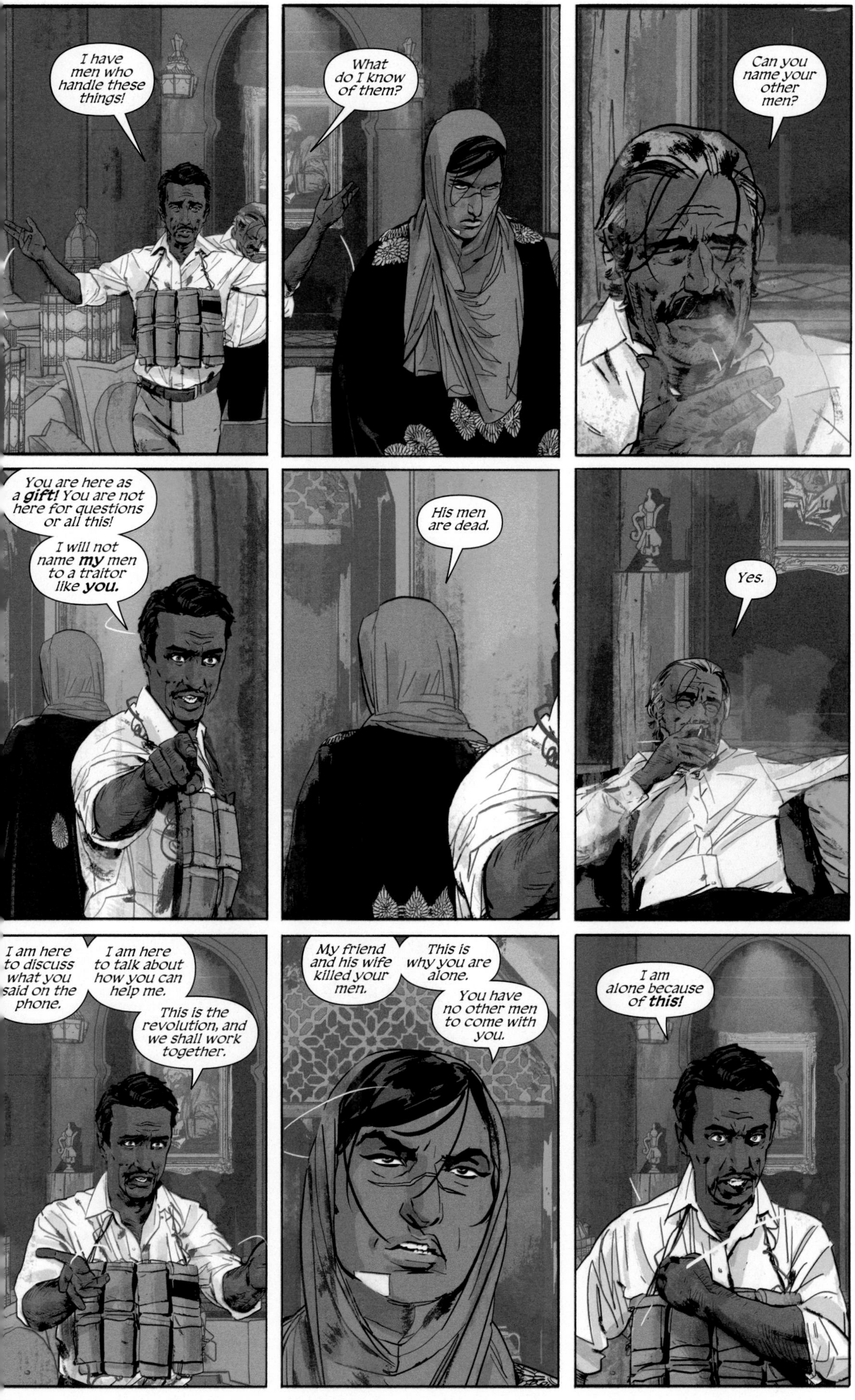
I have men who handle these things!
What do I know of them?
Can you name your other men?
You are here as a gift! You are not here for questions or all this!
I will not name my men to a traitor like you.
His men are dead.
Yes.
I am here to discuss what you said on the phone.
I am here to talk about how you can help me.
This is the revolution, and we shall work together.
My friend and his wife killed your men.
This is why you are alone.
You have no other men to come with you.
I am alone because of this!

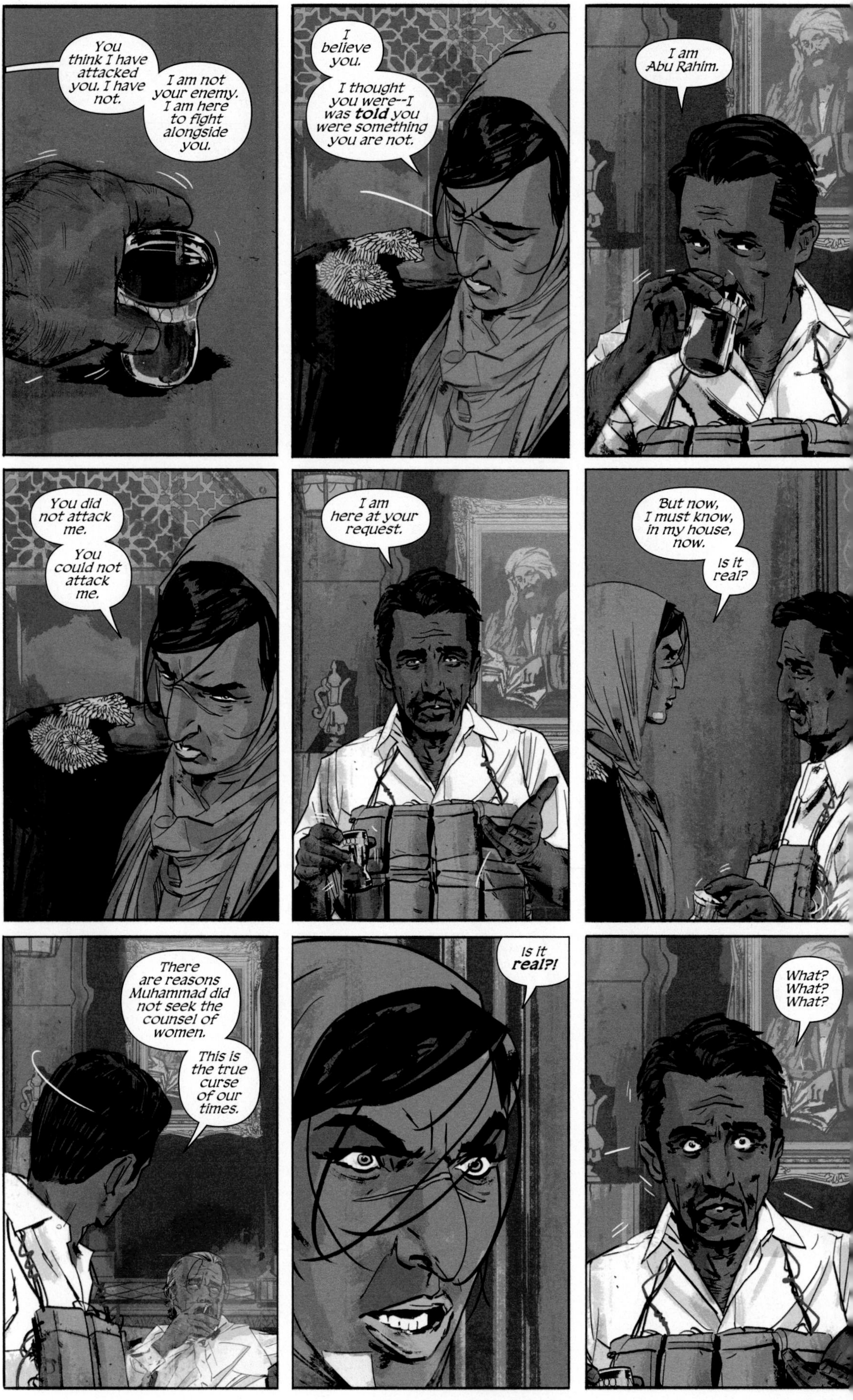
You think I have attacked you. I have not.
I am not your enemy. I am here to fight alongside you.
I believe you.
I thought you were--I was **told** you were something you are not.
I am Abu Rahim.
You did not attack me.
You could not attack me.
I am here at your request.
But now, I must know, in my house, now.
Is it real?
There are reasons Muhammad did not seek the counsel of women.
This is the true curse of our times.
Is it **real?!**
What? What? What?

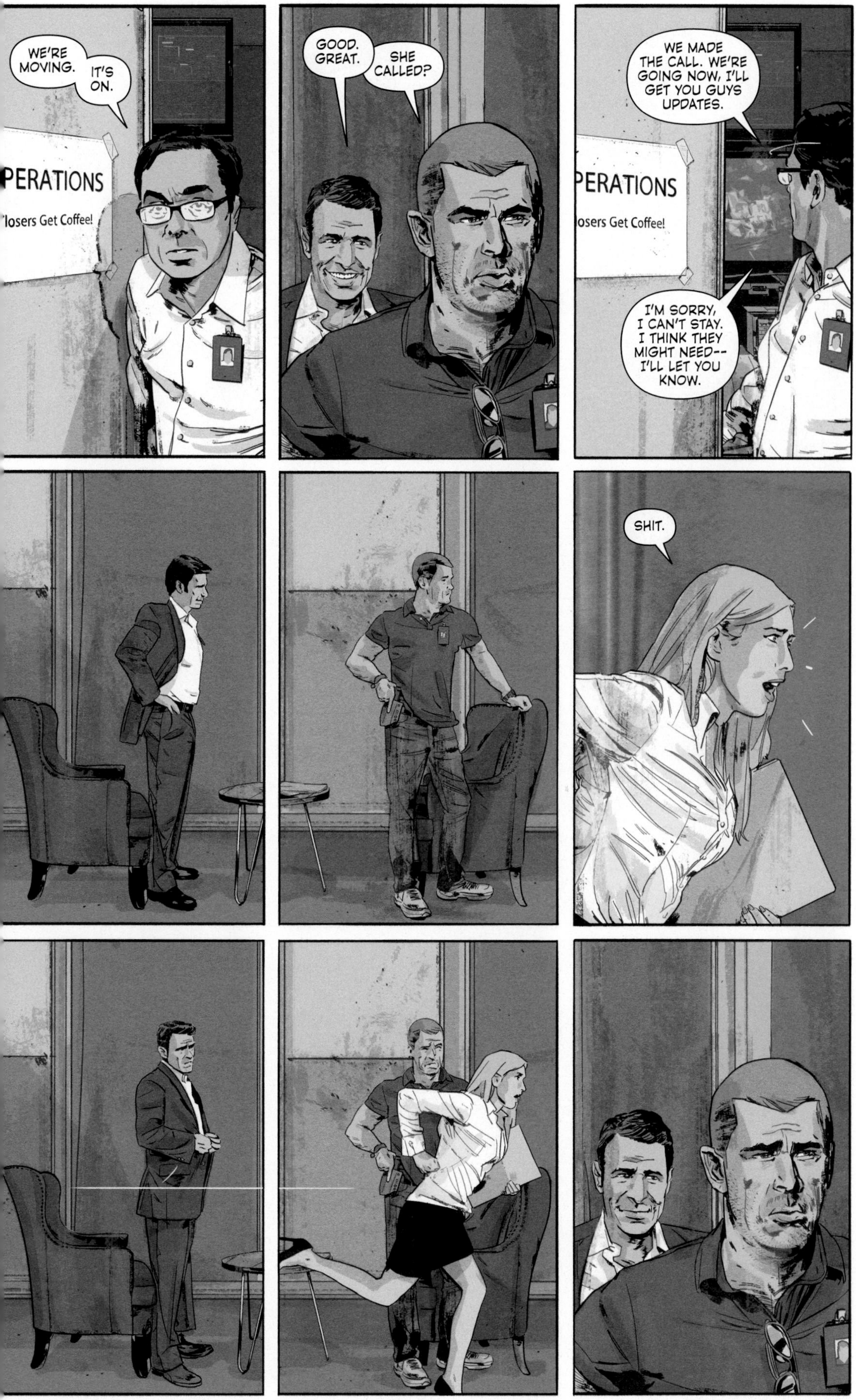
WE'RE MOVING.
IT'S ON.
PERATIONS
losers Get Coffee!
GOOD. GREAT.
SHE CALLED?
WE MADE THE CALL. WE'RE GOING NOW, I'LL GET YOU GUYS UPDATES.
PERATIONS
osers Get Coffee!
I'M SORRY, I CAN'T STAY. I THINK THEY MIGHT NEED-- I'LL LET YOU KNOW.
SHIT.

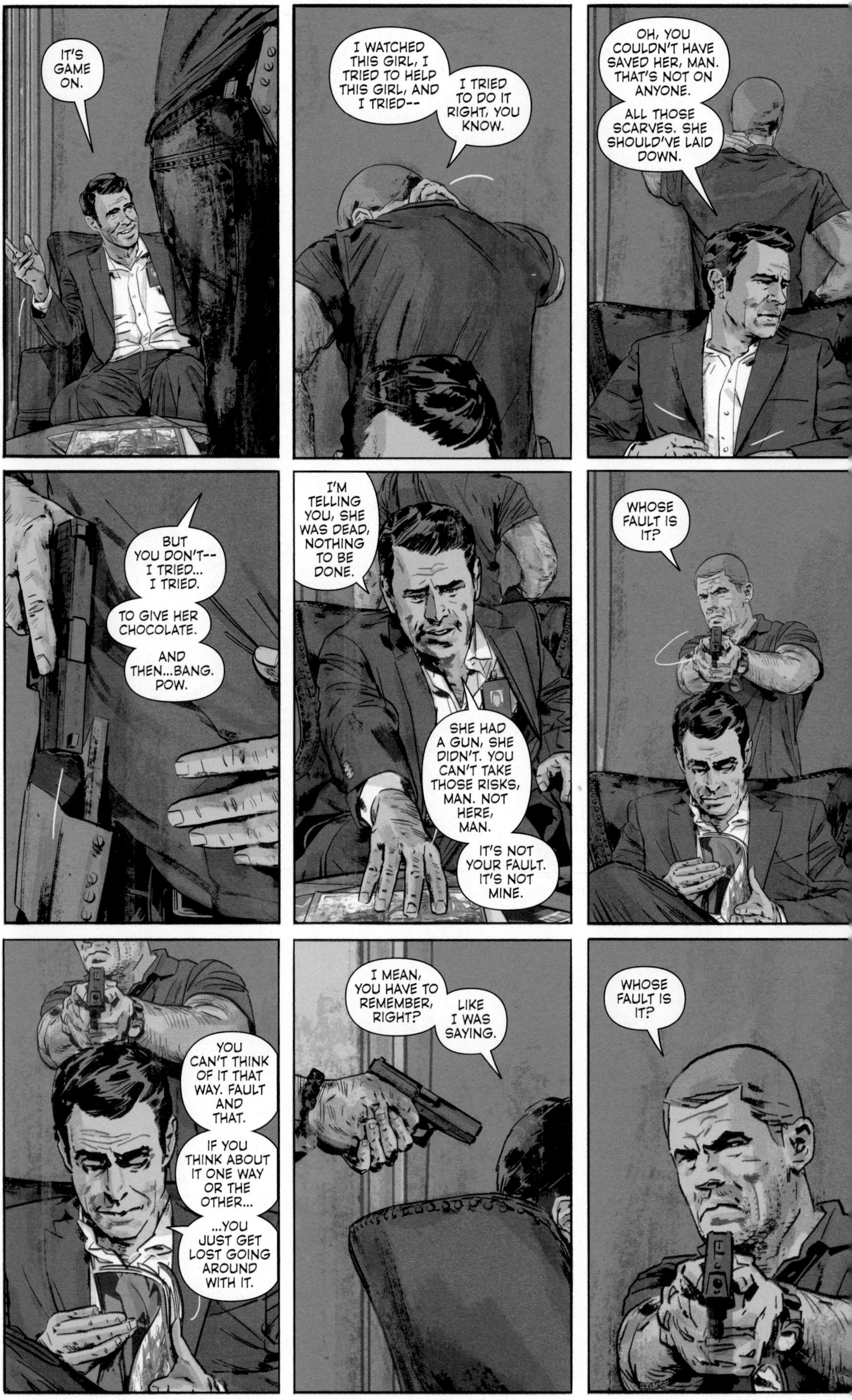

IT'S GAME ON.
I WATCHED THIS GIRL, I TRIED TO HELP THIS GIRL, AND I TRIED--
I TRIED TO DO IT RIGHT, YOU KNOW.
OH, YOU COULDN'T HAVE SAVED HER, MAN. THAT'S NOT ON ANYONE.
ALL THOSE SCARVES. SHE SHOULD'VE LAID DOWN.
BUT YOU DON'T-- I TRIED... I TRIED.
TO GIVE HER CHOCOLATE.
AND THEN...BANG. POW.
I'M TELLING YOU, SHE WAS DEAD, NOTHING TO BE DONE.
SHE HAD A GUN, SHE DIDN'T. YOU CAN'T TAKE THOSE RISKS, MAN. NOT HERE, MAN.
IT'S NOT YOUR FAULT. IT'S NOT MINE.
WHOSE FAULT IS IT?
YOU CAN'T THINK OF IT THAT WAY. FAULT AND THAT.
IF YOU THINK ABOUT IT ONE WAY OR THE OTHER...
...YOU JUST GET LOST GOING AROUND WITH IT.
I MEAN, YOU HAVE TO REMEMBER, RIGHT?
LIKE I WAS SAYING.
WHOSE FAULT IS IT?

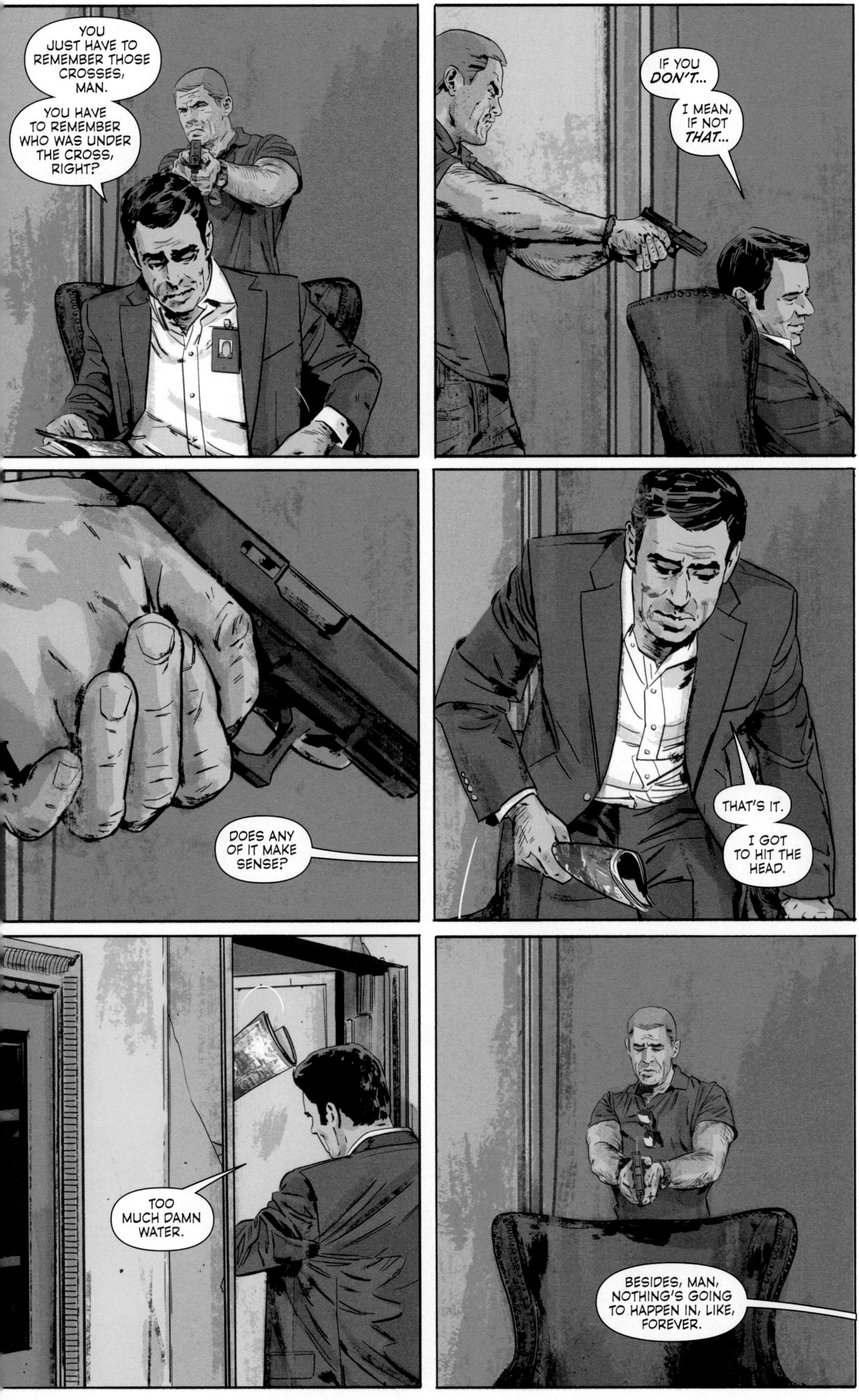
YOU JUST HAVE TO REMEMBER THOSE CROSSES, MAN.
YOU HAVE TO REMEMBER WHO WAS UNDER THE CROSS, RIGHT?
IF YOU *DON'T*...
I MEAN, IF NOT *THAT*...
DOES ANY OF IT MAKE SENSE?
THAT'S IT.
I GOT TO HIT THE HEAD.
TOO MUCH DAMN WATER.
BESIDES, MAN, NOTHING'S GOING TO HAPPEN IN, LIKE, FOREVER.

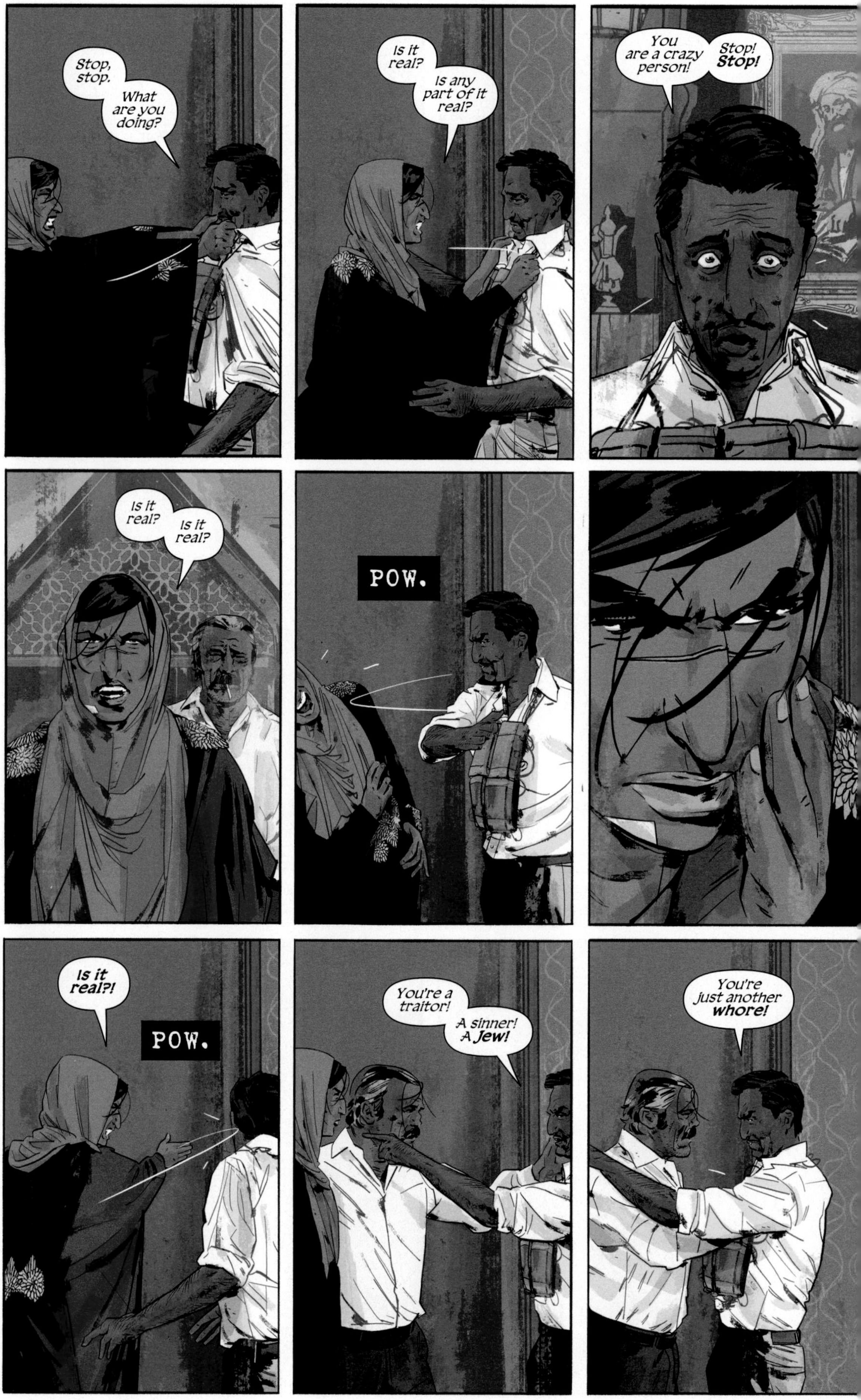
Stop, stop.
What are you doing?
Is it real?
Is any part of it real?
You are a crazy person!
Stop! Stop!
Is it real?
Is it real?
POW.
Is it real?!
POW.
You're a traitor!
A sinner! A Jew!
You're just another whore!

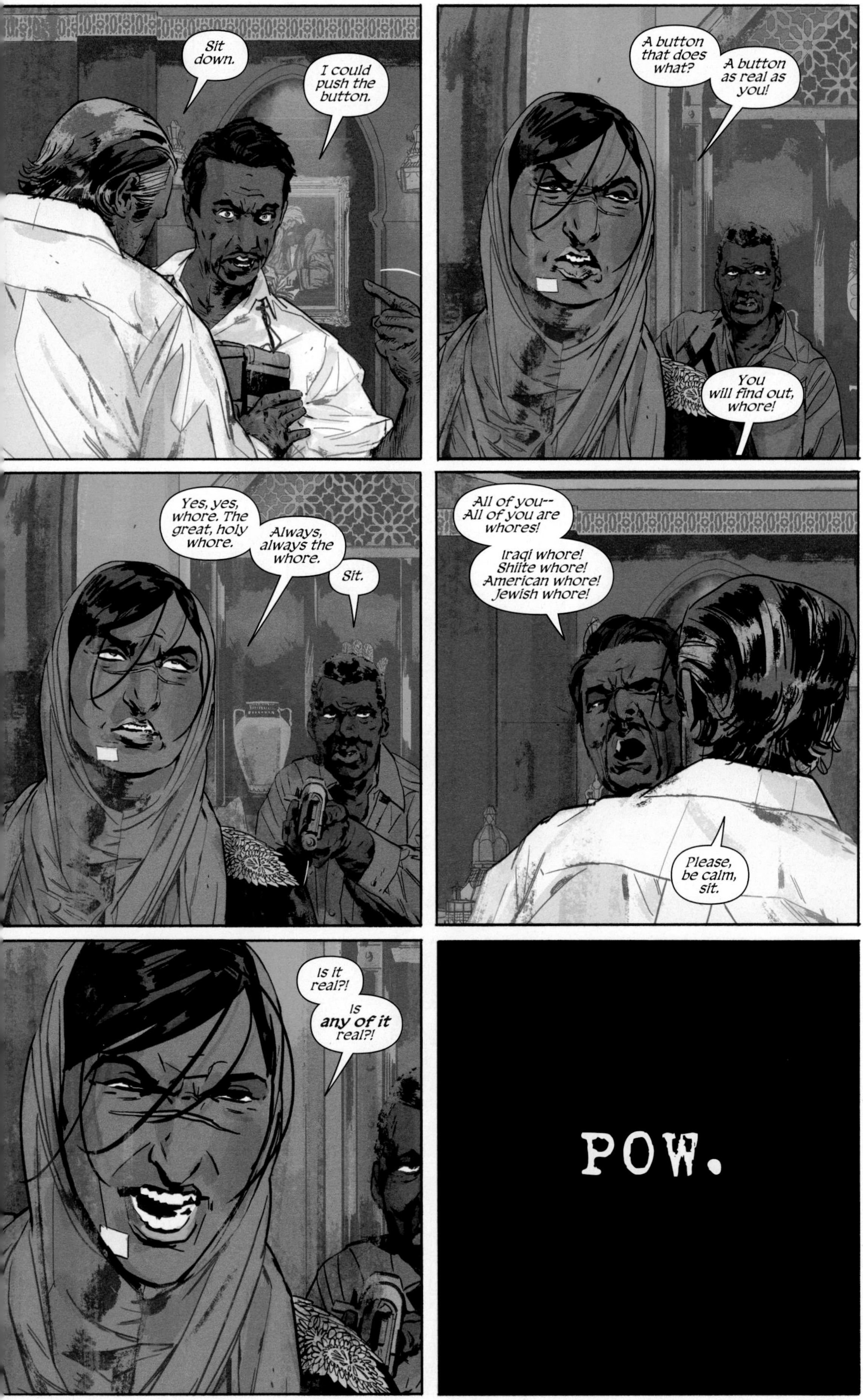
Sit down.
I could push the button.
A button that does what?
A button as real as you!
You will find out, whore!
Yes, yes, whore. The great, holy whore.
Always, always the whore.
Sit.
All of you-- All of you are whores!
Iraqi whore! Shiite whore! American whore! Jewish whore!
Please, be calm, sit.
Is it real?!
Is **any of it** real?!
POW.

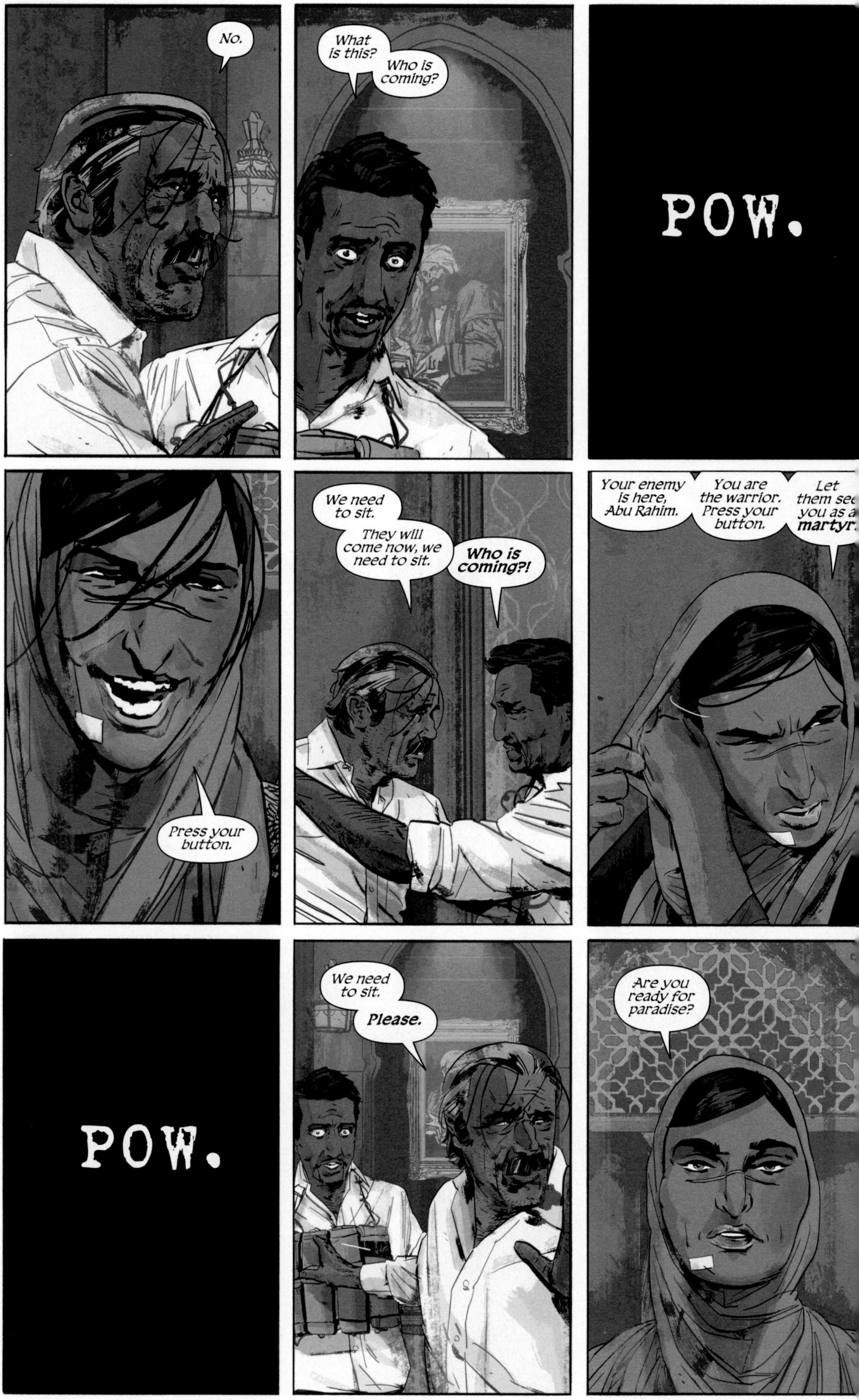

No.
What is this?
Who is coming?
POW.
Press your button.
We need to sit.
They will come now, we need to sit.
Who is coming?!
Your enemy is here, Abu Rahim.
You are the warrior. Press your button.
Let them see you as a martyr.
POW.
We need to sit.
Please.
Are you ready for paradise?

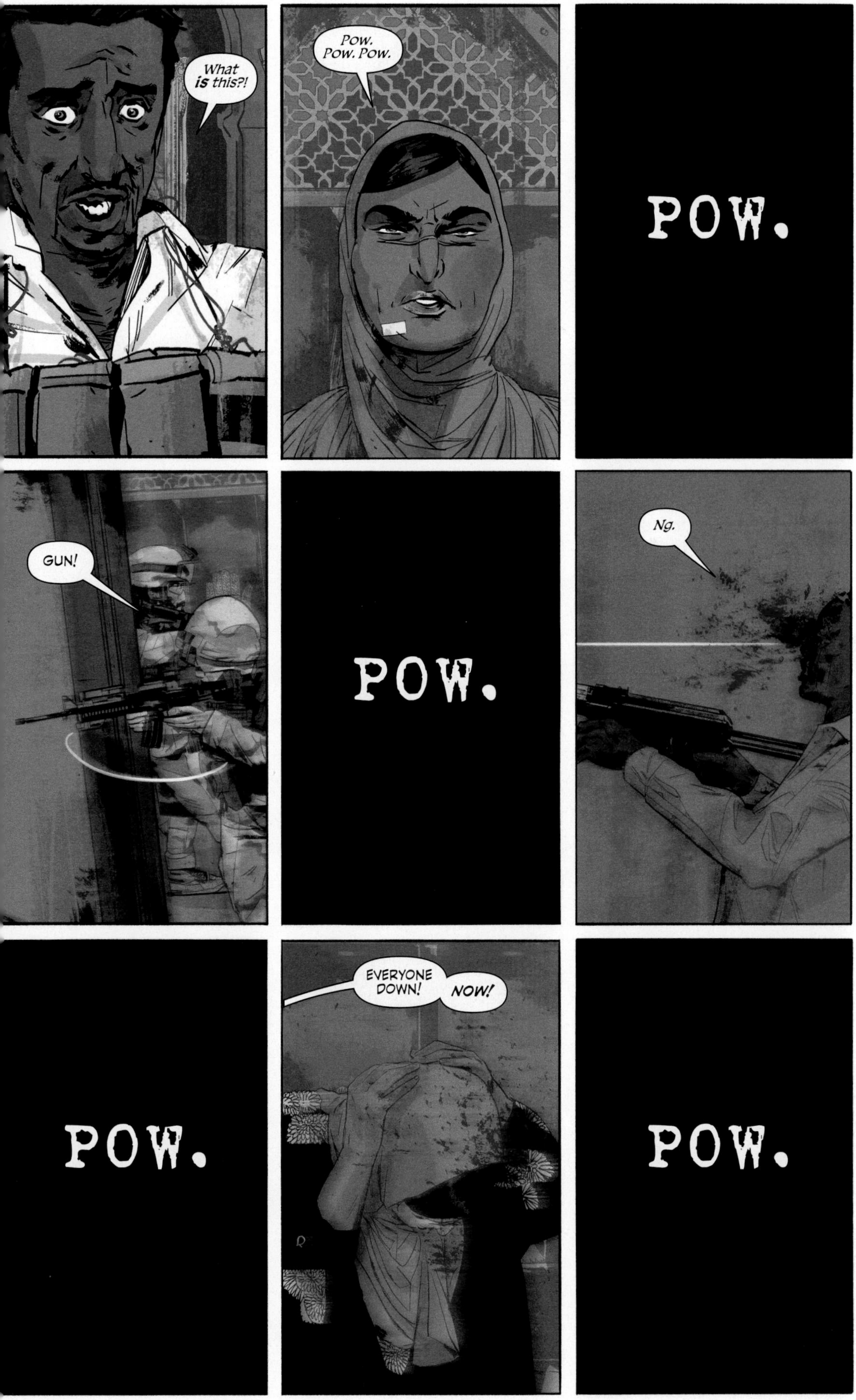

What is this?!
Pow. Pow. Pow.
POW.
GUN!
POW.
Ng.
POW.
EVERYONE DOWN!
NOW!
POW.

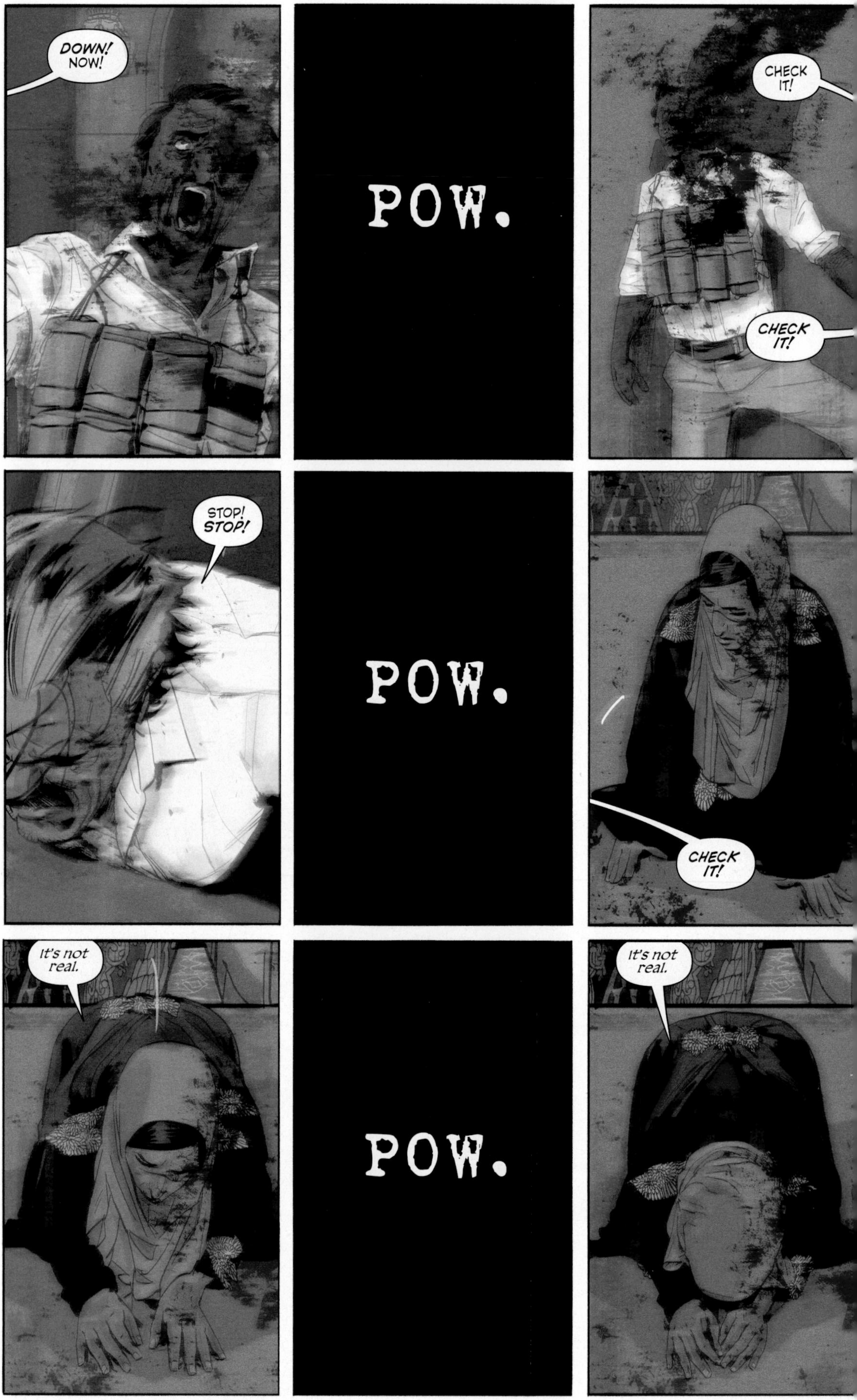
DOWN! NOW!
POW.
CHECK IT!
CHECK IT!
STOP! STOP!
POW.
CHECK IT!
It's not real.
POW.
It's not real.

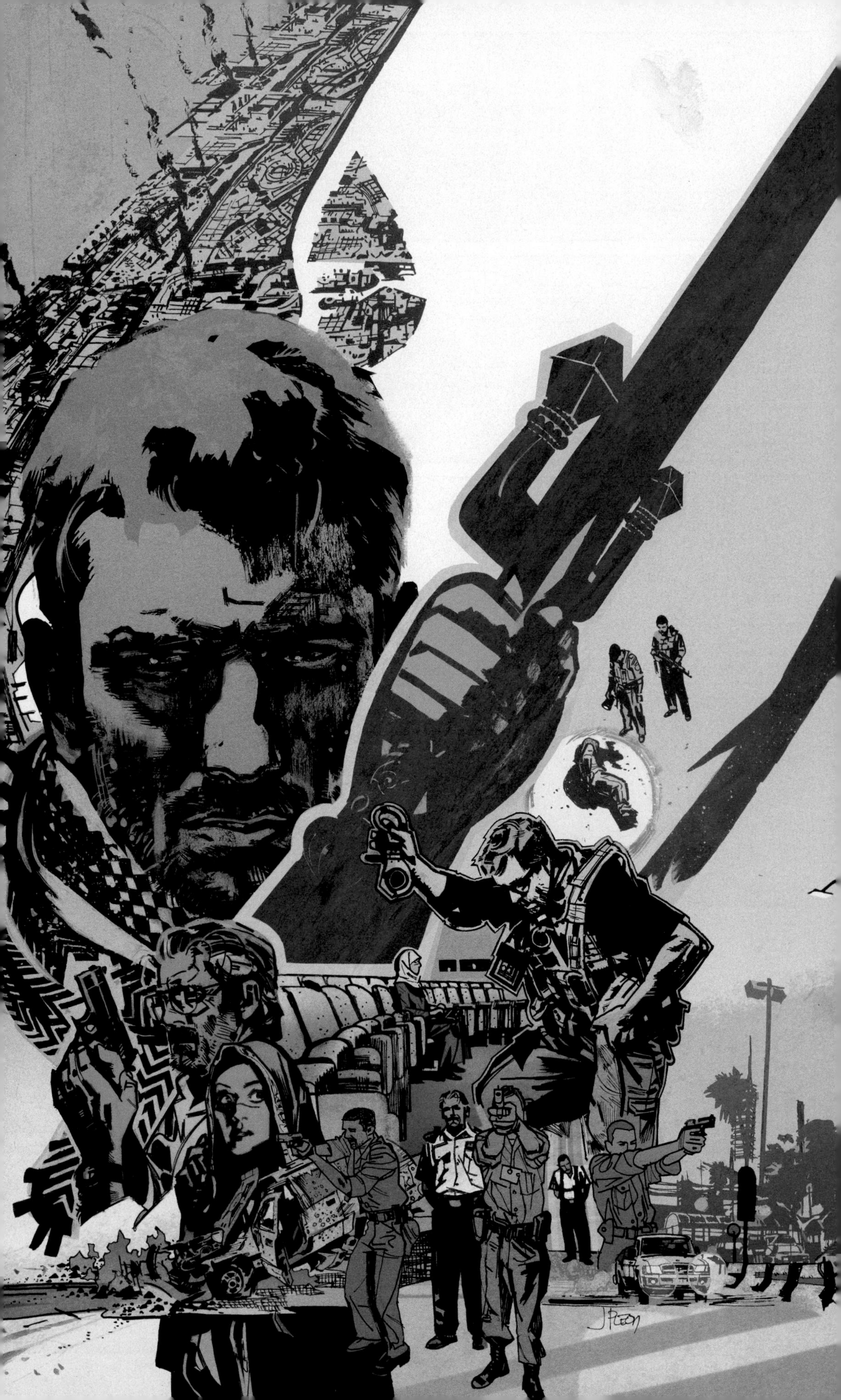

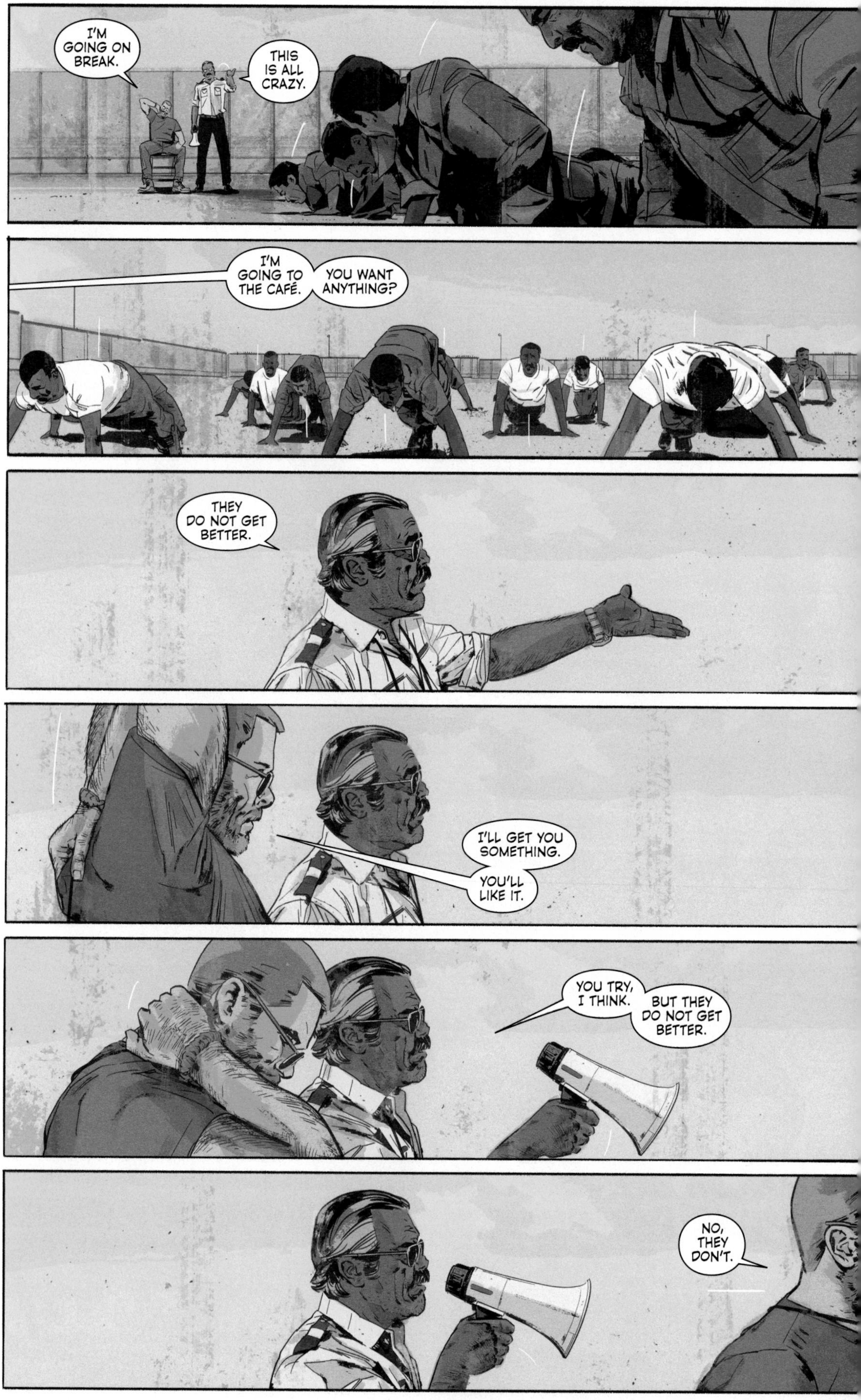
I'M GOING ON BREAK.
THIS IS ALL CRAZY.
I'M GOING TO THE CAFÉ.
YOU WANT ANYTHING?
THEY DO NOT GET BETTER.
I'LL GET YOU SOMETHING.
YOU'LL LIKE IT.
YOU TRY, I THINK.
BUT THEY DO NOT GET BETTER.
NO, THEY DON'T.

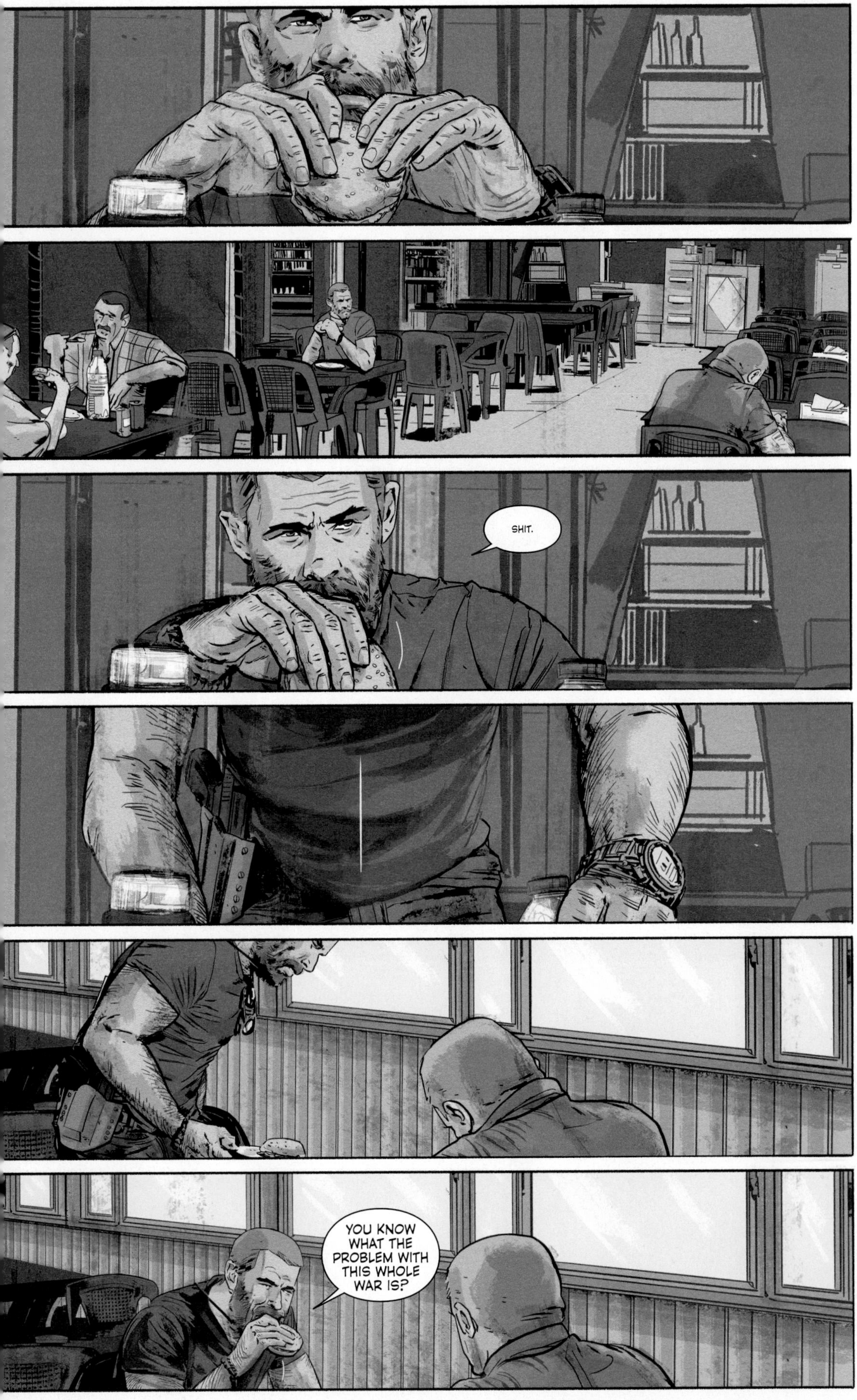
SHIT.
YOU KNOW WHAT THE PROBLEM WITH THIS WHOLE WAR IS?

Jim from Ops.

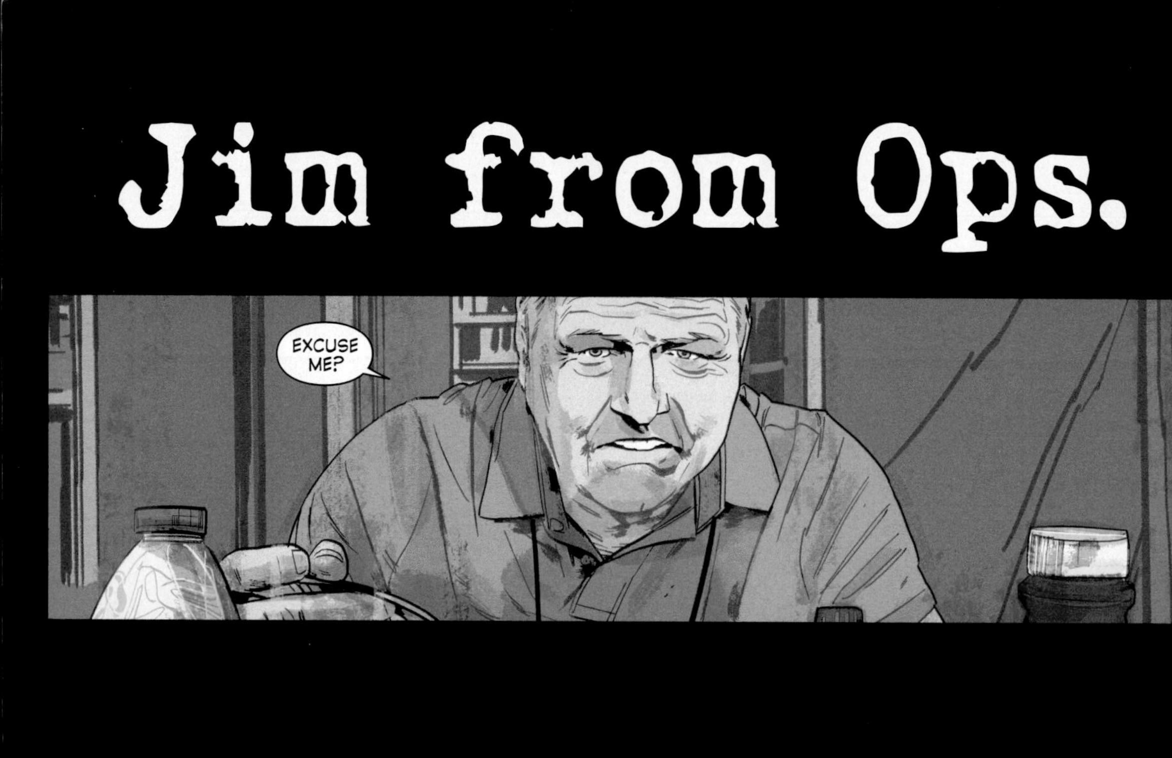
EXCUSE ME?

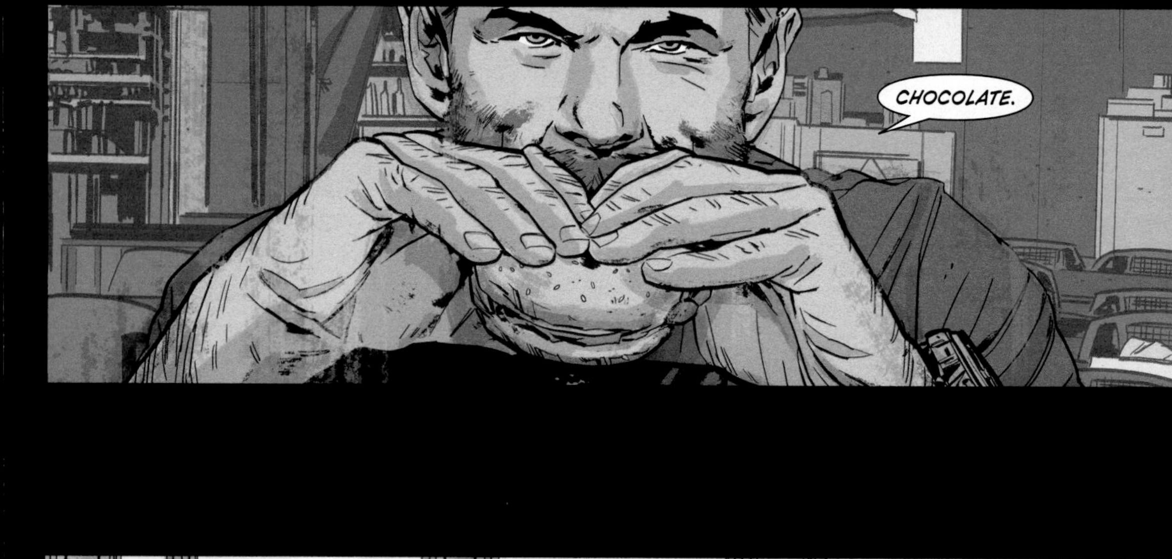
CHOCOLATE.

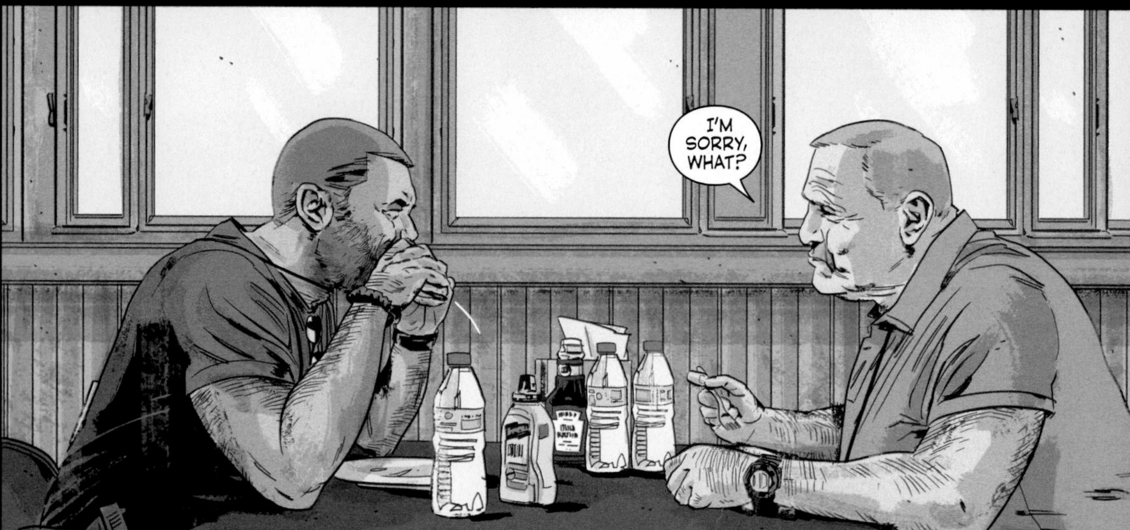
I'M SORRY, WHAT?

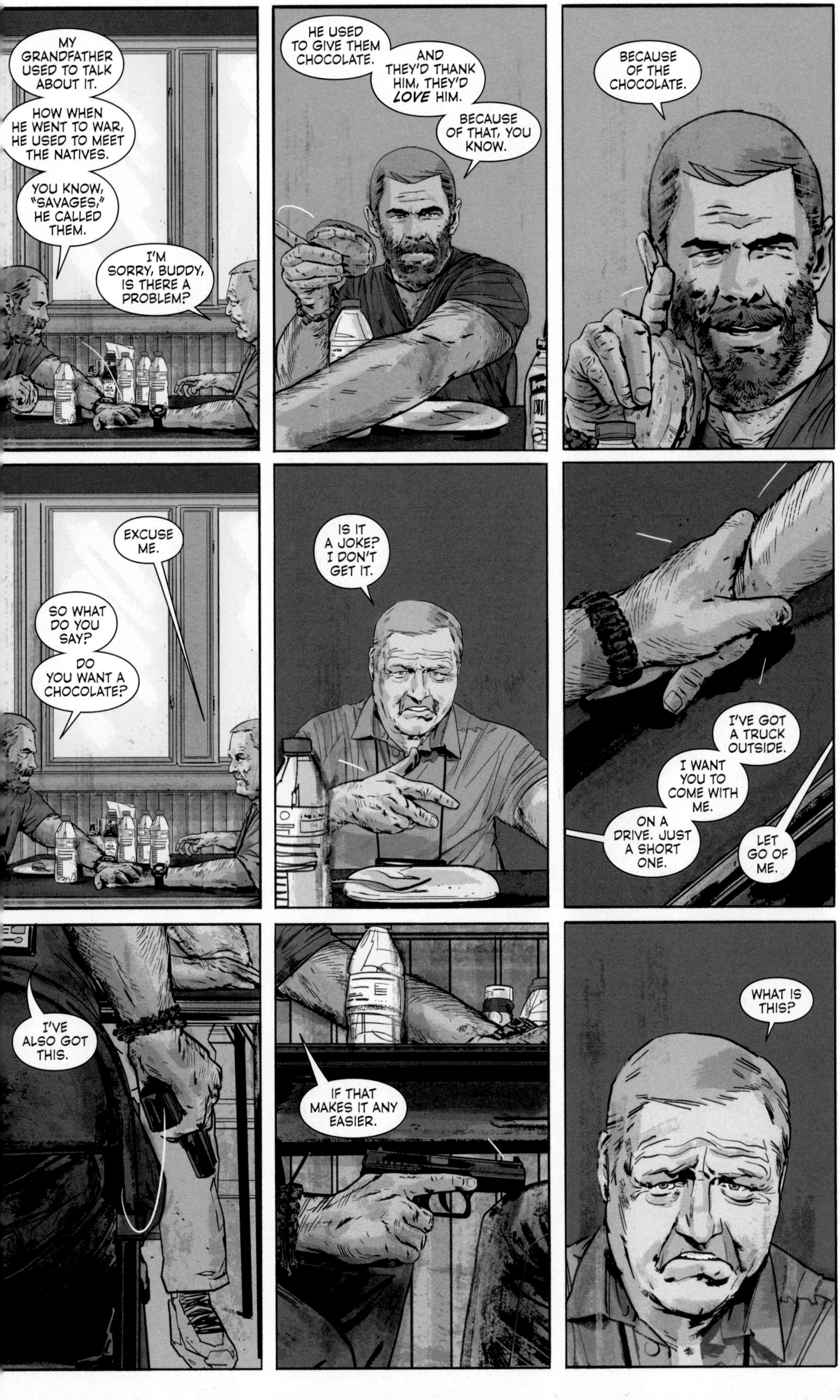
MY GRANDFATHER USED TO TALK ABOUT IT.
HOW WHEN HE WENT TO WAR, HE USED TO MEET THE NATIVES.
YOU KNOW, "SAVAGES," HE CALLED THEM.
I'M SORRY, BUDDY, IS THERE A PROBLEM?
HE USED TO GIVE THEM CHOCOLATE.
AND THEY'D THANK HIM, THEY'D *LOVE* HIM.
BECAUSE OF THAT, YOU KNOW.
BECAUSE OF THE CHOCOLATE.
EXCUSE ME.
SO WHAT DO YOU SAY?
DO YOU WANT A CHOCOLATE?
IS IT A JOKE? I DON'T GET IT.
I'VE GOT A TRUCK OUTSIDE.
I WANT YOU TO COME WITH ME.
ON A DRIVE. JUST A SHORT ONE.
LET GO OF ME.
I'VE ALSO GOT THIS.
IF THAT MAKES IT ANY EASIER.
WHAT IS THIS?

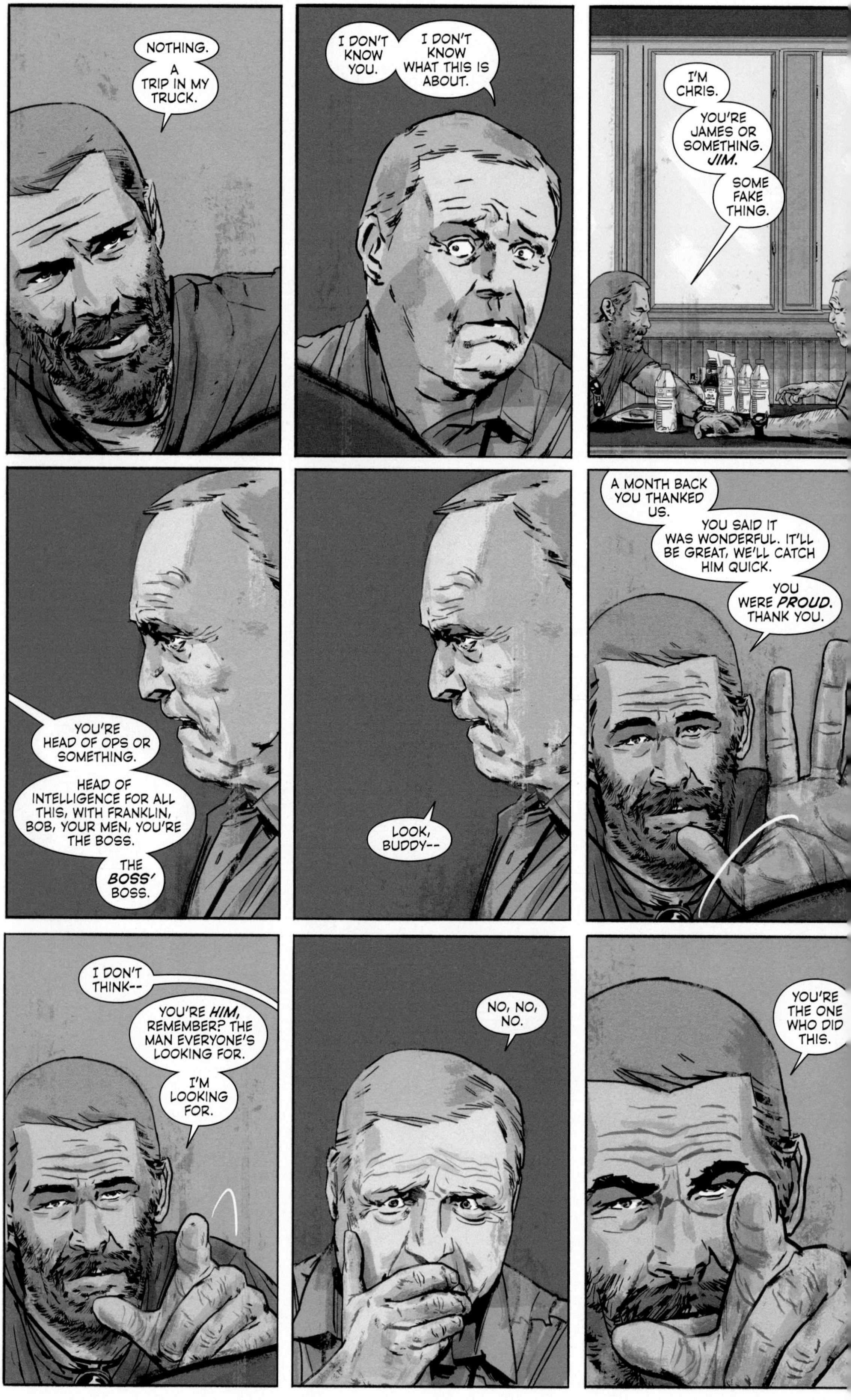
NOTHING.
A TRIP IN MY TRUCK.
I DON'T KNOW YOU.
I DON'T KNOW WHAT THIS IS ABOUT.
I'M CHRIS.
YOU'RE JAMES OR SOMETHING. JIM.
SOME FAKE THING.
YOU'RE HEAD OF OPS OR SOMETHING.
HEAD OF INTELLIGENCE FOR ALL THIS, WITH FRANKLIN, BOB, YOUR MEN, YOU'RE THE BOSS.
THE BOSS' BOSS.
LOOK, BUDDY--
A MONTH BACK YOU THANKED US.
YOU SAID IT WAS WONDERFUL. IT'LL BE GREAT, WE'LL CATCH HIM QUICK.
YOU WERE PROUD. THANK YOU.
I DON'T THINK--
YOU'RE HIM, REMEMBER? THE MAN EVERYONE'S LOOKING FOR.
I'M LOOKING FOR.
NO, NO, NO.
YOU'RE THE ONE WHO DID THIS.

...have video today of the four contractors in Fallujah. They show them in their car and--after being burned in the car--being dragged.
"The Americans are saying the men are Blackwater employees, delivering food. The Jihadist and these people are claiming they are **CIA.** Doing operations."
MAR. 31 2004
The council has been asked for any information or contacts we may have that will help in retrieving the bodies.
BUZZ BUZZ
If you do have such information, please report it to the council. Do not pass on this information directly as we wish to avoid confusion and repetition.
CHRISTOPHER
Moving on to item forty-two. We have a delivery of air-conditioning units scheduled for arrival at Checkpoint Three today.

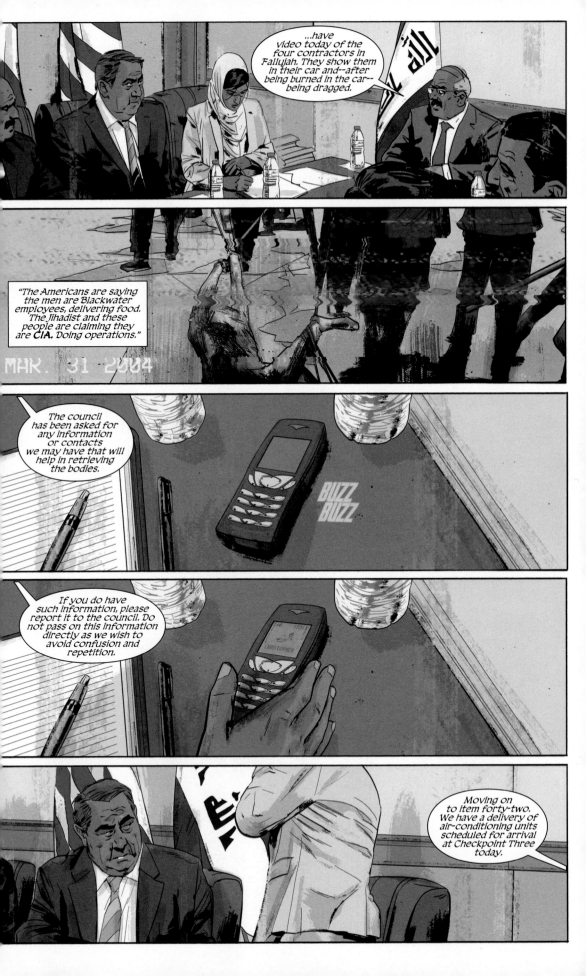

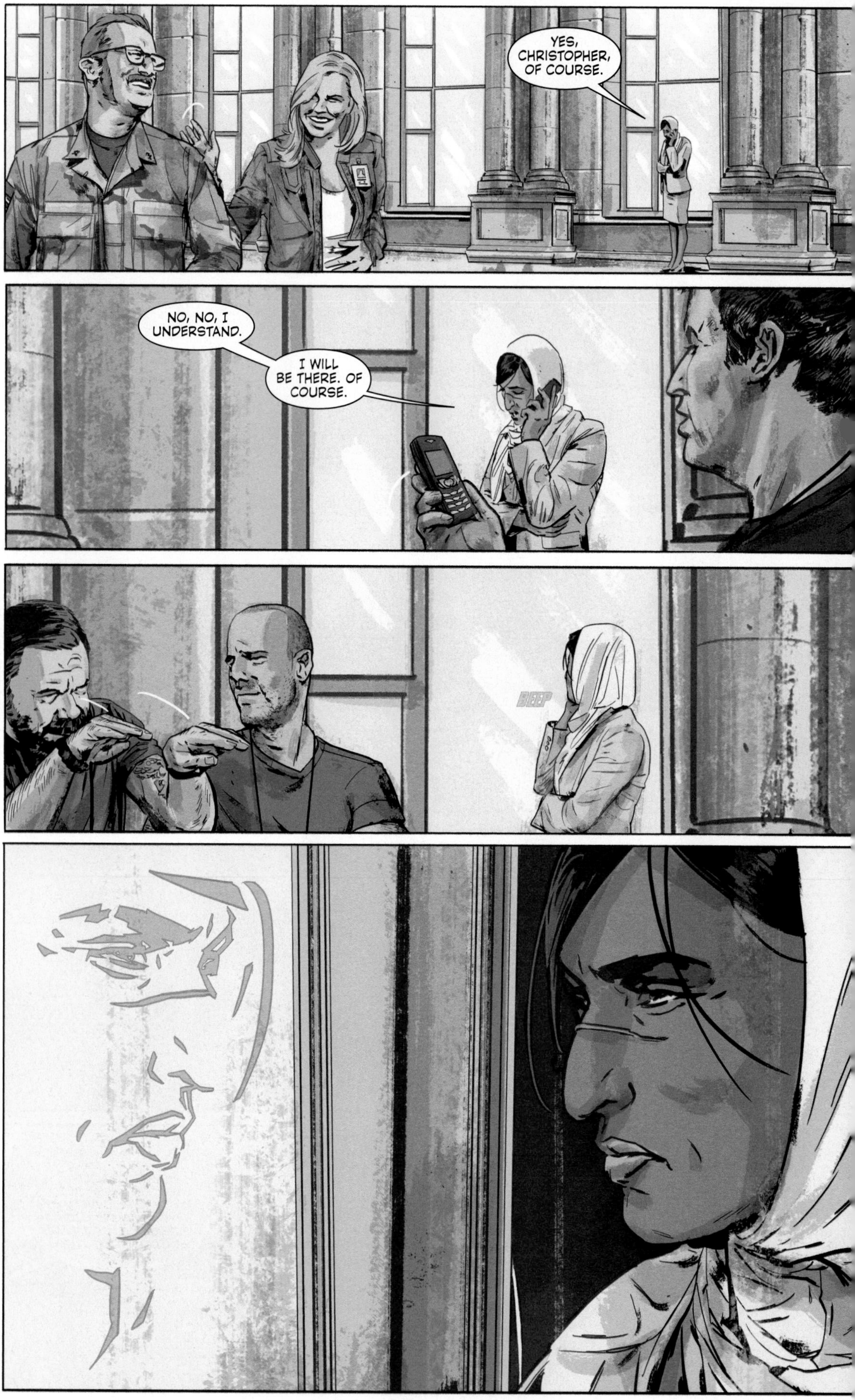
YES, CHRISTOPHER, OF COURSE.
NO, NO, I UNDERSTAND.
I WILL BE THERE. OF COURSE.
BEEP

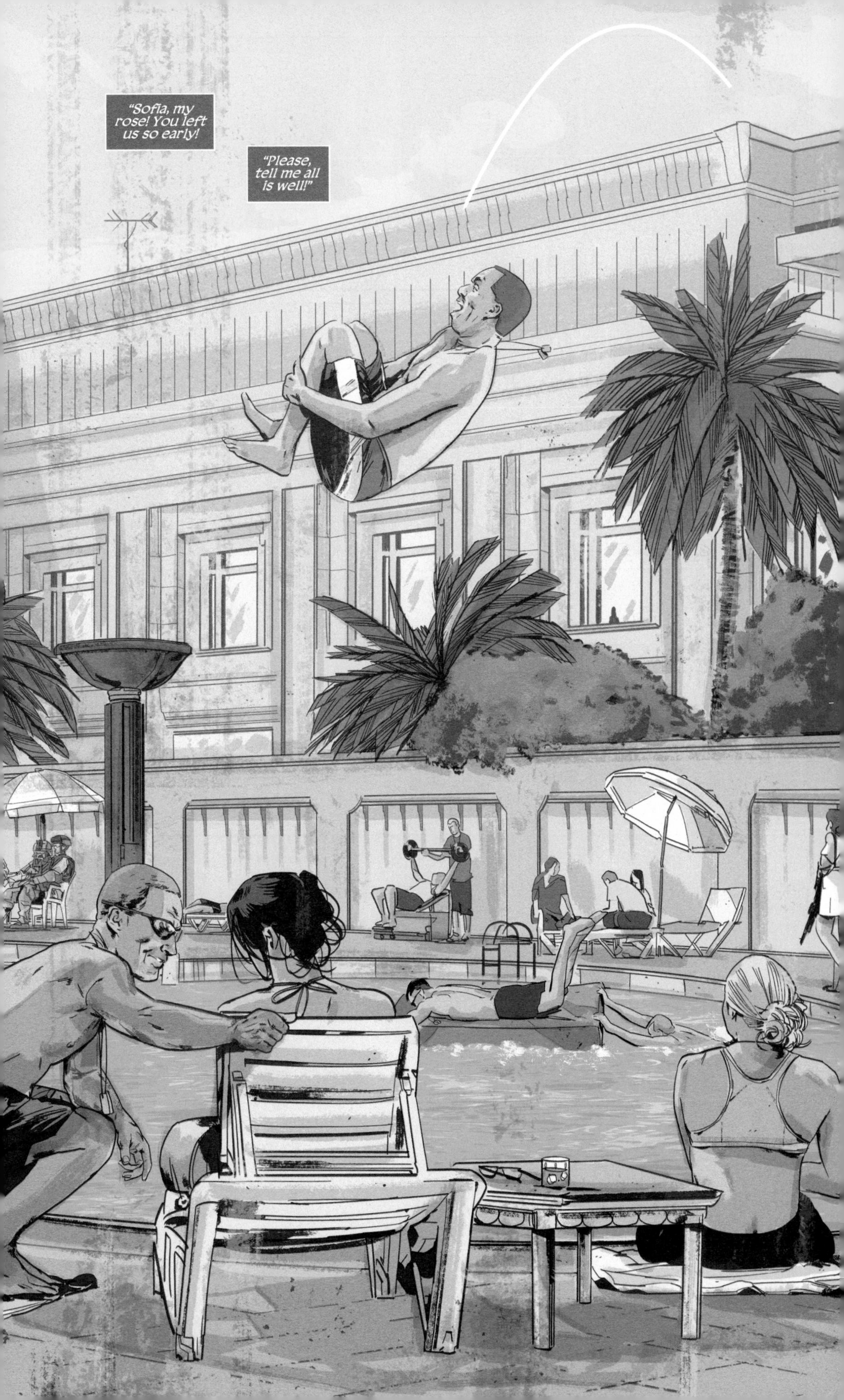
"Sofia, my rose! You left us so early!
"Please, tell me all is well!"

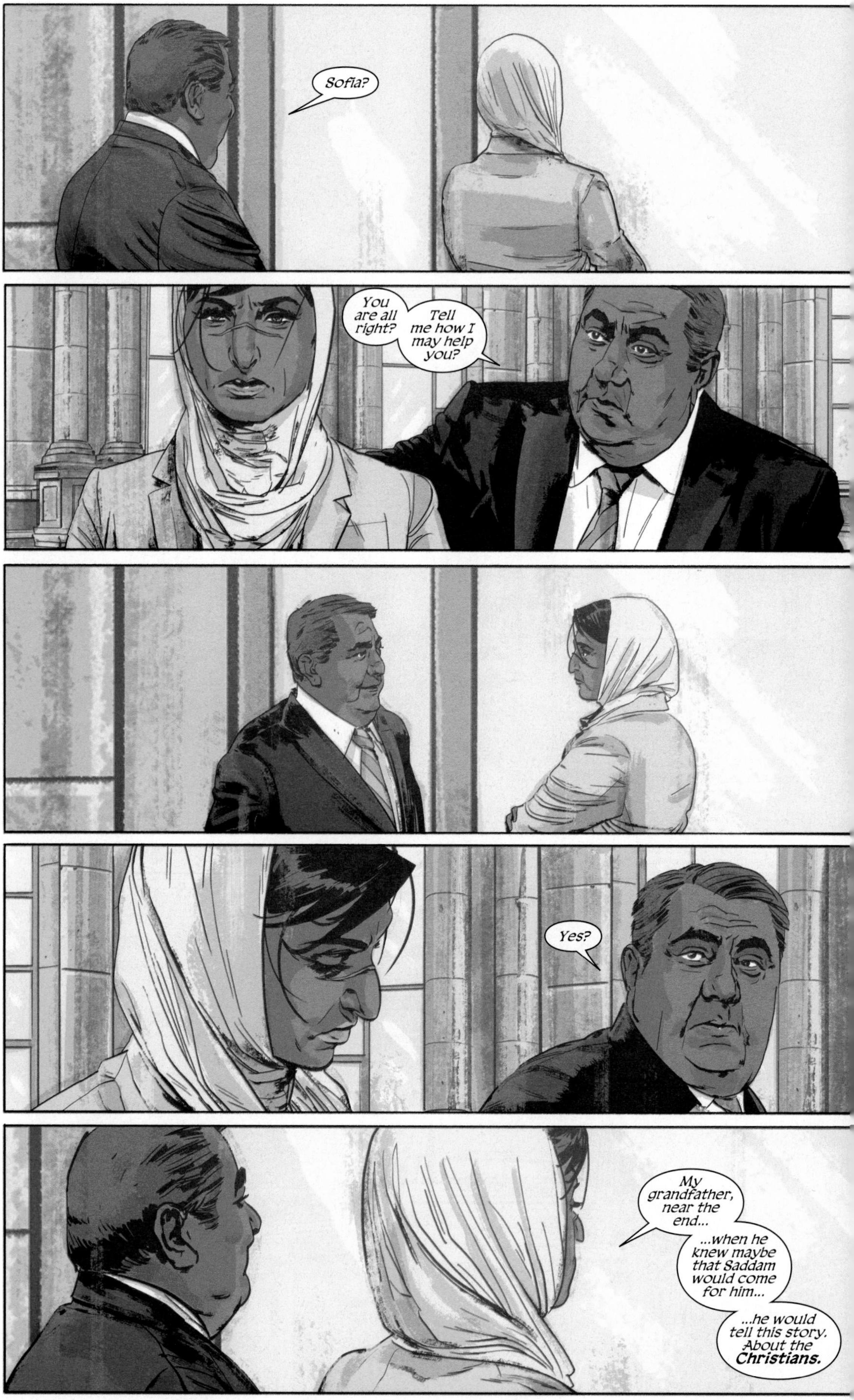
Sofia?
You are all right?
Tell me how I may help you?
Yes?
My grandfather, near the end...
...when he knew maybe that Saddam would come for him...
...he would tell this story. About the **Christians.**

"Hundreds of years ago, there was a Muslim who wanted to join Christianity...

"...and he told his Christian friend he was converting...

"...and his first act of converting was to go to Rome, the capital of the Christians.

"The friend was upset.

"He knew that the capital was full of sin.

MAR. 31 2004

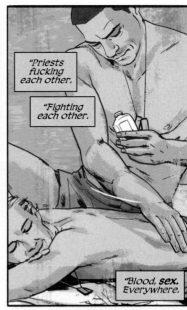

"Priests fucking each other.

"Fighting each other.

"Blood, *sex.* Everywhere.

"All the sins of Babylon.

MAR. 31 2004

"When the convert returned, the friend expected him to recant his conversion.

"The friend greeted the convert and expected this.

"But the convert said...

"...'No, no, no. My faith is all the stronger now!'

MAR. 31

"The friend was surprised.

"And he asked how this could be.

"And the convert said:

"Any religion, **anything,** that still has believers in a land such as this...

"...Well, **this...**

MAR. 31 2004

"...'This thing must be true.'"

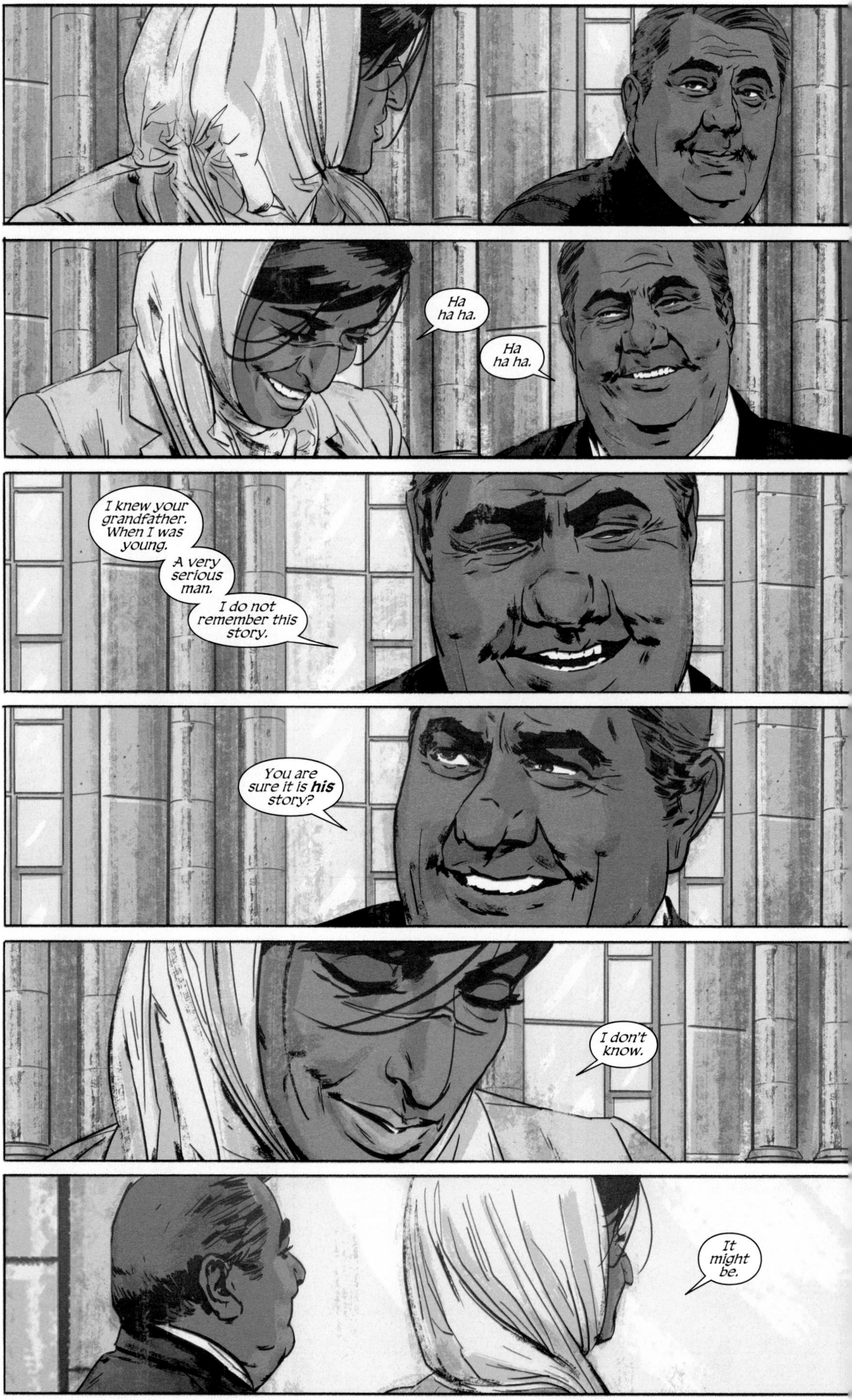
Ha ha ha.
Ha ha ha.
I knew your grandfather. When I was young.
A very serious man.
I do not remember this story.
You are sure it is **his** story?
I don't know.
It might be.

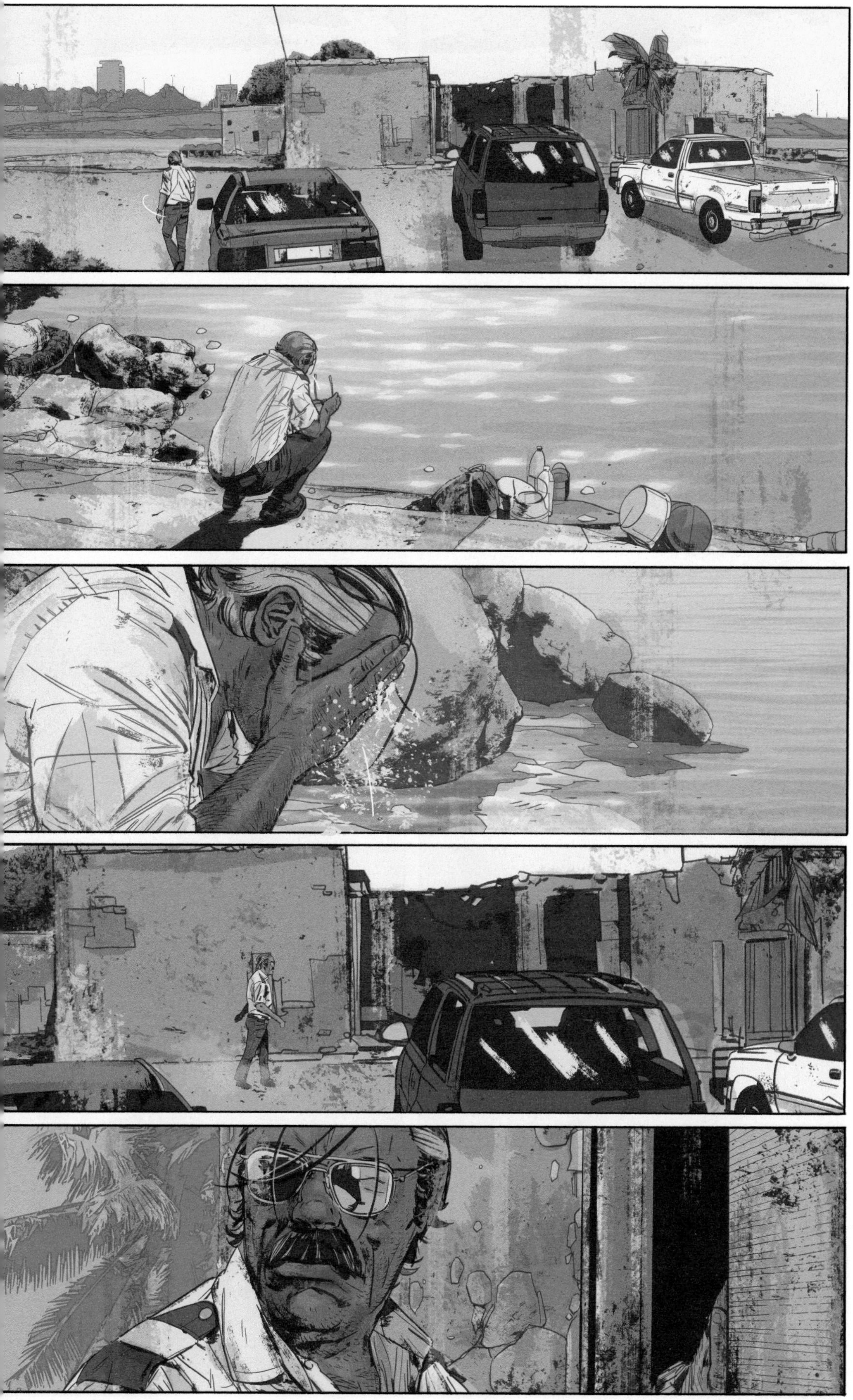

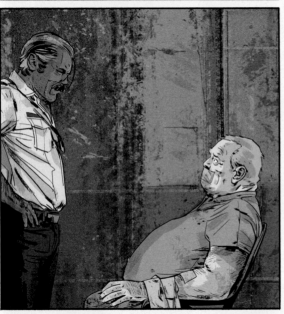

RRIF

THIS IS
WRONG.

YOU
GOT IT
WRONG.

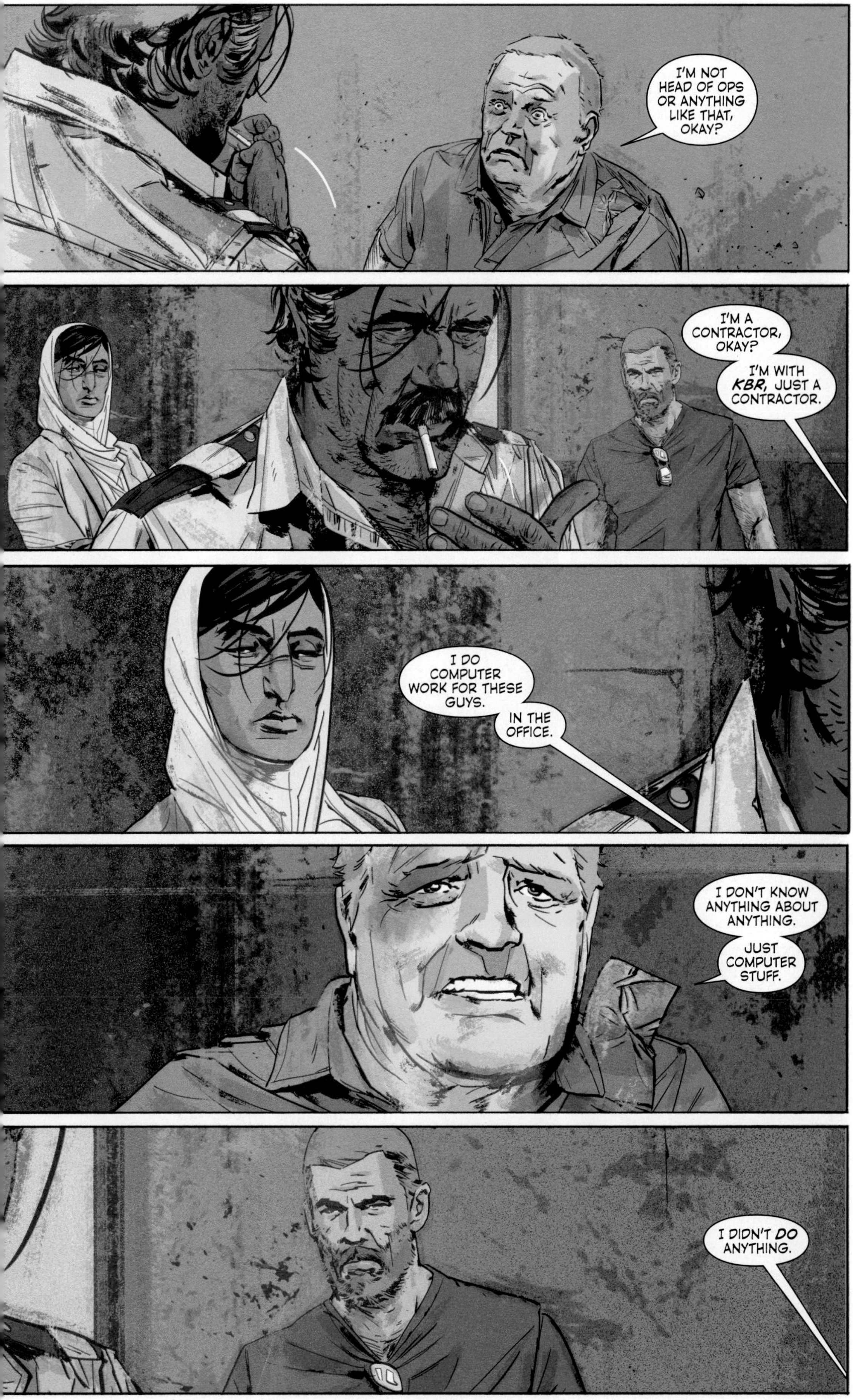
I'M NOT HEAD OF OPS OR ANYTHING LIKE THAT, OKAY?
I'M A CONTRACTOR, OKAY?
I'M WITH KBR, JUST A CONTRACTOR.
I DO COMPUTER WORK FOR THESE GUYS.
IN THE OFFICE.
I DON'T KNOW ANYTHING ABOUT ANYTHING.
JUST COMPUTER STUFF.
I DIDN'T DO ANYTHING.

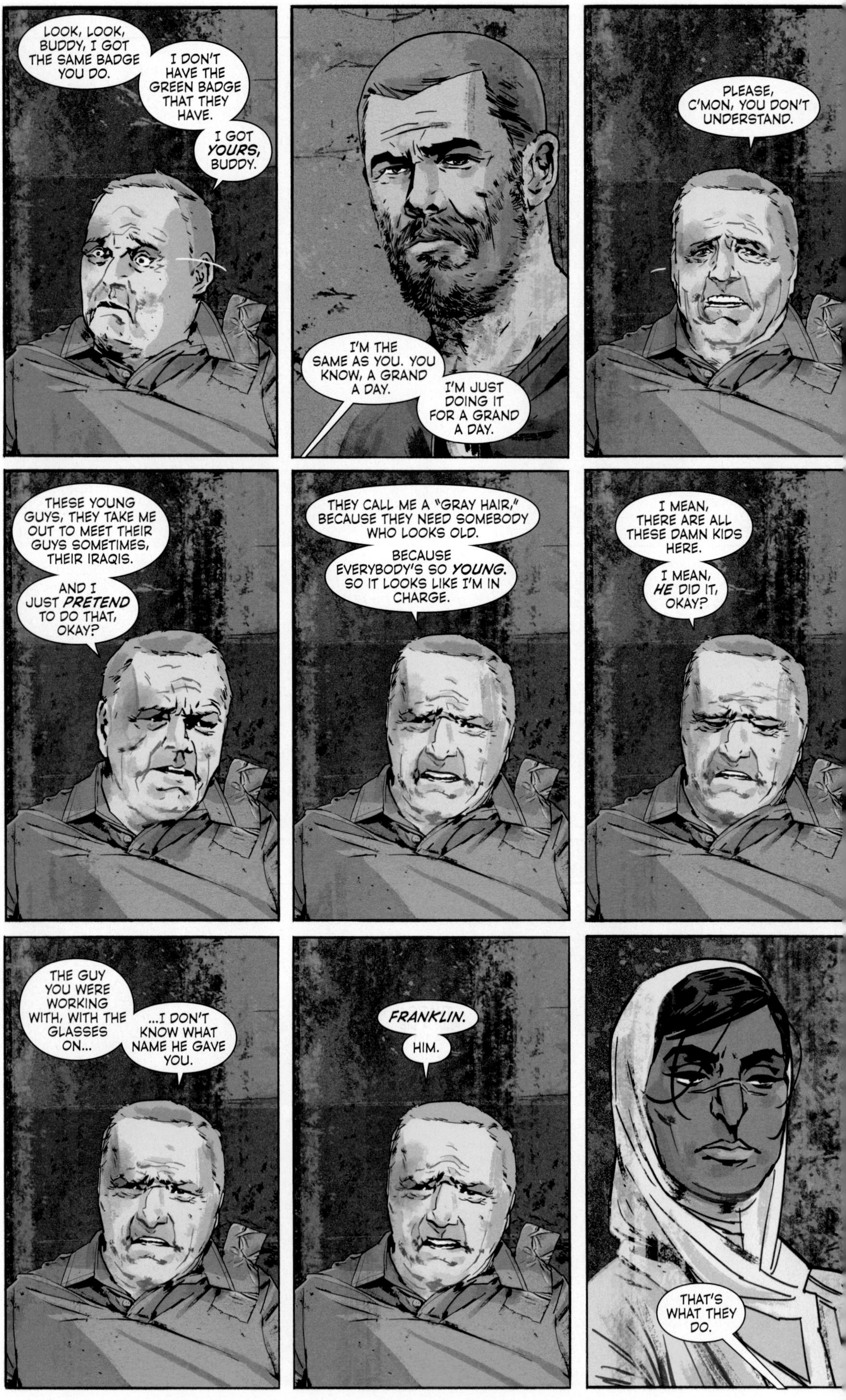
LOOK, LOOK, BUDDY, I GOT THE SAME BADGE YOU DO.
I DON'T HAVE THE GREEN BADGE THAT THEY HAVE.
I GOT *YOURS,* BUDDY.
I'M THE SAME AS YOU. YOU KNOW, A GRAND A DAY.
I'M JUST DOING IT FOR A GRAND A DAY.
PLEASE, C'MON, YOU DON'T UNDERSTAND.
THESE YOUNG GUYS, THEY TAKE ME OUT TO MEET THEIR GUYS SOMETIMES, THEIR IRAQIS.
AND I JUST *PRETEND* TO DO THAT, OKAY?
THEY CALL ME A "GRAY HAIR," BECAUSE THEY NEED SOMEBODY WHO LOOKS OLD.
BECAUSE EVERYBODY'S SO *YOUNG.* SO IT LOOKS LIKE I'M IN CHARGE.
I MEAN, THERE ARE ALL THESE DAMN KIDS HERE.
I MEAN, *HE* DID IT, OKAY?
THE GUY YOU WERE WORKING WITH, WITH THE GLASSES ON...
...I DON'T KNOW WHAT NAME HE GAVE YOU.
FRANKLIN.
HIM.
THAT'S WHAT THEY DO.

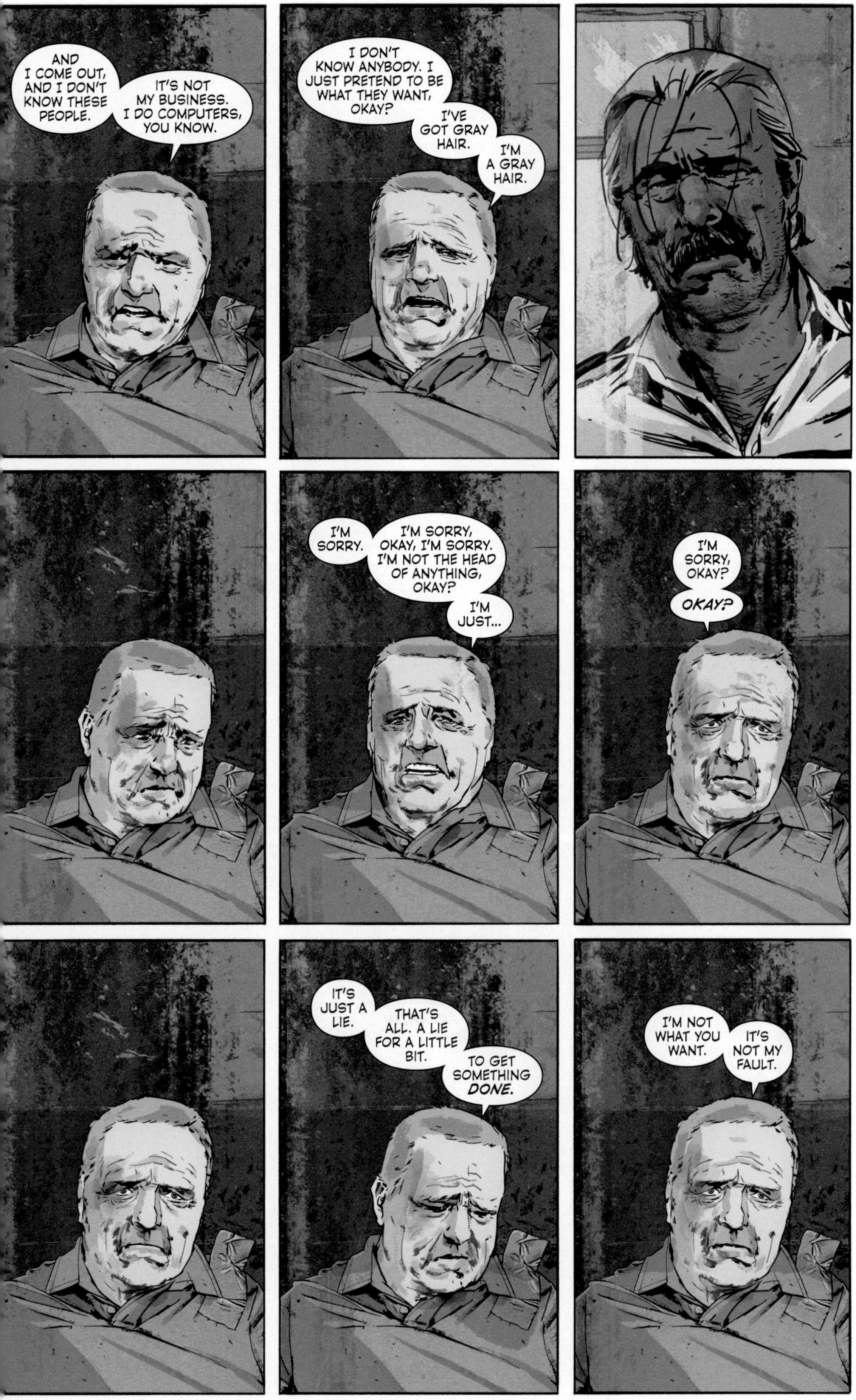
AND I COME OUT, AND I DON'T KNOW THESE PEOPLE.
IT'S NOT MY BUSINESS. I DO COMPUTERS, YOU KNOW.
I DON'T KNOW ANYBODY. I JUST PRETEND TO BE WHAT THEY WANT, OKAY?
I'VE GOT GRAY HAIR.
I'M A GRAY HAIR.
I'M SORRY.
I'M SORRY, OKAY, I'M SORRY. I'M NOT THE HEAD OF ANYTHING, OKAY?
I'M JUST...
I'M SORRY, OKAY?
OKAY?
IT'S JUST A LIE.
THAT'S ALL. A LIE FOR A LITTLE BIT.
TO GET SOMETHING DONE.
I'M NOT WHAT YOU WANT.
IT'S NOT MY FAULT.

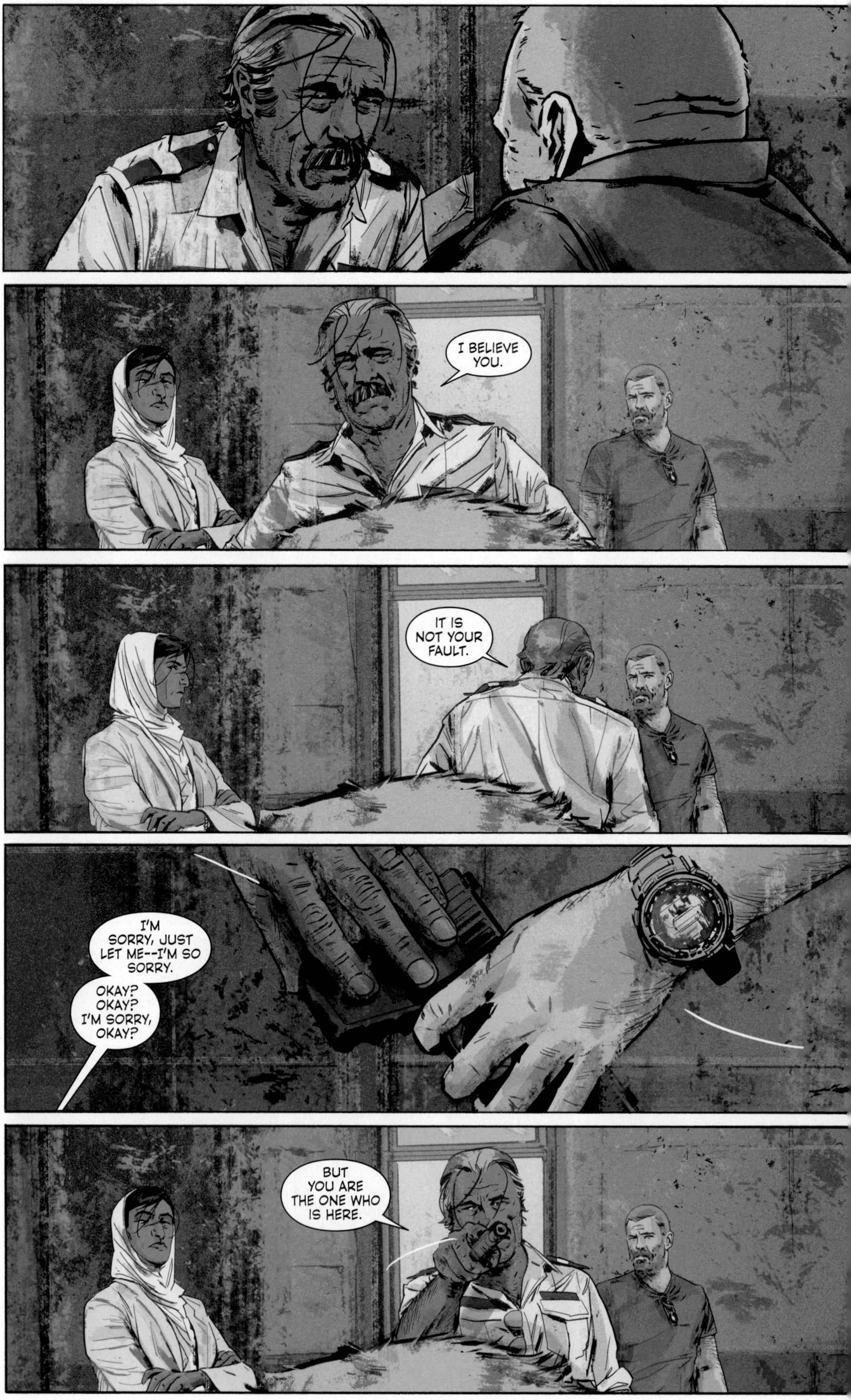
I BELIEVE YOU.
IT IS NOT YOUR FAULT.
I'M SORRY, JUST LET ME--I'M SO SORRY.
OKAY? OKAY? I'M SORRY, OKAY?
BUT YOU ARE THE ONE WHO IS HERE.

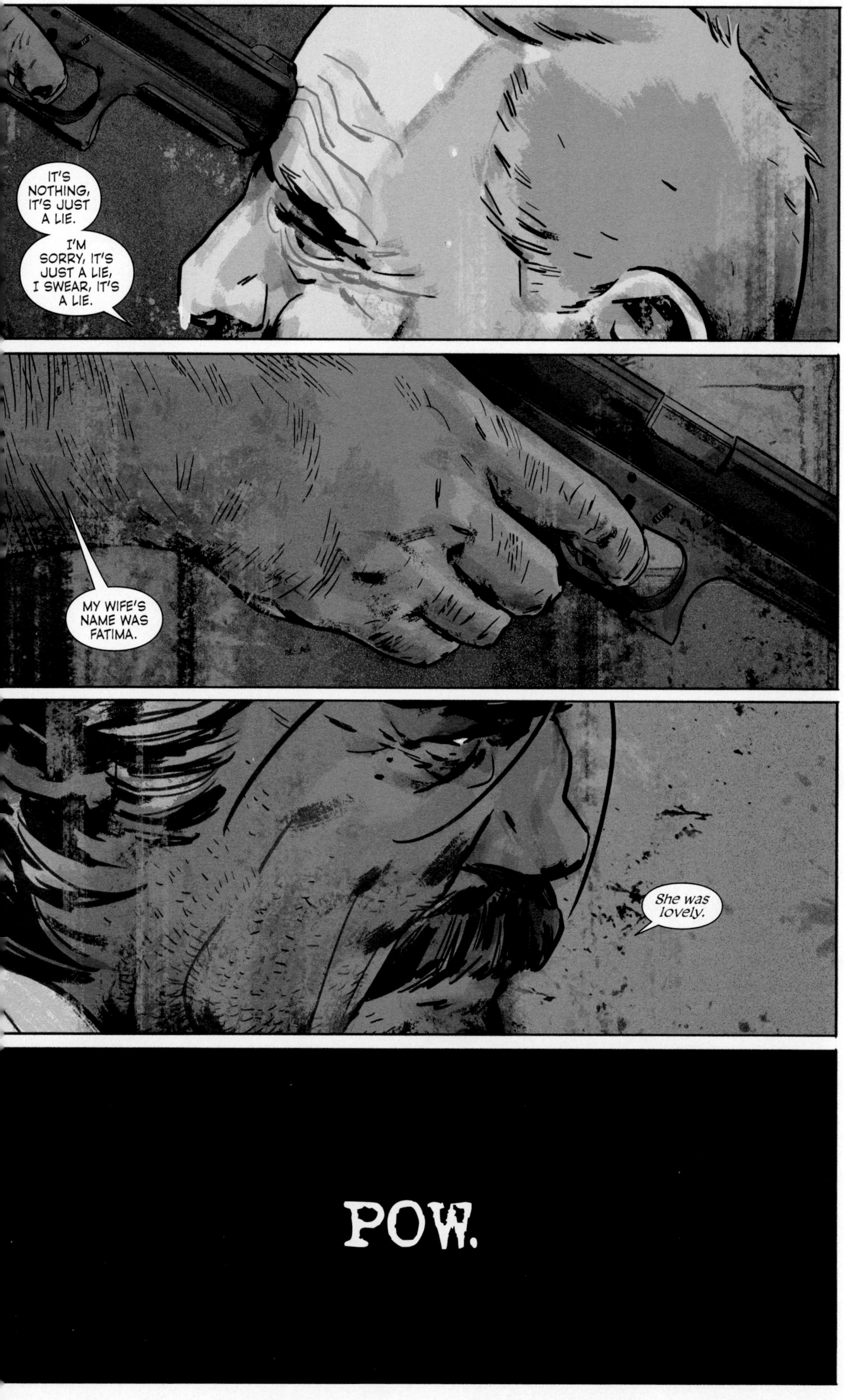
IT'S NOTHING, IT'S JUST A LIE.
I'M SORRY, IT'S JUST A LIE, I SWEAR, IT'S A LIE.
MY WIFE'S NAME WAS FATIMA.
She was lovely.
POW.

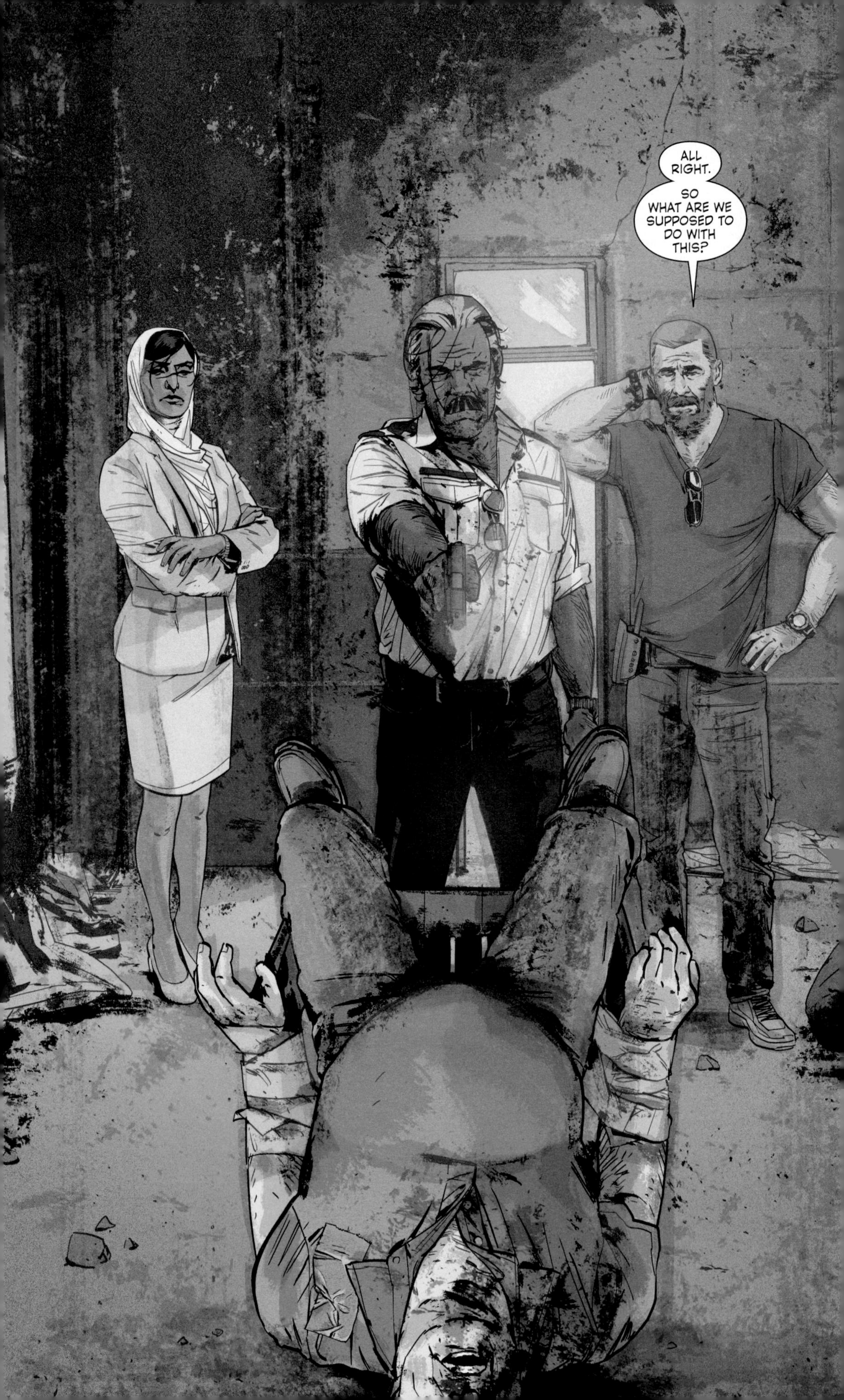
ALL RIGHT.
SO WHAT ARE WE SUPPOSED TO DO WITH THIS?

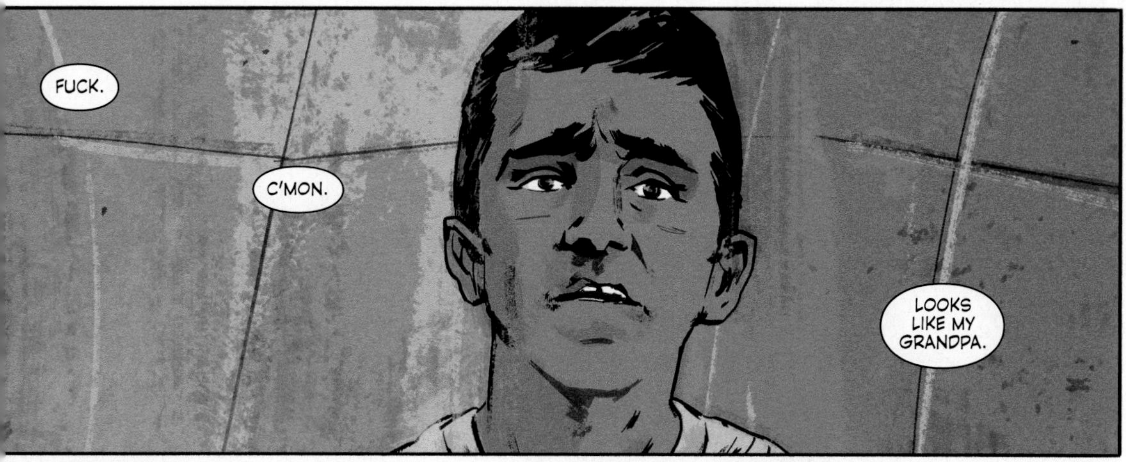
FUCK.
C'MON.
LOOKS LIKE MY GRANDPA.

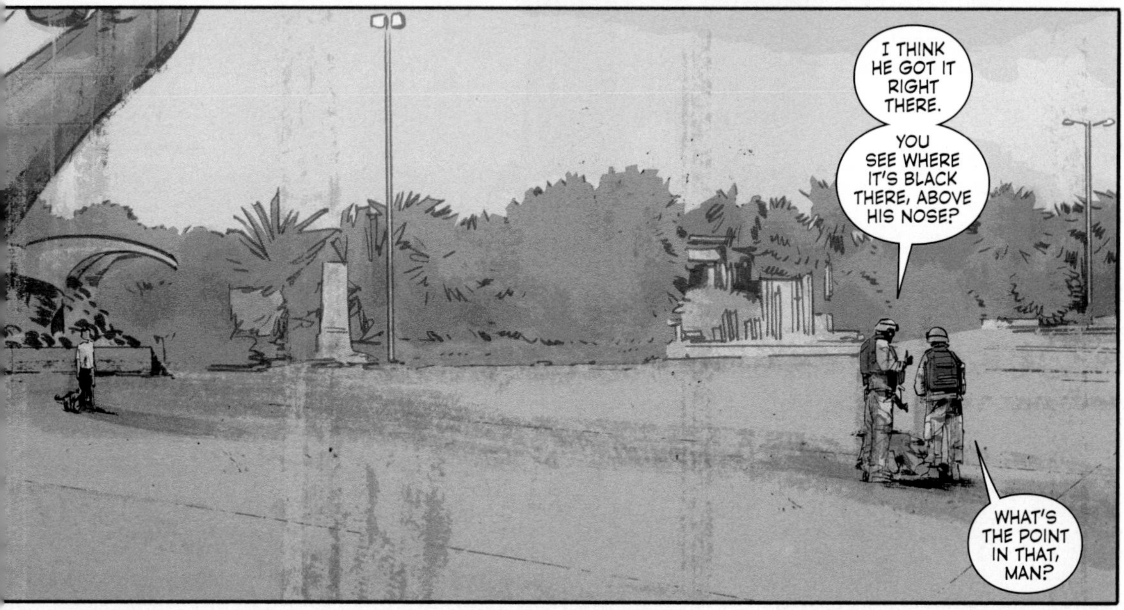
I THINK HE GOT IT RIGHT THERE.
YOU SEE WHERE IT'S BLACK THERE, ABOVE HIS NOSE?
WHAT'S THE POINT IN THAT, MAN?

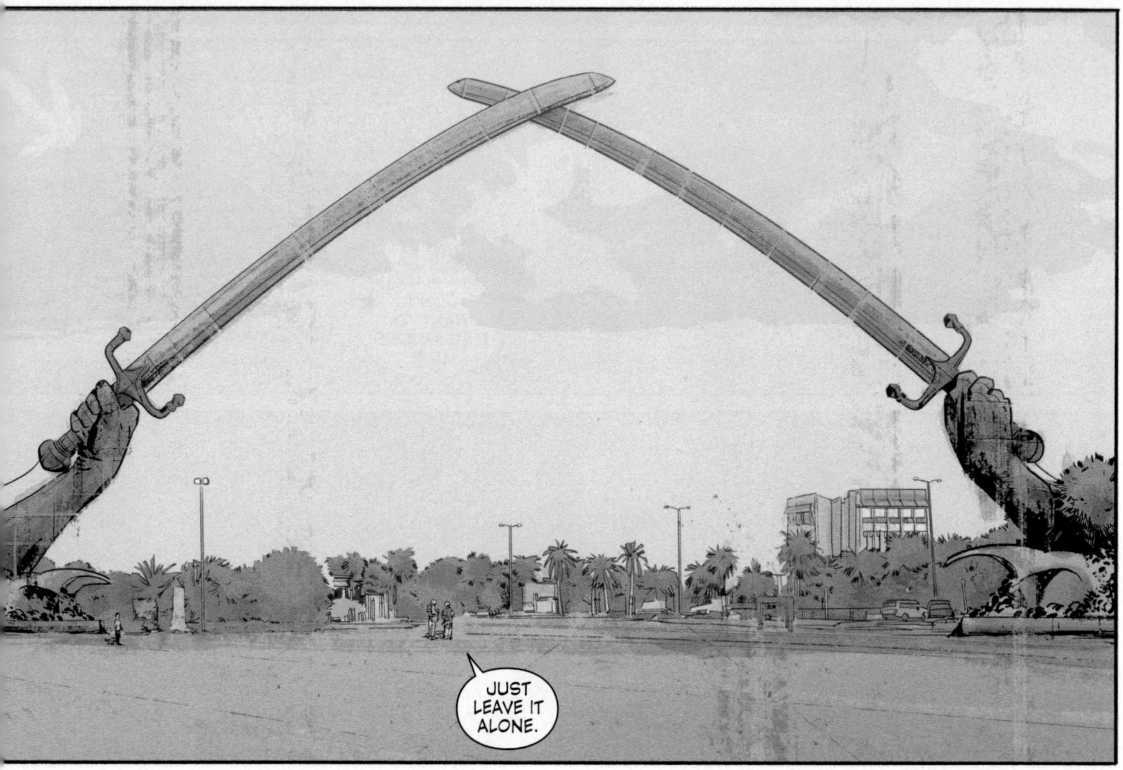
JUST LEAVE IT ALONE.

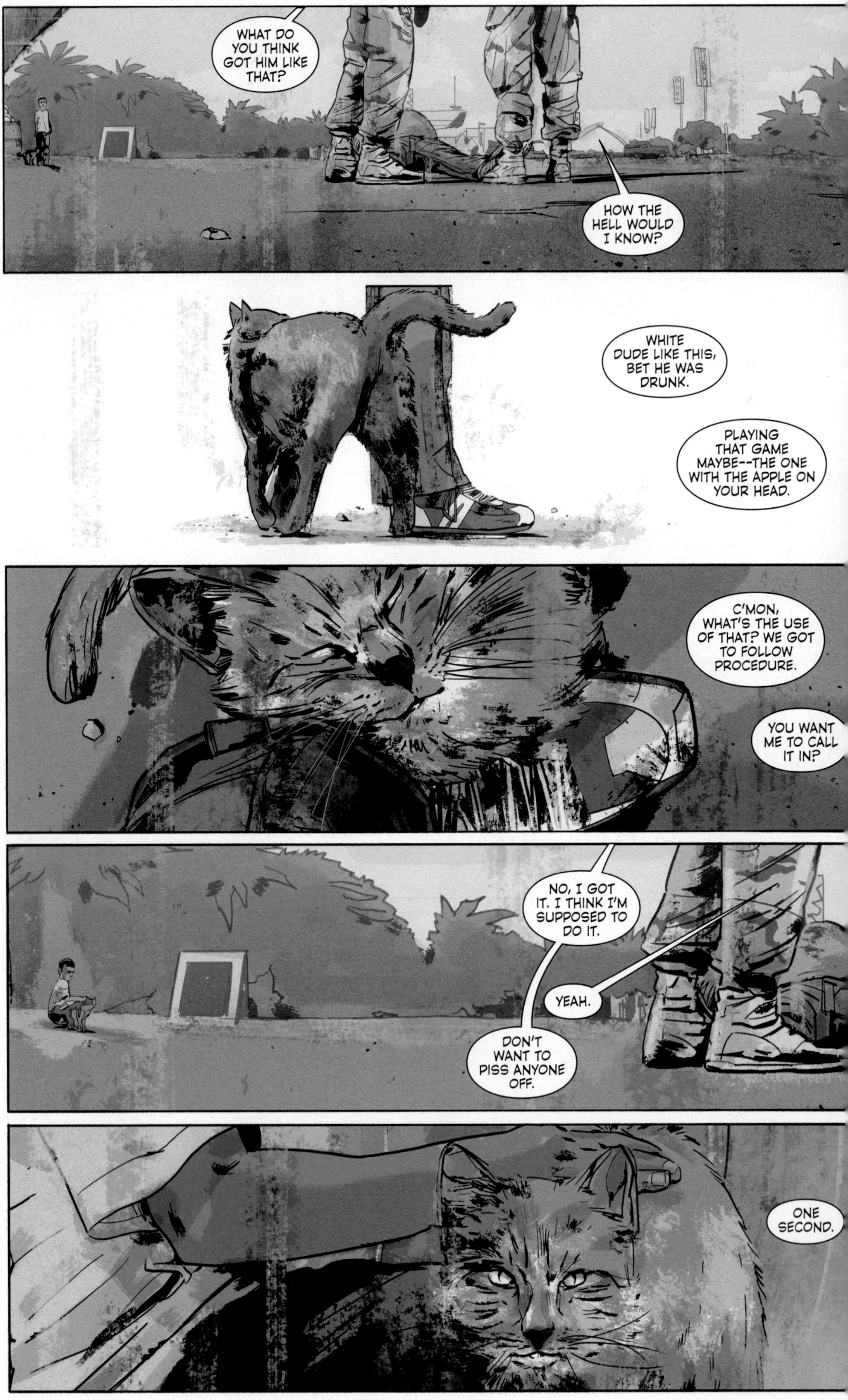
WHAT DO YOU THINK GOT HIM LIKE THAT?
HOW THE HELL WOULD I KNOW?
WHITE DUDE LIKE THIS, BET HE WAS DRUNK.
PLAYING THAT GAME MAYBE--THE ONE WITH THE APPLE ON YOUR HEAD.
C'MON, WHAT'S THE USE OF THAT? WE GOT TO FOLLOW PROCEDURE.
YOU WANT ME TO CALL IT IN?
NO, I GOT IT. I THINK I'M SUPPOSED TO DO IT.
YEAH.
DON'T WANT TO PISS ANYONE OFF.
ONE SECOND.

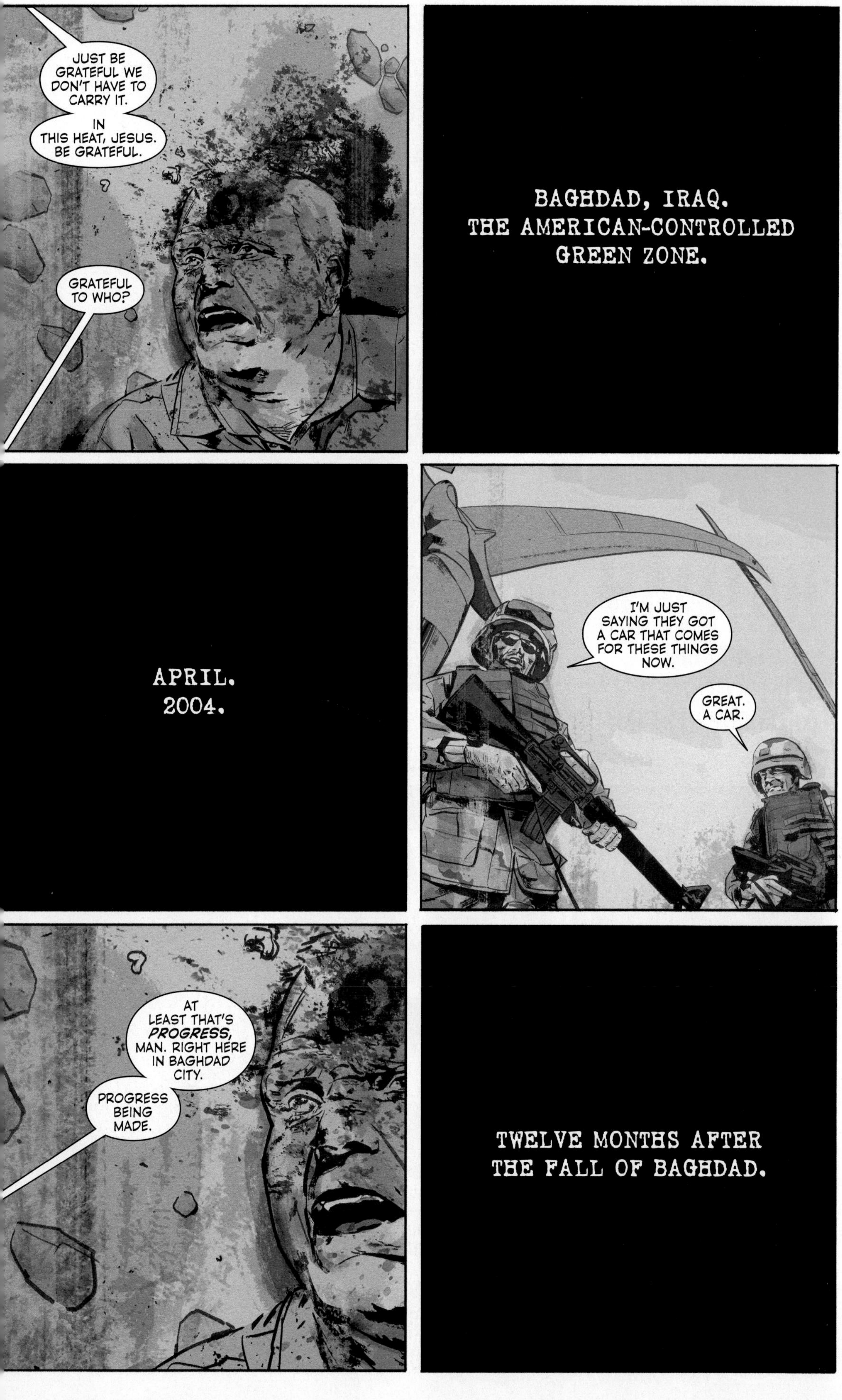
JUST BE GRATEFUL WE DON'T HAVE TO CARRY IT.
IN THIS HEAT, JESUS. BE GRATEFUL.
GRATEFUL TO WHO?
BAGHDAD, IRAQ. THE AMERICAN-CONTROLLED GREEN ZONE.
APRIL. 2004.
I'M JUST SAYING THEY GOT A CAR THAT COMES FOR THESE THINGS NOW.
GREAT. A CAR.
AT LEAST THAT'S *PROGRESS*, MAN. RIGHT HERE IN BAGHDAD CITY.
PROGRESS BEING MADE.
TWELVE MONTHS AFTER THE FALL OF BAGHDAD.

DC UNIVERSE REBIRTH

BATMAN

VOL. 1: I AM GOTHAM
TOM KING
with DAVID FINCH

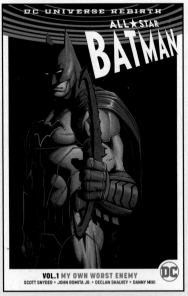

**ALL-STAR BATMAN VOL. 1:
MY OWN WORST ENEMY**

**NIGHTWING VOL. 1:
BETTER THAN BATMAN**

**DETECTIVE COMICS VOL. 1:
RISE OF THE BATMEN**